Internment during the
Second World War

Philosophical Foundations of the Cognitive Science of Religion

A Head Start

Robert N. McCauley

with

E. Thomas Lawson

BLOOMSBURY ACADEMIC
LONDON • NEW YORK • OXFORD • NEW DELHI • SYDNEY

BLOOMSBURY ACADEMIC
Bloomsbury Publishing Plc
50 Bedford Square, London, WC1B 3DP, UK
1385 Broadway, New York, NY 10018, USA

BLOOMSBURY, BLOOMSBURY ACADEMIC and the Diana logo
are trademarks of Bloomsbury Publishing Plc

First published 2017
Paperback edition first published 2019

A catalogue record for this book is available from the British Library.

Library of Congress Cataloging-in-Publication Data
Names: Pistol, Rachel, author.
Title: Internment during the Second World War :
a comparative study of Great Britain and the USA / Rachel Pistol.
Description: London ; New York : Bloomsbury Academic, 2017. |
Includes bibliographical references.
Identifiers: LCCN 2017006374 | ISBN 9781350001428 (hb) |
ISBN 9781350001435 (epub)
Subjects: LCSH: Germans–Great Britain–Evacuation and relocation, 1940–1945. |
Italians–Great Britain–Evacuation and relocation, 1940–1945. |
World War, 1939–1945–Prisoners and prisons, British. |
World War, 1939–1945–Concentration camps–Great Britain. |
Japanese Americans–Evacuation and relocation, 1942–1945. |
World War, 1939–1945–Prisoners and prisons, American. |
World War, 1939–1945–Concentration camps–United States.
Classification: LCC D801.G7 P57 2017 | DDC 940.53/1741–dc23
LC record available at https://lccn.loc.gov/2017006374

ISBN: HB: 978-1-3500-0142-8
PB: 978-1-3501-0604-8
ePDF: 978-1-3500-0141-1
ePub: 978-1-3500-0143-5

Typeset by Newgen Knowledge Works Pvt Ltd., Chennai, India

To find out more about our authors and books visit
www.bloomsbury.com and sign up for our newsletters.

In memory of David Cesarani

Contents

Illustrations

Acknowledgements

The idea for this book originated over a decade ago in conversation with my late colleague David Cesarani at Royal Holloway, University of London. I am indebted to David for his advice, knowledge, understanding, and humour this past decade as I have completed this monograph. David was an incredible friend, and I know that his memory will continue to influence me in my future research. It was a privilege to have worked so closely with him on many projects, and to have learned from someone with so much experience. Thanks are also due to David's family, Dawn, Daniel, and Hannah, for all the meals and laughter they have provided over the years. Thank you to Dawn in particular for being such an inspiration. I would like to thank Tony Kushner and Charmian Brinson for their help and constructive feedback on the content of this book, particularly in the run-up to publication. Thanks to Wendy Ugolini, who met with me on a trip to Edinburgh, and offered me advice and the use of some of her interview transcripts. Many thanks must go to the History Department at Royal Holloway for their unswerving support over the past twelve years, and also to my colleagues at the University of Exeter in the months running up to publication.

During the course of my research, I was generously funded by the Friendly Hand Charitable Trust for my two research trips to the United States, and I am truly grateful for their support which allowed me to gather the documentation needed to discuss the experiences of those interned in America. While in America, I spent many hours in the Special Collections at the University of California, Los Angeles (UCLA),and several weeks at the Bancroft Library at the University of California, Berkeley (UC Berkeley). Many thanks to Amy Wong and to the staff at Special Collections at UCLA, and a particular thank you to David Kessler and to the staff at the Bancroft Library, UC Berkeley. Thanks are also due to Angela Sutton, who guided me around Tule Lake; John Hopper, who showed me the fantastic work of the Amache Preservation Society; Rob Reif for his help at Manzanar; and Kathy Ritchie and Patricia Wakida, who I met at the Japanese American National Museum. I would like to thank Royal Holloway for awarding me a College Research Scholarship, and for granting me the funds to undertake a research trip at the Manx National

Archives, which was essential to the project. The staff at the Manx National Archives were very supportive and their assistance has been very much appreciated. Special thanks to Alan Franklin, Wendy Thirkettle, and Yvonne Cresswell for their help and for providing me access to the many documents I needed to examine. I am indebted to the kindness of John McKenzie, and Cara and Selu Mdlilose, who extended tremendous hospitality to me during my visit, and who kindly drove me around the island so that I could visit the former internment sites. Thank you to Caroline and Dan McKenzie for introducing me to John, Cara, and Selu.

Through David Cesarani, I was fortunate to get to know a wonderful group of people who have been a great source of encouragement and friendship. Special thanks must go to Rachel Century, along with Vivi Lachs, Larissa Allwork, Dan Tilles, Ed Marshall, Kazia Person, Doerte Letzmann, Bob Sherwood, Shane Nagle, and Russell Wallis. Thanks also to Christina Davidson, Miranda Roush Schmidt, and Jenny Clubbe for their company during my time in Berkeley, and for a memorable first Independence Day in the United States. For their encouragement over the years and belief in me I must thank Ann Baker, Katrina Asbury, Rob Blackburn, Laura Blake, Caroline Buchan, Nicola Buntin, Lottie Butcher, Oliver Chapman, Paul Crawford, Vicky Davis, Adriana Dragu, Christie Dunnahoe, Alex Elbourn, Indra Fallon, Elena Fitkov-Norris, Stuart Fitz-Gerald, Dawn-Marie Gibson, Peter Hamilton, Chris Hand, Damien Hansen, Laura Hathaway-Jenkins, Ray Jones, John Kitching, Lucy and Rob Moore, Phil Molyneux, Dan Russell, Sarah Shiells, Jay Singh, Heather and Lenin Soares, Shaun Suddards, Emmett Sullivan, Rose and Nuno Teixeira, Kylie and Mark Thomas, Val Thorne and Liz Wilkinson. Thank you to the Brand family for introducing me to David Brand; to Martha Tuninga and Sumiko Kobayashi; and to Gaby Koppel for giving me access to the letters written by her aunt during internment. Special mention and appreciation go to Sarah Rawlins, Sue Tucker, Andy Christley, Mandy Lauw, Clara and Harriet Scott, and Carys, Andrew, Henry, and Ben Dickinson. While there is not room here for me to list all the people who have travelled this journey with me, I would like you all to know – whether named or not – how much I have appreciated your support.

I could not have undertaken this project without the support of my family in the United Kingdom and in the United States. Thank you, Matt, Tim, Lydia, Micah, Anayah, the Wallaces, the Troncosos, and the Valadezes. Special mention must go to my parents, to whom I am forever grateful. My father, Dan, has travelled across California, Oregon, and Colorado with me, and has now visited three former internment camp sites in America as a result of my research. My mother, Julie, has always believed in the importance of this book. Not only have they supported and encouraged me at every step of the way, but they have been there through all of the ups and downs, and have nursed me post-emergency surgery, and in the final months of the preparation of this book when I was fully incapacitated in a hip-to-ankle cast with a broken leg. I cannot thank you enough.

Introduction

The topic of this book could not be timelier. In both Great Britain and the United States of America, much is being made in the political sphere of the issues of race, immigration, and the rights of foreigners residing in each nation. It is impossible to consider the treatment of enemy aliens during the Second World War without exploring the treatment of foreigners in preceding centuries. As the first chapter of this book discusses, protests over immigration and calls for restriction are invariably heightened during times of economic discontent. Throughout history, immigration is perceived negatively whenever a country is experiencing economic problems. The financial crisis of 2007–2008 and the subsequent recession and austerity measures hark back to the economic crises of the late 1800s, and the Wall Street Crash of 1929. Both countries have been in this position before, but arguably little has been learned. Current events are therefore not surprising, but are disappointing for the lack of attention paid to the history of the preceding centuries. It is, therefore, of even greater importance to be aware of the way foreigners have been treated in Great Britain and the United States of America, both in peace and war, in order to avoid repeating the mistakes of the past.

Evidence of the turmoil both Britain and America are experiencing is found in recent political events, not dissimilar to those experienced during the 1930s and 1940s. Great Britain unexpectedly voted to leave the European Union, and the Leave campaign triumphed using a campaign of fear, which included massive distortion of facts surrounding foreigners and immigration. Nigel Farage, former leader of the UK Independence Party (UKIP), unveiled a billboard during the campaign that showed a picture of Syrian refugees fleeing their homeland, for which he was reported to the police for inciting racial hatred – not only was the image in incredibly poor taste, but it harked back to Nazi propaganda footage of migrants.[1] While UKIP tried to distance itself from the comparisons made between their rhetoric and that of the Nazis, there can be no mistaking the message UKIP was trying to portray – that immigrants are parasites, not refugees, and that many of them are trying to take advantage of Western countries. Such sentiments have been oft repeated in Britain, such as when eastern Europeans arrived in Britain because of Russian persecution in the late nineteenth century, and when Jewish refugees sought asylum in Britain during the 1930s. The 'Brexiters' consistently campaigned for the idea of 'taking the country back'. Gisela Stuart, Labour member of Parliament and spokesperson for the Leave campaign, claimed that the only way to 'take back control' on immigration was to leave the European Union, because of concern that 'no matter how great the pressure on schools, hospitals and housing becomes or how much wages in our poorest communities are pushed down', the needs of ordinary British people would not be met.[2] The problem with such arguments is that they encourage a 'them and us' mentality, which feed xenophobic and racist attitudes. Proof that this attitude engenders violence was tragically given when Jo Cox, member of Parliament for Batley and Spen in West Yorkshire, was gunned down by a man who gave his name in court as 'Death to traitors, freedom for Britain'.[3] In the days following the vote to Leave, thousands of stories were posted on social media that showed how those who were not white, or who spoke with an accent, were harassed, threatened, and told to 'go home'.[4] In the first few days following the EU referendum, hate crimes increased in Britain by as much as 57 per cent.[5] Regardless of nationality, no one should suffer insult or injury as a result of their nationality or skin colour. As the grieving family of Jo Cox said during this tragic and turbulent time, it is necessary for the British public 'to focus on that which unites us and not which divides us'.[6] This is a message needed not just in Britain, but across the globe, as men, women, and children are imprisoned and killed for the sake of their race or religion.

Both Great Britain and the United States of America are currently nations divided, and in America, immigration and the presence of foreigners is also being used as an explanation for social and economic problems. Refugees from the Middle East have been brought up in debates about the threat of terrorism. Since the tragedy of September 11, 2001, there has been a fear of anyone of Middle Eastern appearance, or more specifically, anyone who appears Muslim. Much in the same way that Japanese and Japanese Americans were targeted because of the way they looked, those who appear Muslim are subject to increased scrutiny and discrimination. This follows a long history in America of discrimination based on skin colour, particularly experienced by the African American community. There have been many atrocities committed in the name of Islam, and since 9/11, many have been charged and found guilty of 'jihadi terrorism'.[7] The problem America faces is that the attacks that have taken place in the past fifteen years have been perpetrated by American citizens. In the Orlando massacre – the largest mass killing on American soil since 9/11 – the gunman was an American citizen. The growth of technology and accessibility via the World Wide Web of terrorist literature and chatrooms where vulnerable children and teenagers are groomed for violence is perhaps the most serious threat to American national security that exists today. However, the issue is not as simple as America being targeted by these individuals. Those most vulnerable to such grooming are those who live on the edge of society. As the divide between the rich and the poor continues to grow, and the divide between different ethnicities fails to diminish, the number of marginalized individuals in society is increasing. One only has to look at the case of Flint, Michigan, where the residents have been poisoned by the water supply since 2014, and even today lead-filled water continues to enter their homes. Over half the population of Flint are black and 41 per cent live in poverty, forced to exchange food stamps for bottled water.[8] The residents feel that their concerns are not adequately addressed because of the colour of their skin, and because they are poor. Racial inequality is still prevalent in American society, and until this is eradicated, it is highly likely that the rise of extremism will continue.

There is also the issue of what constitutes terrorism. Since 9/11 there have been a number of mass shootings in America, but these are not classed as acts of terrorism in the same way as jihadi terrorist attacks. Often when a white extremist opens fire on schoolchildren, work colleagues, cinemagoers, shoppers, or those against whom he holds a grudge, the debate turns to gun control. The total number of individuals killed due to gun crimes in America far outweighs the numbers of those killed through acts of terrorism.[9] That is not to say terrorism is not a threat, but it shows the distortion of the terrorism debates, which inevitably revolve around race, much as arguments about national security did during the Second World War. President Donald Trump, to take the highest profile example, made immigration and terrorism the foundation of his presidential campaign. After the Orlando massacre, Trump said, 'The bottom line is that the only reason the killer was in America in the first place was because we allowed his family to come here', and that 'with the terrorists, you have to take out their families. When you get these terrorists, you have to take out their families'.[10] Such comments are redolent of the campaign waged against the families of Japanese immigrants during the Second World War. Trump supporters have even gone so far as to link present-day America with Japanese American internment by inappropriately claiming that Second World War internment forms a legal precedent for the creation of a Muslim registry.[11] The need for a true understanding of the history of Japanese American internment has never been greater.

Trump's campaign slogan is 'Make America Great Again' – the implication being that the alleged 'weakness' of America is due to the number of legal and illegal migrants resident, and not any other social or economic issues. Trump's website proclaims the need for immigration 'reform', the main plank of his policy being the insistence that Mexico pay to build a wall to strengthen American borders. According to Trump, 'the Mexican government has taken the United States to the cleaners. They are responsible for this problem, and they must help pay to clean it up'.[12] Trump has labelled Mexicans as 'dirty', 'criminals', and 'rapists', racial slurs that his supporters are quick to endorse, in the same way that the terms 'Japs' and 'yellow peril' were readily used by Americans in the nineteenth and early twentieth centuries. There have been hundreds of thousands of deportations of illegal immigrants from American soil during the twentieth century, but as Michael Chertoff, the former secretary of Homeland Security under President George W. Bush, said regarding Trump's ambitious deportation plans: 'I can't even begin to picture how we would deport 11 million people in a few years where we don't have a police state, where the police can't break down your door at will and take you away without a warrant'.[13] Once again, this harks back to the treatment of Jews in Europe during the 1930s and 1940s, and the treatment of enemy aliens during the Second World War. There is a difference between illegal and legal immigration, but the problem of giving power for blanket arrests is that this power can so easily be abused. During the Second World War, German, Austrian, and Italian enemy aliens were considered on a case-by-case basis, while the wholesale internment of all Japanese along with their families, who were mostly American citizens, was a blatant contradiction of constitutional privilege. The concept of internment is not controversial in the sense of being a recognized solution to dealing with enemy aliens in a time of war, but when that becomes an excuse to lock away American children, it shows how power can be abused.

This is a period of isolationism, where both Britain and America are calling for tougher border control. Right-wing politicians in both nations believe that the only way to protect a country is to keep out foreigners. There are many different issues involved in the immigration debate, such as illegal versus legal immigration; however, there is very little distinction made between these categories when talking about immigration, leaving all foreigners victim to negative connotations. Not since the 1930s and 1940s has there been such hatred directed at foreigners living in Britain, with calls for foreigners and non-whites to 'go home'. In America, there have been various times during the twentieth century when immigrant or refugee groups have been targeted by racists, and the Civil Rights Movement and the Black Lives Matter movement demonstrate how unequal American society continues to be in the present day. The fact that individuals are still targeted and stereotyped as a threat to be feared because of the colour of their skin shows how little progress has been made in the past century. The issues of racial inequality and the inherent fear of the 'other' are just as prevalent in modern-day society as they were in the early twentieth century. The First World War was a conflict between nation-states, whereas the Second World War was a conflict based more on ideology than nationality. The lack of greater understanding of this issue caused the detention of tens of thousands of individuals who would have gladly fought for the Allied powers from the beginning of the conflict. Ultimately, as shown in Chapter 3, many internees in both countries were admitted or drafted into the Armed Forces, and the heroic efforts of these former internees is impressive. As the chapter also discusses, many of the former internees have contributed incredibly positively to their adoptive nations post-war, or in the case of those of Japanese ancestry, they have gone on to achieve greatness in spite of their treatment by their country of birth. There is much to be learned from the actions and reactions of the internees to their incarceration, and the sacrifices they and their families have made cannot be overlooked.

This monograph is the first transatlantic comparison of Second World War internment. Greg Robinson has written an excellent comparative history of North American internment, and Roger Daniels has also considered the treatment of enemy aliens in both the United States and Canada.[14] This work aims to build on their work, among others, to further demonstrate how Allied countries treated enemy aliens. The United States has a written Constitution and Bill of Rights, whereas Great Britain governs by an unwritten code, which makes the comparison of internment in the two nations significant from both a legal and social standpoint. The benefits of comparative history are immense. As Marc Bloch believed, 'history cannot be intelligible unless it can "succeed in establishing explanatory relationships between phenomena"'.[15] Comparative history is 'a way to determine what needs to be known, and social analysis not at least implicitly comparative is hard to imagine. There is really no other way to identify historical eras or recognize historical change'.[16] It is also a means of 'isolating the critical factors or independent variables that account for national history'.[17] This book is written primarily from a social and cultural standpoint, and the experiences and memories of the internees themselves form a key part of the internment discussion. There are as many different experiences of internment as there were internees, but by telling the internees' stories readers will hopefully understand the human sacrifices behind the history.

For the purpose of this book, the main comparison of internment lies between the internment of German, Austrian, and Italian internees in Great Britain, and those of Japanese ancestry in the continental United States of America and Hawaii, though those of German, Austrian, and Italian descent in America are not forgotten in this comparative internment study, and neither are the few Japanese internees who were detained on the Isle of Man. This book compares the internment experiences of those already resident in Great Britain and the continental United States at the outbreak of hostilities, though it is recognized that, certainly in the case of America, internees were also 'imported' from other locations outside of the United States.

Although it may seem a more obvious approach to compare Germans interned in the United States with Germans interned in Great Britain, it is not as revealing a comparison as would first appear. Japan attacked the United States on American soil, and a huge amount of American anger was directed at those of Japanese ancestry. In Britain, the greatest threat from attack stemmed from the continent, and most of the anger was aimed at Germans, Austrians, and Italians. This book is, therefore, a comparison of similar enemy alien groups who, while they may not have shared the same nationality, shared the same discrimination and backlash from their perceived country of birth's actions. The harshest penalties were imposed on those who originated from countries that were considered to be the greatest threat. That is not to say that the other groups of enemy aliens did not also suffer, but that these groups disproportionately bore the brunt of calls for mass arrests and incarceration.

For the purpose of this study, prisoners of war are not considered, as this is a topic entirely deserving of another monograph. Internees are civilians who are detained because of their nationality during times of conflict for reasons of national security and fears of espionage, not for having been captured while bearing arms during the conflict. Prisoners of war are, therefore, a separate entity to internees. This book also does not offer in-depth analysis of British citizens detained by means of Defence Regulation 18B. This is because many of the British citizens who were detained under 18B had actively spoken out or participated in events that were against British war interests.[18] However, there were also examples of British subjects of Italian origin detained under 18B, and these arrests were, in large part, a result of their foreign ancestry. No direct comparison can be made between the internment of British men and women, who included members of the British Union of Fascists, and the internment of Japanese American citizens, who were mostly children or young people interned solely because of their nationality. It is, therefore, a more equal comparison to consider Japanese American children and young adults alongside the German and Austrian children and young adults who were interned on the Isle of Man.

Regarding terminology, when discussed as a whole, those of Japanese ancestry living in the United States are collectively known as the Nikkei. The first generation of immigrants from Japan who settled in America are the Issei, and their American-born children are the Nisei. Nisei who were sent to Japan as young children or teenagers who then returned to America are the Kibei. Children of Nisei and Kibei are the Sansei, or 'third generation'. In Britain, the detention of enemy aliens was commonly known as internment, and will be referred to as such. However, in the case of the United States of America, many different terms have been used to describe the forced removal of Nikkei from the West Coast of America and their subsequent detention in euphemistically termed 'Relocation Centers'. Wherever the word 'relocation' or 'evacuation' is used, it is with the understanding that it describes a movement of persons forced by the US government to leave their homes and livelihoods with no adequate compensation or information as to what would happen to them in the short or long term. Relocation was not a choice and had neither the best interests of the Nikkei nor the security of the West Coast behind it.

This work makes use of the rich primary source material located in the National Archives at Kew, the Manx National Archives in Douglas, the Isle of Man, the Bancroft Library at the University of California, Berkeley, and Special Collections located at the University of California, Los Angeles. A large number of interviews have been recorded in an attempt to preserve the voices of those who were interned, and this work draws upon those held at the Imperial War Museum, the Japanese American Relocation Digital Archive (JARDA), the German American Internee Coalition, and also several interviews conducted by the author with former internees and family members from the United States and Great Britain. The author has also had the privilege of including never before seen source material from letters written by a sixteen-year-old refugee interned in Rushen Camp, which have been used courtesy of Gaby Koppel. Several of the former internment camps in both Britain and America have been visited, and use will be made of first-hand knowledge regarding the historical preservation of these sites.

In this book, oral history and documentary sources are taken to complement each other. Consideration has also been given to the concept of 'myth making', and the influence of generations of history. As Paul Thompson has noted, 'Telling one's own life story requires not only recounting directly remembered experience, but also drawing on information and stories transmitted across the generations, both about the years too early in childhood to remember, and also further back in time beyond one's own birth.'[19] This is particularly significant with the immigrant communities discussed in this monograph where, during the war particularly, cultures collided between the country of an individual's birth and the customs of British and American society. A large part of identity in immigrant families comes from the stories transmitted from previous generations to reinforce ideas of heritage and culture. These stories are combined with the experiences of families as they settle in a new land and are faced with combinations of prejudice, acceptance, and different cultural norms. This makes the experiences of the internees all the more complex, especially as former internees reconstructed their lives in a post-conflict environment.

Internment as presented in this monograph follows an essentially chronological structure with some thematic sections. The first chapter examines the legal precedents for the mass incarceration of enemy aliens and patterns of anti-alienism during the nineteenth and twentieth centuries in Britain and the United States. Chapter 2 focuses on the experiences of the internees and how they created 'homes' in the most unlikely of places. The release process and how the former internees set about rebuilding their lives and ultimately gained redress in the United States is covered in the third chapter. The final chapter deals with the historical memory and commemoration of the former sites of internment. The conclusion juxtaposes and explores the parallel and intertwining themes, analysing the similarities and differences between the practices and experiences of internment in the two countries.

The Origins of Internment

Anti-alien legislation in Britain

To understand the internment of aliens during the Second World War, it is first necessary to consider the treatment of aliens in the preceding centuries. The treatment of aliens is usually characterized by fear and suspicion of the foreign 'other'. That fear is often based on economic or security issues, and it is perhaps no surprise that anti-alien legislation has revolved around these two problems. In 1793, Parliament passed the 'Regulators of Aliens Act', based on fears of infiltration by Republican agents following the French Revolution.[1] As a result of the Act, all foreigners had to register and carry a certificate on their person at all times while in Britain. Merchant seamen and domestic servants were, however, exempt from the Act. Aliens were required to register with the local magistrate wherever they chose to reside, and if they wished to move, they had to obtain a 'passport' from the magistrate or else face imprisonment followed by deportation.[2] The 1793 Act set a precedent for monitoring aliens arriving at and residing within Britain's shores.

Regulations of Aliens Acts in 1816 and 1826 continued the practice of registering aliens, though exempted categories grew to include necessary immigrants, such as those in domestic service, and political necessities such as foreign ambassadors. Aliens had to notify the authorities where they lived twice a year, but these restrictions were relaxed somewhat in 1836, when aliens were merely required to produce their passports upon arrival in Britain and answer a short landing questionnaire. They were then free to remain in the country as long as they wanted.[3] Supposedly, aliens were monitored following their arrival in Britain, but as the nineteenth century progressed, fewer and fewer ships submitted lists of aliens brought into the country outside the Port of London. This laxness in practice, coupled with a prolonged economic depression in the 1870s and a dramatic increase of immigration in the 1880s led to demands for a revival of the 1836 Act in May 1890.[4] As often repeated in history, a decline in economic prosperity led to a reconsideration of immigration policy and the effects of immigration on the native population. The economic problems of the late nineteenth century, therefore, led to significant changes in immigration policy in the early twentieth century.

During the 1880s and 1890s, the largest immigrant group by far to enter Great Britain were eastern European Jews fleeing persecution in their homelands. Many of these immigrants settled in the East End of London, and the London borough of Stepney soon developed the largest immigrant population in the country.[5] Criticism was levelled at the immigrant community due to their tendency to form 'a society apart, with standards derived from other sources than England'. As immigrant numbers increased, so did anti-alien feeling, ultimately resulting in anti-alien rallies and calls for restriction.[6] The tensions arose from the fact that the conditions in the neighbourhoods in which the immigrants settled were already poor. The increase in numbers in these already impoverished areas exacerbated the terrible living conditions of the East End. The problem was so severe that in 1898 and 1899 two Parliamentary committees reported 'general agreement that pauper immigration [was] an evil and should be checked', as well as a 'tendency of destitute foreigners to reduce still lower the social and material condition of our poor'.[7] The situation was set to get even worse, however, from 1900 with the so-called exodus from Rumania, the 1903 Kishinev outrage, and the pogroms that were a result of the Russo-Japanese War of 1904 and the Russian Revolution of 1905.[8] The fact that those fleeing persecution abroad and seeking refuge in Britain were Jewish meant that the refugee 'problem' was considered to be a 'Jewish problem'. The Anglo-Jewish community offered charitable aid where appropriate and repatriated those unable to support themselves, but this was not considered enough to deal with the issue, and political parties – particularly those on the right – campaigned on issues of curbing immigration. Based on the findings of a Royal Commission on Alien Immigration the previous year, an Aliens Bill was introduced to Parliament in 1904. It was feared that if immigrants continued to enter Britain in large numbers, the nation's 'health' and 'efficiency' would suffer.[9] In 1905, therefore, the watershed of British immigration policy, the Aliens Act, was passed. Despite the fact it was less restrictive than the recommendations of the Royal Commission, and much watered down from the 1904 Bill debated in Parliament, the Aliens Act was designed to specifically target destitute immigrants fleeing Russia and its neighbouring countries.

The language of the 1905 Aliens Act may have sounded similar to previous immigration Acts, but the meaning of the term 'immigrant' had changed. Now an immigrant was only considered to be 'an alien steerage passenger' arriving in Britain who was not in possession of an onward paid ticket to another destination, or who failed to convince immigration officers that he or she would leave Britain within a reasonable time.[10] Immigrants from the middle or upper classes were not affected by the Act, and from the start of the twentieth century there began to be a marked difference in the way different classes of immigrants were viewed. From this time on, immigrants were considered as either 'desirable' or 'undesirable'. 'Undesirable immigrants' were those who had insufficient means to support themselves, or those suffering from mental or physical illnesses who might become a 'charge upon the rates or otherwise a detriment to the public'.[11] The only exception was in cases of immigrants entering the country

> solely to avoid prosecution or punishment on religious or political grounds or for an offence of a political character, or persecution, involving danger of imprisonment or danger to life or limb, on account of religious belief, leave to land [would] not be refused on the ground merely of want of means, or the probability of his becoming a charge on the rates.[12]

Thus, refugees continued to be granted asylum in Britain, despite the exclusionist tone of the 1905 Act.

The early twentieth century was a time of exclusionist policies across the globe. The policies of the United States will be considered later, but other European countries and the British dominions were already, or well on the way to, discriminating against certain types of immigrants. Twice in the nineteenth century Germany attempted to expel all alien Poles, in 1886 and 1890. Having failed to do so, Germany then introduced identity cards in 1907 to control this immigrant group.[13] In 1901, Australia introduced the 'White Australia' policy that stayed in force until 1973, and in 1910 Canada followed suit with a law that lasted till 1962.[14] The 1905 Act also masked national disquiet regarding the arrival of German gypsies in 1904 and the deportation orders that forcibly despatched several hundred gypsies back to mainland Europe between 1905 and 1906.[15]

It is possible that the 1905 Aliens Act did, to an extent, achieve its intended goal as it deterred pauper immigration between 1906 and 1910.[16] The greatest effect of the Act was as a psychological deterrent to those considering Britain as a destination. After the Act was passed, many eastern Europeans decided to bypass Britain as an option and instead headed directly to America.[17] In reality, comparatively few immigrants were turned away from British ports in the years following the act. Between 1906 and 1913 a total of 7,594 aliens were refused the right to immigrate into Britain, and refusals never reached much more than 1,000 per year.[18] The number of aliens properly inspected by immigration officers also fell in the years following the Act – in 1906, 71 per cent of alien immigrants arriving at British ports were inspected compared to 59 per cent in 1910.[19] By 1914, the threat of the Aliens Act seemed to have worn off and immigration levels had returned to the average 5,000 a year Britain had experienced from 1881 to 1905.[20] The foundation had been laid, however, for further exclusionist legislation, and it was with little difficulty that new strictures were passed into law.

With the declaration of war against Germany in 1914, and the precedent of the 1905 Aliens Act, it was perhaps unsurprising that the rise of anti-alienism intensified to a point where more legislation was passed. As David Cesarani noted regarding the growth of anti-alienism during this time: 'Anti-alienism developed a momentum, dynamic and logic of its own. The existence of a statute and the administrative machinery to enforce it provided the basis for continuity. Politicians and civil servants began to amass experience in operating anti-alien measures and laid down precedents for future development. Anti-alienism was carried forward by the inexorable workings of the Home Office bureaucracy.'[21] The 1914 Act placed strict controls over registration, movement, and deportation of aliens in order to prevent the possibility of enemy aliens sabotaging the war effort.[22] For reasons of national security, immigrants could be denied the right to land, could be deported if already landed, and had to register with the police.[23] As the war progressed, these measures were not considered strong enough, and all male enemy aliens resident in the British Isles were interned.

The 1914 Act was originally intended as a temporary measure, but after the First World War it was renewed in the form of the 1919 Aliens Restriction (Amendment) Act.[24] The 1914 Aliens Restriction Act can be seen largely as a sign of the times, as the Defence of the Realm Act was passed in the same year, which rendered civilians liable to court martial instead of trial by jury, as well as the introduction of the death penalty for assisting the enemy.[25] However, the 1919 (Amendment) Act demonstrated just how strong anti-alien feeling was by the end of the war.[26] Cleansing the country from foreigners was a popular political campaigning tool that won many votes. Lloyd George set the scene in his election pledge in September 1918 when he claimed that Germans had 'forfeited claims to remain' in the United Kingdom.[27] The 1919 (Amendment) Act was, therefore, particularly harsh, and the discussion surrounding it had a decidedly racist overtone.[28] No former enemy aliens were allowed to land in the United Kingdom for three years after the Act's passage without permission from the Secretary of State, and if so granted, aliens were not allowed to remain for more than three months without applying for an extension to remain.[29] The 1919 (Amendment) Act resulted in the expulsion of over 30,000 Germans, Austrians, Hungarians, and Turks.[30] Never before had a movement been made to expel such a vast number of foreigners at one time, regardless of the time they had been resident in the United Kingdom. The 1919 (Amendment) Act marked a huge departure from previous policy with its blatant hostility towards wartime 'enemies' of the United Kingdom, a hostility shared by the other victorious Allied nations. Long gone was the Britain renowned for its belief in 'unquestioning refuge and tolerance'.[31]

The years preceding internment

Britain in the 1930s had no legal obligation to grant refuge to those seeking asylum.[32] The 'watchword of British policy was to admit only such refugees as could be conveniently disposed of … whether what was at stake was refuge or rescue'.[33] During the 1930s refugees from Germany started to arrive, although Britain was not always the destination of choice – of the 150,000 who had fled Germany by the end of 1937, only 5,500 came to Britain.[34] It was only after *Kristallnacht*, in 1938, that the numbers of refugees dramatically increased; during the early 1930s the majority of those arriving in Britain were fleeing political persecution, but as the decade progressed, the number of Jewish refugees increased exponentially. The British approach to the refugees was a mixture of 'antipathy, ambivalence and sympathy'.[35]

Visas had been abandoned between Britain, Germany, and Austria in 1927, but as the numbers of refugees increased, visas were reinstated in 1938 in an attempt to stem the flow.[36] Passport officers abroad complained about the 'poor type of refugee for whom authorizations for visas are being issued', and the government believed it was allowing in a number of 'mentally and physically defectives' who would become public charges.[37] Even the Board of Deputies of British Jews agreed that 'if a flood of the wrong type of immigrants were allowed in there might be serious danger of anti-Semitic feeling being aroused'.[38] One might have thought that with such concerns over the quality of refugee the British would welcome professionals, but the admission of skilled workers met with almost as many objections as that of the unskilled. As early as 1935, the British Dental Association warned that if Jewish dentists were legally debarred (whether for racial or other reasons) from practicing dentistry in Germany, then they would not be able to practice in Britain either.[39] Sixty-one dentists were granted admission to the British Dental Register in 1936 but no further dentists were to be admitted unless they were individuals 'of outstanding eminence'.[40] The British Medical Association took an even harder line by refusing to admit any specialists and were only prepared 'on humanitarian grounds' to admit fifty German and twenty Austrian general practitioners 'whose activities [were] less likely to attract attention'.[41] This despite the fact that in a total of 45,000 practicing doctors in Britain, the admission of 200 or 300 refugees would have meant an increase of less than 1 per cent to their number. As one member of the Home Office noted, 'it would seem contrary to the traditions of this humane and liberal profession to refuse this small measure of help to their professional brethren who are the victims of a mediaeval persecution'.[42] Not all professions took such a negative approach to the foreigners, however – architects, particularly in London, were keen to endorse a 'generous policy' towards the refugees that included exemption from examinations and inclusion on the architects' register provided they were otherwise suitably qualified.[43] The academic world was also generous in their help to professional brethren, offering positions at British universities to German and Austrian academics where possible, and even organized tours of American universities for academics to help them find roles in the United States.[44] Numerous schemes were arranged in order to offer hope to those abroad but these schemes could not satisfy the vast numbers of those trying to escape Germany.[45] German youths were to be offered agricultural training in preparation for potentially moving to one of the colonies, but such plans were not popular with Britain's dominions.[46] The dominions feared that Britain's unwanted refugees might be forced upon them, a fear which was not entirely unfounded as will be shown later. Australia, for example, believed it was going to be overrun by foreign doctors trained in Great Britain but forced out of the country after completion of their qualifications.[47] Canada was equally unwilling to take British 'rejects', despite British hopes to the contrary.

Although there were protests from several prominent professions refusing employment to refugees, general public opinion was that refugees should not be sent back to Germany unless they were 'criminally undesirable'.[48] Norway and Belgium were prepared to offer sanctuary to German refugees and allowed them indefinite leave to remain, provided they did not come to the adverse notice of the police.[49] Britain had already accepted, as of early 1938, at least 10,000 refugees, a marginal figure considering the size of the country. As conditions for the Jews in Germany worsened, the Home Office recognized that granting asylum was a necessity, and that once admitted to the country it should be assumed that refugees would become permanent residents.[50] However, debates still raged over the suitability of refugees, and visas were to be granted to only those who could prove they had friends or relatives in Britain or were of international repute in their field.[51] The government approach to Jewish refugees stumbled, time and again, over the problem of what to 'do' with the refugees, rather than their plight.[52] Britain was, however, more liberal in its approach to granting visas to transmigrants. Many transmigrants travelled as far as Britain, and then decided to settle for any one of a multitude of reasons, including problems with their onward transit, particularly to the United States of America. In 1939, Britain still had hopes that the United States would relax its immigration laws and ease the pressure on numbers arriving in Britain. However, the United States never did, meaning countless individuals and families were left stranded in Britain if they were lucky, or continental Europe where, even if an American visa was to be granted, it was often too late.[53] One striking example of the British government being lenient in the granting of visas can be found in the case of the Kitchener Camp near Sandwich, in Kent. Here, at a former First World War embarkation camp, 4,000 men who were either in transit or were training for occupations abroad were housed between February 1939 and March 1940. The camp, funded by the Central British Fund for German Jewry, wanted to give opportunities for men to leave Germany as they felt women already had the opportunity by applying for positions as domestics. The British government allowed the men into the country on the guarantee of the Central British Fund, a show of leniency from the standard policy of admission, which was based on individual means.[54]

The numbers of those seeking refuge in Britain grew continually during the 1930s until, on the outbreak of war, an estimated 80,000 German, Austrian, and Czechoslovakian refugees had been admitted to the country.[55] A significant number of these refugees were maintained by refugee organizations, and there were at least 15,000 such cases at the beginning of the war.[56] The strain this put on charitable organizations was lessened, to some extent, by a government scheme that matched pound for pound the contributions from private benefactors.[57] Aid was thus guaranteed through the Central Committee for Refugees to help support those in need of immediate assistance at the beginning of the war, although it was a heavy financial burden to be borne even with government pledges. However, when war broke out, the concern switched to what would happen to the tens of thousands of refugees who were now considered enemy aliens.

First World War internment

In order to understand the situation of enemy aliens during times of war, the First World War provides a particularly good example. When war was declared in 1914, approximately 60,000 German nationals were resident in Great Britain. These Germans were, for the most part, economic migrants of the late nineteenth century.[58] Only three days after war was declared with Germany, the General Staff decided that all male enemy aliens between the ages of seventeen and forty-two should be interned for the duration of the war. However, the decision of the General Staff was overturned and instead only those who were deemed to be an immediate threat to the security of the nation were imprisoned.[59] Despite a lack of suitable internment camps, by May 1915 there were 19,000 internees.[60] Prime Minister Asquith publicly announced on 13 May 1915 that 'all adult males ... should, for their own safety, and that of the community, be segregated and interned, or, if over military age, repatriated'.[61] Certain cases of women and children were also subject to repatriation unless there were reasons of justice or humanity for them to remain. The Home Office desired to repatriate all German female adults unless they gained their nationality through marriage, and those who did not obtain an exemption notice from a special tribunal were advised to leave the country voluntarily or face deportation.[62] There was a significant difference between the enemy aliens of the First World War and those of the Second, as the bulk of the latter consisted of refugees from Nazi oppression. It was in the interests of genuine refugees to assist the British war effort for self-preservation, if nothing else. It was therefore hoped that the mass internment of the First World War could be avoided.

Tribunals

In 1939, a tribunal system was instituted in order to ascertain which enemy aliens were friendly to Britain and which were potential threats to national security. The hope was that by screening enemy aliens resident in Britain it would be possible to avoid detaining genuine refugees. Sir John Anderson, then Home Secretary, stated publicly that 'the plans prepared are based on the principle that effective steps must be taken to render harmless all aliens who may be hostile to this country, but there should be no unnecessary interference with other foreigners, of whom many are anxious to help this country'.[63] The tribunals were to be established

[with] the assistance of nearly a hundred men with legal experience to review all cases of Germans and Austrians who are in this country. Each of these gentlemen will sit as a tribunal to review all cases in the area assigned to him. In London there will be several tribunals for areas in which there are large numbers of Germans and Austrians. No tribunal will have more than about 500 cases to examine, and it will therefore be possible to complete the review rapidly. The police will make arrangements for seeing that particulars of each case are brought before the tribunal. The Voluntary Committees which have been befriending refugees will assist the tribunals by giving the information which they have about individual aliens, and it has been arranged with the Refugee Joint Consultative Committee that they will send to each tribunal an accredited representative to act as a liaison officer who will obtain and present this information.[64]

The police were responsible for arranging the date of each alien's tribunal and ensuring the relevant persons attended. Males were given highest priority, females second, and the sick and elderly last, though families were seen as a unit.[65] Each tribunal was given discretion on whether to interview every enemy alien. It was hoped that there would be sufficient information provided by refugee organizations, the police, and security forces, that time could be saved on each decision if an interview did not take place. However, guidelines did state that if the recommendation for internment were to be made, then 'the Alien *should* be interviewed'.[66] Monitoring of the enemy alien population by MI5 was rudimentary at best, and until 1935 had focused almost exclusively on those with left-leaning sympathies. It was only from 1935 that pro-Nazis started to be monitored in MI5's card index files.[67] It was with some suspicion then that many anti-Nazi enemy aliens were viewed, because Communists were still considered one of the greatest threats to national security. Italians were also viewed with suspicion, particularly after the Italian invasion of Abyssinia in 1935–36.[68]

One of the biggest problems the tribunals had to overcome was the language barrier. Immigrants who had fled to Britain immediately preceding 1939 had often not planned to leave their home country, and often did not speak much English. In many cases it was necessary to have an interpreter present in order to adequately present the alien's case, which was encouraged by the Home Office, although this was not always possible.[69] In London, for example, it was much easier to procure an interpreter than in it was in other parts of the country due to the many refugee organizations located in Bloomsbury House.[70] The major problem with the tribunals, however, was the lack of consistency in classifying enemy aliens as either 'A' – requiring immediate internment as the alien constituted a threat to national security; 'B' – not to be interned immediately but subject to travel and property restrictions; and 'C' – a genuine refugee who should remain at liberty. There were huge variations in the way judges gave their classifications. In Cheltenham, for example, the judge qualified all of his 'C' classifications, which actually made them count as 'B' and therefore led to multiple cases of internment.[71] In some cases individual family members received different classifications. Hilda Ogbe, for example, was classified 'B' along with her mother, but her brother was counted as a 'C'.[72] Hesitancy, an inability to adequately express oneself in English, left-leaning political beliefs – all of these could sway the verdict of a tribunal away from 'C' towards 'B', and occasionally even 'A'. Many judges were more likely to be swayed to a 'C' classification if an alien could speak fluently in English, a trait more useful to a spy than to a genuine refugee. As one young enemy alien described his tribunal:

> This was … presided over by Judge Thesinger, a reasonably well-regarded judge and brother of a much better known actor. This geriatric gaggle set to in the finest Colonel Blimp tradition: what school had I been to (Cheltenham; very sound), did I play soccer or rugby there (rugby, of course; very good), did I play squash (I did; splendid), was I a member of the Officer Training Corps (forgot it was Cheltenham; silly question, of course, ha-ha) … It went on in that vein until it came to references, and I handed over [General Sir Ernest] Swinton's little note … it was reverently passed from hand to hand … and I was promptly certified as a 'friendly alien'. It should perhaps have occurred to me then that a screening process that would theoretically have allowed me to have long telephone chats with Hitler that very night might create problems at some later stage.[73]

The tribunals tended to keep interviews with enemy aliens short. One enemy alien, a member of the Communist Party and known to the police as an 'agitator', remembered being asked only 'Where is your passport?' at his tribunal. When he replied that he did not know he was classified 'A' and taken into custody.[74]

If an enemy alien was classified as 'B', it meant travel restrictions and certain other prohibitions, such as being forbidden from owning a camera or a set of binoculars. Police permits were required to travel more than a few miles from the alien's home and it was considered 'a slur on one's character' by many refugees not to be given a designation of 'C', which was interpreted as a label of innocence.[75] Regardless of classification, no enemy alien was permitted to live in a 'protected area', designated by the government around coastal areas and other places of military significance.[76] Any enemy alien residing in a protected area had to relocate and register their new address with their nearest police station.

Despite these inconveniences, however, the majority of enemy aliens were still at liberty – a marked difference from the same stage of the First World War. Many, though, believed that it was only a matter of time before they would be rounded up, and they were ultimately proved right. The speed at which France and the Low Countries fell to the Germans in May 1940 caused widespread panic in Britain. Unable to believe that the German Armed Forces were capable of such quick victories, rumours quickly spread that the invading German Army was greatly assisted by Germans living within France, Belgium, Luxembourg, and the Netherlands who formed a Fifth Column. The belief in a Fifth Column gained credence at all levels of British society. Home Intelligence Reports gathered in 1940 between mid-May and mid-July found that throughout the country the fear of an army of Fifth Columnists was prevalent.[77] However, there was still hope that those classified as genuine refugees by a tribunal would remain at liberty and be able to assist in the British war effort.

In the early stages of the war there was no need to bring Italians before the tribunals, as Italy did not declare war against Great Britain until June 1940. However, when Italians resident in Britain became enemy aliens in 1940, the tribunals had all but been wound down and Italians were, therefore, denied the opportunity to present their cases to the authorities. Many of the Italians living in Britain had been resident for a great many years and were business owners, well established in their communities. In June 1940, Italian businesses suffered from vandalism and attacks, and these were particularly violent in Scotland.[78] Many businesses were also located in protected areas, causing huge problems for families forced to relocate further inland.[79] The experiences of the Italian community can therefore be seen as quite distinct from the Germans and Austrians, as the majority had lived in Britain for decades and were not fleeing persecution on the continent. Their loyalty to Britain could not be ascertained without a tribunal, and without this opportunity Italians were considered en masse, as will be further explored in the next chapter.

Anti-alien legislation in America

Like Great Britain, the United States of America also introduced a number of immigration laws in the century before the Second World War. Immigration was actually encouraged by Abraham Lincoln and the Republican Party in the 1860s, who declared that immigration 'should be fostered and encouraged by a liberal and just policy'.[80] However, less than twenty years later America passed a law discriminating against certain types of immigrant because of their race.

Between 1850 and 1882, Chinese immigration to America dramatically increased. Motivated by dire economic conditions at home, Chinese immigrants poured into the United States as news of high wages for labourers reached China during the Californian gold rush. Chinese immigration continued unchecked until calls for exclusion led to a complete halt in 1882.[81] The Chinese were never welcomed as anything more than cheap labour in the United States. Chinese immigrants were specifically denied the opportunity to naturalize in the 1870 Act because of their so-called undesirable qualities.[82] According to Republican senators in the run up to the passage of the 1882 Chinese Exclusion Act, the Chinese were 'Alien in manners, servile in labor, pagan in religion … fundamentally un-American', as well as 'a cancer in [America] that will eat out its life and destroy it'.[83] In the words of the 1882 Act itself, it was 'the opinion of the Government of the United States [that] the coming of Chinese labourers to [America] endanger[ed] the good order' of society.[84] In San Francisco, the Chinese constituted one-quarter of the city's population and yet made up one-third of the workforce.[85] The majority of those who immigrated to America began as contract labourers, in effect a new group of enslaved workers to replace emancipated African Americans. Tensions mounted as workers protested that they were being undercut by the Chinese and therefore it was not a fair job market. As early as 1867, bills aimed at restricting Chinese immigration were presented to the legislature.[86] In 1879, Congress passed the Fifteen Passenger Bill, designed to prevent ships carrying more than fifteen Chinese passengers from entering the United States. Despite the fact that the Fifteen Passenger Bill went on to be vetoed by the president, its passage was significant as the 'first immigration restriction law aimed at a particular nationality ever drafted, debated, and passed by Congress'.[87] It was to come as no surprise then that only three years later the Chinese Exclusion Act was approved by the House of Representatives by a large majority.[88] The significance of the 1882 Chinese Exclusion Act cannot be underestimated. For the first time in American history a federal law had been passed 'banning a group of immigrants solely on the basis of race or nationality'.[89] Once the Chinese Exclusion Act had been placed on the statute books there was a precedent for further exclusionist immigration law with a racial bias. The Act made 'discrimination more acceptable, more apparent, and more prevalent throughout the nation. All sections of the country, East and West, North and South, united in Congress to promote discrimination and legitimize segregation openly'.[90] The Chinese Exclusion Act prevented any further Chinese immigration with the exception of a very small number of teachers, students, and merchants.[91] The door had been closed for the Chinese, and it was only a matter of time before more exclusionist laws aimed at other races were passed.

The next group to be targeted by the American legislature were the Japanese. During the 1880s, a number of Japanese travelled to Hawaii to work on the plantations. When Hawaii was annexed by the United States in 1898, Japanese immigrants were then able to travel freely to mainland America. Once there, the Japanese toiled as farm labourers until they could work themselves up to owning or leasing their own tract of land. The industriousness of the Japanese community meant that even though they usually farmed poor pieces of agricultural land, they managed to produce bumper levels of crops. American farmers resented the way Japanese farmers maximized the yields on their land, and this antagonism led to calls for restriction on Japanese immigration on the West Coast. The way America viewed Japan also began to change at this time, especially after Japan's victories over China in 1895 and Russia in 1905. America began to view exclusion as a way of controlling potential enemies, and as Japan increased in military strength, an agreement was struck in order to prevent unskilled workers being granted passports by the Japanese government.[92] The so-called 1907 Gentlemen's Agreement was the first of several anti-Japanese laws passed, including the 1913 Alien Land Law, which prevented any Japanese individual from owning land in California, and a 1915 law, which made even the leasing of land by Japanese illegal.[93]

It was not only the Chinese and Japanese to which America objected as immigrants at this time. America sought to weed out those considered 'undesirable', and a number of laws were passed to this effect. In 1891 an Act was passed denying entry to 'paupers, polygamists, and persons suffering from loathsome and contagious diseases'; in 1903, epileptics, prostitutes, professional beggars, and anarchists were added to the list of those to be kept out.[94] In 1917, chronic alcoholics, vagrants, 'persons of constitutional psychopathic inferiority', and those convicted of a crime involving 'moral turpitude' found themselves excluded.[95] However, despite the plethora of categories for exclusion, there was no corresponding increase in the levels of those denied permission to land.[96] However, three months after the passage of the 1917 Act, all aliens over the age of sixteen who could not read a short paragraph in English or another language or dialect, were denied entry to the United State unless the immediate relative of someone already resident in America, though it is important to note that there was an exemption for those that could prove they were fleeing religious persecution.[97] The 1917 Immigration Act also created the Asia-Pacific Triangle – no longer was immigration banned just from China and Japan, but also from India.[98] Until 1934, the only Asians allowed into the United States were Filipinos, as the Philippines were American territory until the Philippine Independence Act.[99]

Even though the examination of aliens entering the United States had been made more thorough and rigorous, those calling for restriction were still not satisfied. Four years after the Asiatic Barred Zone was created, the beginnings of what was to become known as the 'Quota System' or 'National Origins' Act was introduced. That such an Act came about was the result of a great wave of anti-alien hysteria that swept the nation. In 1920, Italian miners were beaten, stoned, and had their property razed to the ground in southern Illinois.[100] In the same year Henry Ford launched an anti-Jewish campaign in the Midwest.[101] With an economic depression corresponding with an increase in immigration at the beginning of the 1920s, the stage was set for further anti-alien legislation.[102] Much was also written at the time arguing that if 'yellow' or 'brown' races mixed with the 'Nordic' races, a mongrel race would be created.[103] In 1924, the quota system was officially accepted before coming into full practice in 1929. The generally accepted belief at the time was that there had been a golden era of immigration, pre-1880, where families from Northern and Western Europe had come to America, established themselves, assimilated well, dispersed themselves around the country, and practised a variety of trades including farming. Unfortunately, so the belief went, these immigrants had been replaced sometime in the 1880s and 1890s with Southern and Eastern European males who were transient, unskilled labourers, who congregated on the East Coast and did not assimilate.[104] The desire was for a return to an era where the immigrants were 'desirable', assimilable, and fitted more easily with the American ideal. The 1924 Act was, therefore, based on the 1890 census, as the numbers in this group were more favourable to old immigrant groups from northern and western Europe, and would also 'promote racial harmony' as it constituted the countries from which the colonists and other early settlers had originated.[105] The use of the 1890 census naturally led to many nations expressing dissatisfaction at their quota allocations. Despite the fact that German, Scandinavian, and Irish immigration had, during the 1920s, outnumbered the British by almost three to one, Great Britain was given a quota larger than the totals of all other countries in northwest Europe combined.[106] In order to protect the quota system, visas started to be issued abroad, by consular officials, meaning that immigrants could not board a ship unless already in possession of a visa.[107] No more than 10 per cent of each nationality's quota of visas were to be granted in any calendar month, and couples married 'by reason of a proxy or picture marriage' – a specifically Japanese practice – were denied entry.[108] By the 1930s, an era of American history had come to an end: 'After three centuries of free immigration America all but completely shut her doors on newcomers. The Statue of Liberty would still stand in New York harbour, but the verses on its base would henceforth be but a tribute to a vanished ideal.'[109]

The years preceding internment

Despite restrictions on immigration, anti-alien feeling still ran high. Asians may have been prevented from entering the United States by law, but this did not mean that Americans were happy to coexist with Asians already in the country. To focus on relations between Caucasians and the Japanese specifically, there was no distinction so far as the majority of the population was concerned between the Issei immigrants and their Nisei children who were American citizens. As citizens, it might have been hoped that they would enjoy the same opportunities as their Caucasian neighbours, but this was far from reality. As Yoshiko Uchida wrote in her moving memoir of being a Japanese American in California before the war and of her subsequent internment:

> There was nothing I could do about being left out, but I could take precautions to prevent being hurt in other ways. When I had outgrown my father's home haircuts and wanted to go to a beauty parlor, I telephoned first to ask if they would take me.
>
> 'Do you cut Japanese hair?'
> 'Can we come swim in the pool? We're Japanese.'
> 'Will you rent us a house? Will the neighbours object?'
> These were the kinds of questions we asked in order to avoid embarrassment and humiliation. We avoided the better shops and restaurants where we knew we would not be welcome. Once during my college years, when friends from Los Angeles came to visit, we decided to go dancing, as we occasionally did at the Los Angeles Palladium. But when we went to a ballroom in Oakland, we were turned away by the woman at the box office who simply said, 'We don't think you people would like the kind of dancing we do here.'[110]

The Japanese understood their position in what was still a very much racially segregated society. While racial discrimination and segregation was most prevalent in the South, it was not limited solely to that region. The Supreme Court still upheld the notion that the 'constitutional promise of equal protection of the law for all Americans regardless of race, creed or color' required 'only that the states or the federal government provide equal though segregated facilities for the separate races'. In the South, African Americans were educated in segregated schools, worked in segregated jobs, and lived in segregated areas. Jim Crow laws meant that African Americans were effectively prevented from voting and Southern customs meant that the 'color line' was observed almost everywhere.[111] Even baseball teams were segregated, and when war was declared in 1941, African American soldiers were forced to serve in separate units from Caucasian soldiers. The idea of discrimination based solely on one's skin colour was deeply entrenched in the American psyche.

Underlying the American fear of the Japanese was their fear of the so-called Yellow Peril. Americans were fearful of those who looked different and whom they could not understand. Films such as *Patria* and *Shadows of the West*, produced around 1917, portrayed Japanese immigrants as 'sneaky, treacherous agents of a militaristic Japan seeking to control the West Coast'.[112] As a result of such prejudice and the fact that Issei were unable to naturalize, the Japanese found it necessary to create their own community organizations in order to form support networks. Some of these were religious organizations, such as Buddhist or Christian churches, and others were social or political groups. Wishing their children to know something of their parents' homeland, Nisei children were encouraged to attend Japanese school where they were taught about Japanese language and culture. Some Issei went further and sent their children to Japan for periods of education, and such children were known as Kibei. While to Caucasians the Japanese appeared as one unified group, within the Japanese community there were three distinct identities. The Issei were living by Japanese standards and mores, attempting to forge the best lives possible for them and their families; the Kibei were in a unique position halfway between the Issei and Nisei in their outlook, but fitted fully into neither group; and the Nisei wanted to assimilate into American society as much as possible. With the desire to be accepted by the country where they had grown up and of which they were citizens, the Nisei established their own organizations after the First World War: the American Loyalty League in San Francisco and the Progressive Citizens' League in Seattle. These two organizations then merged into the Japanese American Citizens League (JACL). As is clear from the titles of the organizations, Nisei felt a need to identify themselves with American culture and emphasize their American citizenship.

The types of jobs available to the Issei were limited, given the anti-alien feeling towards Asian immigrants. Issei were originally manual labourers for railroads, lumber companies, canneries, mines, or in agriculture. Initially, the Issei were happy to work for less money than their non-Japanese co-workers, which led to complaints, particularly from the Caucasian labour force. As time progressed, the Issei were able to work their way up to renting agricultural land, and eventually owned land by registering it in the name of their Nisei children. The Issei were highly skilled in intensive farming and were soon producing much more profitable yields than their Californian counterparts, another factor that increased anti-alien antagonism. In 1917, for example, among Californian farmers the average production per acre was less than $42, whereas for the average Issei farmer it was $141. Their productivity was not just limited to California – by 1940 the Issei and Nisei were growing an estimated $2.7 million worth of produce on the West Coast.[113] The fact that the Nikkei often produced more than their Caucasian neighbours, despite the fact that the land leased to them was of a very poor standard, led to further increases in anti-Japanese sentiment on the West Coast. Japanese immigrants did not solely work in agriculture though; many were shopkeepers, although Japanese businesses were more often patronized by the Nikkei, rather than by Caucasians. Where the Japanese really struggled to enter employment was in the professions. This was despite the fact that the Nisei consistently achieved the highest marks in their classes. As one Nisei student recalled when he was trying to apply for the same college courses to which his Caucasian friends were applying:

> The teacher told me outright in a very nice way that there was not much of a chance for an Oriental to get a job in these fields [such as engineering or medicine] ... I began to see that they took us a little differently and we were not quite American in their eyes in spite of things they taught us in the classes about equality and so forth.[114]

Some Nisei were able to qualify as teachers but were often unable to obtain a teaching position, as Caucasian schools only wanted Caucasian teachers. The Nisei grew increasingly frustrated at the fact that even though many of them had a college education they were still in practice barred from entering white-collar professions. By 1940, only 960 persons of Japanese ancestry in California were in white-collar professional roles, and of those the majority were employed in the federal civil service.[115] Perhaps the dichotomy of the Nisei situation is best summed up by a Nisei herself:

> We Nisei were, in effect, rejected as inferior Americans by our own country and rejected as inferior by the country of our parents as well. We were neither totally American nor totally Japanese, but a unique fusion of the two. Small wonder that many of us felt insecure and ambivalent and retreated into our own special subculture where we were fully accepted.[116]

Ironically, it was the industrious ethic of the Japanese community that antagonized the West Coast Caucasians to such an extent where they believed more was needed to be done to prevent those of Japanese ancestry from owning and farming land, or having any influence outside the Japanese community. The Caucasian community felt threatened and were prepared to go to any lengths to solve the perceived 'Japanese problem'.

An innate mistrust of the Japanese was also common among the American elite in the early years of the twentieth century. Franklin Delano Roosevelt, along with many of his contemporaries, developed a wariness towards Japan in the decades preceding his presidency. This feeling of trepidation was caused by the realization that Japan had the potential to become a serious rival to America in terms of both economic and military strength.[117] Restrictions on Japanese immigration were seen to be fair as the Japanese 'were known to have strong taboos against inter-marriage and did not wish their distinct cultures to be polluted by racial mixing'.[118] Roosevelt was not considered to be extreme in his views towards the Japanese, and indeed respected many Japanese individuals. However, he also believed that 'people of Japanese ancestry remained innately Japanese no matter where they lived – even if they were born and raised entirely in the United States, spoke only English, and absorbed American customs', a belief that was to drastically shape his handling of Japanese and Japanese Americans during the Second World War.[119]

Pearl Harbor

As in Britain, there was some monitoring of potentially hostile individuals under-taken in the years preceding the war by the Federal Bureau of Investigation (FBI) as America had no desire to become embroiled in a European conflict, and, like Britain, believed the 'Red Terror' was a greater threat than the Far Right. The Department of Justice (DoJ) and FBI monitored enemy aliens in the United States of America from the outbreak of war in Europe in 1939, and lists were compiled of those with links to potentially hostile governments. In the autumn of 1941, the monitoring of the Japanese community was given greater impor-tance by the FBI when it became clear the Japanese government was using its ambassadors to transmit data concerning the American Armed Forces. The FBI reassured the president that lists had already been prepared documenting those believed to be a security threat in time of conflict, but even so Roosevelt com-missioned a highly classified intelligence report to discover where the loyalties of the Nisei would lie were America and Japan to go to war. The author of that report, Curtis B. Munson, concluded,

The Issei ... is considerably weakened in their loyalty to Japan by the fact that they have chosen to make this their home and have brought their children here ... Many would take out American citizenship if allowed to do so ... the Nisei ... are universally estimated from 90 to 98% loyal to the United States if the Japanese educated element of the Kibei is excluded.[120]

Indeed, this had long been the conclusion of the FBI, tasked with monitoring the Japanese population for several years. Despite the overwhelming consensus of the intelligence services, the Munson Report was not made known outside the highest circles of the State, War, and Navy departments until 1946, and was not referred to at all after the attack on Pearl Harbor. Indeed, to many in the higher echelons of the military and government, the fact that no evidence of espionage or sabotage had been found in the Japanese population was seen to be proof that it was guaranteed to happen.[121]

At dawn on 7 December 1941, Japan launched a surprise attack on the American naval base and Army airfields at Pearl Harbor, Hawaii. After only a few hours of bombing, over 3,500 Americans lay dead or wounded, 6 battleships had sunk or run aground, and 149 American airplanes had been destroyed. By contrast, Japan lost a mere 29 planes with their pilots.[122] On the same day as the Pearl Harbor attack, Japan also struck the Malay Peninsula, Hong Kong, Wake Island, Midway Island, as well as the Philippines, where many more American aircraft were destroyed.[123] The most senior commanders in the Armed Forces had believed that the Japanese Army, Navy, and Air Force were vastly inferior to their American contemporaries and therefore an attack on US soil was considered impossible.[124] As historian Greg Robinson has noted: 'The Japanese bombing of Pearl Harbor did more than sink ships and kill soldiers; it left a deep wound in the American psyche. The surprise attack provoked nationwide anger and a desire for revenge against Japan which far surpassed American bitterness against Germany or Italy.'[125]

Pearl Harbor triggered the first arrests, and within forty-eight hours several thousand persons were apprehended by the FBI.[126] The FBI and the Office of Naval Intelligence (ONI) had created what became known as the 'ABC list' and this was the basis for the arrests. Enemy aliens were categorized into 'A' or those who were considered immediately dangerous; 'B' or potentially dangerous; and 'C' or those merely suspected of entertaining pro-Japanese views. Unlike the tribunal system in Britain, no attempt was made to interview the enemy aliens before they were assigned a category as it was feared it would take too long for the Army to accomplish this.[127] Collaboration was sought from the JACL when forming the ABC list. The JACL wanted to demonstrate loyalty to the American cause, hence the willingness to cooperate with the intelligence agencies. However, this 'fatally compromised' the JACL's position in the community during the war.[128] The idea that tribunals would take too long to accomplish for the Nikkei was proved nonsense when the Attorney General was able to deem 600,000 Italians, a much larger number than the Nikkei population, as non-threatening over a period of ten months.[129]

Arrests took place based on the ABC lists on both the East and West Coasts. The primary targets of the round up on the East Coast were Germans, while on the West Coast they were males of Japanese ancestry who were prominent in the Japanese community. Law enforcement officials investigated all enemy aliens, raided houses for contraband, and made arrests of those considered 'suspicious'.[130] The FBI based its decisions to arrest on which organizations it felt were pro-German, pro-Italian, or pro-Japanese. As early as October 1941, before Japan had even joined the conflict, FBI agents visited Little Tokyo in Los Angeles to question members of the Japanese community and seize documents.[131] However, despite these interviews and having Japanese documents in their possession, the FBI's information was not always accurate and, therefore, many organizations which served purely a social networking need were targeted. This led to arrests taking place because

> some were members of the so-called 'bad societies' which in reality were not – these memberships may be attributed to forced social obligations, prominence in that certain locality for the solicitation of funds, or the use of their names as convenience on the basis of these organizations without consent of the individual–a common procedure or method used by many organizations in the solicitation of funds.[132]

Leaders of Buddhist temples, Japanese schoolteachers, and leaders in the business community were popular targets for the FBI.[133] In the German community the majority of those arrested had actually fought for the German army against America during the First World War, unlike the Japanese, some of whom had fought *for* America during World War One.[134]

Executive Order 9066

Despite the belief that Japanese Americans were as Japanese as their parents, the fact that they were also American citizens could not be denied. The Nisei should, theoretically, have been safe during wartime because their right to freedom was guaranteed by the constitution. In order for any type of movement to be made against them an executive order had to be signed by the president authorizing a temporary loophole in constitutional rights. Any order that allowed for the possibility of detaining American citizens would have provoked national outrage, so the need to avoid in-depth Congressional or Senate debates was paramount. The fact that America was engaged in a global conflict made it easy to paint Executive Order 9066 in a patriotic light, protecting the nation's security. When the White House asked Congress to legislate that any violation of an order given by a military commander under Executive Order 9066 would be a federal offence, they did so, almost without question, seemingly oblivious to the fact that such legislation would restrict the rights of American citizens.[135] Executive Order 9066 was passed 19 February 1942, and gave Secretary of War Henry Stimson the authority to designate Military Areas from which commanders could exclude anyone. As a result of these powers, in March 1942 the West Coast was divided into two Military Areas.[136] Although the Japanese had not been excluded from living in these areas, they were encouraged to move, if possible, and if they did not move they were subject to certain restrictions. All enemy aliens were placed under curfew in Military Area No. 1. German and Italian aliens, as well as those of Japanese ancestry, who resided within the area had limits placed on their movements and were banned from possessing certain items from March 1942.[137]

While a curfew was not unusual for individuals with citizenship of a hostile nation, it was remarkable that it was also instituted for the Nisei. Including the Nisei in the category of American 'enemies' was a popular refrain in the media of the time. As one *Los Angeles Times* editorial stated: 'A viper is nonetheless a viper wherever the eggs are hatched – so a Japanese American, born of Japanese parents – grows up to be a Japanese, not an American.'[138] For the Nisei, the fact that none of their Caucasian friends with American citizenship were expected to adhere to a curfew led to several test cases being brought by Nisei individuals against the unconstitutionality of the order. Minoru Yasui, a member of the Oregon bar and a reserve officer in the US Army who worked for the Consulate General of Japan in Chicago, resigned his job at the outbreak of war and attempted to enlist in the Army. Refused acceptance into the US Military he decided to take a stand and was arrested for a curfew violation. Yasui used his legal training to argue that the curfew breached the Constitution when applied to American citizens. While the district judge in the case agreed with Yasui, he was able to get around ruling on the constitutionality by claiming that Yasui's work for the Consulate made Yasui an enemy alien.[139] Although Yasui's citizenship was restored a year later by the Supreme Court, the conviction regarding breach of curfew was upheld. In the spring of 1942 'not even the courts of the

United States were places of calm and dispassionate justice.[140] Remarkably, in the case of Yasui, and the cases of Hirabayashi, Korematsu, and Endo that shall be discussed in the next chapter, there was a marked reluctance of the American Civil Liberties Union (ACLU) to get involved. Despite the ACLU claiming to uphold the rights of racial and political minorities, it had little interest in the legality of how Japanese Americans were treated.[141]

Conclusion

In both Britain and the United States, anti-alien legislation in the century preceding the Second World War framed the way that enemy aliens were viewed at the outbreak of hostilities. From the nineteenth century into the early years of the twentieth century, both Britain and America attempted to impose some form of control over immigration. The introduction of a literacy test in both countries, for example, demonstrated the desire to only allow those with at least a rudimentary education the right to remain. However, the language did not need to be English – any language, provided the aliens could read and write a short paragraph, was acceptable. This did not mean that those speaking a foreign language were not still viewed as a threat. Fear of the 'other', particularly those whose skin was not white, was particularly pervasive during the nineteenth and early twentieth centuries.

The 1905 Aliens Act in Britain was aimed solely at Eastern Europeans, the majority of whom were Jews fleeing persecution. In America, the 1882 Chinese Exclusion Act and the 1907 Gentleman's Agreement explicitly targeted at the Chinese and Japanese respectively. Nor was the 1917 creation of the Asiatic Barred Zone particularly subtle in its wording. However, despite this legislation, Asian immigrants were still often viewed and treated better than African Americans. As one Japanese American explained, 'We were discriminated on the [West] Coast but at least we were able to sit in a bus wherever we felt like sitting. Our discrimination was very different, not as intense as [the discrimination against African Americans] was.'[142] Asian immigrants suffered extensive discrimination, and yet they were able to differentiate between their treatment and the treatment of other racial groups. Discrimination towards immigrants was prevalent in both societies– perhaps more explicitly in the United States, but it was also present in Great Britain. One notable difference between Britain and America, however, was the way that immigrants from Europe were viewed in the years preceding the Second World War. Britain was willing to receive a certain number of refugees, although there was a backlash against the immigration of certain groups from a number of professions, and widespread unease in much of the general public. America, by contrast, was completely inflexible in its approach. As the US Department of State made clear, 'The fact that an alien may be in danger of going to prison or a concentration camp in his country or that he may be threatened with danger is a matter not covered by our immigration laws and the consul cannot consider this as giving any preferential treatment.'[143] The fact that tens of thousands of European refugees were granted at least temporary leave to remain in Britain showed some latitude towards a persecuted people. This rather more generous approach was also in evidence by the institution of a tribunal system to classify enemy aliens on the outbreak of war. When America was shocked into the conflict two years later, it followed suit with the introduction of tribunals, but only selectively – tribunals were suitable for those of European ancestry, but not for those of Japanese ancestry. While in the early months of the war in each respective country enemy aliens were, for the most part, able to retain their liberty with certain prohibitions on areas in which they could reside, how far they could travel, and what they could own, the question remained as to how long such liberties would last. The clues regarding what might happen next were evident in a century's worth of legislature and societal prejudice.

Life in the Camps

Arrest and transit camps in Britain

When Winston Churchill famously gave the order to 'Collar the Lot' in June 1940, internment had already begun. Germans and Austrians had already been arrested due to Fifth Column fears and a belief that it was better to be safe than sorry, and from June, Italians were added to that number. However, formal arrangements had not yet been finalized regarding the long-term housing for several thousand internees, nor was there an obvious timescale. During the First World War, use had been made of the Isle of Man, and this seemed the logical choice again. However, acquisition of properties on the Isle of Man would take time, so other locations were sought on an interim basis. The first step, however, was to apprehend thousands of male enemy aliens across the country, as well as 4,000 female enemy aliens and some of their children. Apprehension took place at either the enemy alien's home or their place of employment, and very little accurate information was given to those who were detained. The procedure was much the same for the Italians when Italy declared war on Great Britain, the main difference being that there was no attempt to hold tribunals to classify Italian nationals. This happened despite the fact that a Home Office report noted that in general 'practically all captured Italian seamen are keen Fascists, whereas the bulk of the Italian civilian internees were anti-Fascist'.[1] The experience of Italians was therefore quite different in many ways from the experience of Germans and Austrians.[2] While the majority of the internees were of German, Austrian, or Italian descent, they were not the only nationalities targeted; after the attack on Pearl Harbor a small number of Japanese men were also interned. Again, not given the opportunity to attend tribunals, the men arrested were 'only officials, journalists, seamen and persons against whom MI5 have a case', as well as a large contingent of seamen.[3]

The arrests more often than not were conducted in the early hours of the morning.[4] Lucky were the ones who had a premonition that their incarceration might not be as short as the arresting policemen and women suggested on the rare occasions where such comments were made. Max-Otto Ludwig Loewenstein, later known as Mark Lynton, was fortunate in that he packed an overnight case with pyjamas, shirts, and some toiletries when he was asked to accompany plain-clothes officers to the station in Cambridge. As he remembered, 'Nothing that had been said prompted me to do so, and I do not know to this day why I did; just as well, though, since I was not to return to Cambridge or to any of my belongings for nine months.'[5] Eugen Stern, an Austrian refugee, wrote, 'Had I known how everything would turn out, I would have brought a bigger suitcase with all the necessary things.'[6] Some were fortunate and given plenty of time to pack their belongings, such as the Dalheim family, a mother and four children who were awoken at 7 o'clock on a May morning in 1940. While the family packed their cases, a policeman searched the father's office. He was rewarded for his efforts with two of the girls offering him a fake chocolate in the hope that he might break his teeth by biting it.[7] The majority of internees who later recalled their experiences could not recollect much or any information being given regarding the likely duration or location of their stay. This made the arrests all the more traumatic for family members who did not know when they would be reunited. Renate Steinert, six years of age at the time of her father's arrest, remembered locking herself in the bathroom when the detectives came to take her father.

> I was asked to come out, and I kissed him goodbye, which was quite dreadful, quite dreadful. I was crying, and my mother was crying, my father was struggling not to cry, and then he was marched off, we didn't know where. The detectives didn't know. They were detectives from Harrow Road police station, what could they know? They wouldn't have known a real enemy alien at fifty paces. So my mother and I were left alone, and there followed weeks of absolute misery, while my mother worried desperately about where my father was. We could get no news.[8]

Some internees were apprehended by kindly policemen and women who did everything in their power to make the process as painless as possible, whereas others were detained by individuals who were ignorant of the identities of those they were arresting, believing the enemy aliens to be foreign spies.

After arrest an internee would first be taken to the local police station. For how long the internee remained there varied from case to case. Fred Uhlman found the policeman in temporary charge of his incarceration an affable fellow who offered to purchase anything Uhlman might need. Fred gave him some money and the policeman returned with some fruit and chocolate.[9] For most internees, no food would be provided from the point of their arrest, early in the morning, to their arrival at a temporary camp late that night. Transit camps came in a number of guises. Anything from vacant land where tents and barbed wire could be erected hastily, to derelict mills, housing estates, and even prisons were utilized in the temporary housing of the interned. For those women unfortunate enough to be interned early on in the process, their home was often Holloway Prison. Austrian writer Elisabeth von Janstein, one of the earliest female internees, remembered the humiliation of the admission procedure, the discomfort of the accommodation, and the fear and uncertainty of the situation.[10] Mothers were separated from their children as the governor deemed it cruel to introduce children to a prison environment.[11] Once the Rushen internment camp had been established on the Isle of Man, however, women and children were more likely to be taken to a transit camp en route to Liverpool, from where they would be shipped to the Isle of Man at the earliest possible opportunity. When the Dalheims were arrested, for instance, they were taken to a school in Bradford where they were provided with food and bedding for the night, before proceeding to Liverpool the following day.[12] Another internee recalled being taken to a newly built but unopened hospital where mattresses that were provided for the women and children stuck to the newly varnished floor.[13] After the immediate panic of the initial round up was over, attempts were made to keep families together and avoid painful separations. The distress of the initial separations was worsened by the experiences that many refugees had fleeing Germany and Austria, and the fear that the same thing could happen again.

For the men who were interned, the accommodation was much more of a mixed bag. One of the first established transit camps was at the Butlins holiday camp at Clacton. Lou Baruch, arrested in the initial round up of enemy aliens, remembers being transported on

> a very pleasant journey with our soldier companions ... we got to Liverpool Street station. The guards were hungry and thirsty and so were we. All our, and their, luggage was piled up as well as their rifles. We sat on the luggage and they asked us, the Category 'A' prisoners to look after their equipment including the arms, whilst they came back with something to eat. Of course we agreed.[14]

Those from the first wave of arrests found themselves at a Warners vacation camp in Seaton. Leo Baruch remembered the huts were unbearably cold and he had 'never been so hungry in [his] life'.[15] As internment progressed and the number of arrests increased, many others were taken to Kempton Park race course in Surrey where the grandstand was used for accommodation.[16] Countless other buildings such as schools and barracks were used as temporary housing.[17] In one instance even the winter quarters of a circus was used.[18] However, the most notorious of transit camps was Warth Mill, near Bury, Manchester, more aptly termed 'Wrath Mill' by its reluctant inhabitants.[19] Warth Mill was a rat-infested former cotton mill that had stood derelict for some years prior to the outbreak of the Second World War.[20] As one internee remembered:

> The rooms were dark, even in those sunny days of July, the floors soaked with the oil which for years had dripped from the looms, the staircases with an open lift shaft were very narrow, the corridors even narrower and damp. In case a fire was started by an incendiary bomb not a single man would have escaped, and had a person forced his way into the open air, the space between the walls and the barbed wire would have been far too small. The hygienic accommodation was of a highly objectionable primitiveness: on the premises were – for about 2000 people – sixty W.Cs – an euphemism for there were just buckets spreading a terrific stench and no water-flushing system.[21]

Even the infirmary failed to offer much more protection than the standard accommodation, being 'a room on the first floor, which looked a bit cleaner but had almost no windows, and leaks in the roof'.[22] From the vantage point of the infirmary, an internee named Lachs took the opportunity to assess the types of 'dangerous' aliens that had been rounded up for internment. He described

> an idiot of 40 years, who could hardly read and write who was not able to do anything for himself and had to be cared for. There was a young boy of 17 who suffered from a mental illness. There was a man with tuberculosis of the legs, one with a heavy heart disease, several with diabetes, one young man had still to suffer from the consequences of injections which he had got against diptheria so that he could hardly move. There was a young technician, a doctor of tech. science, who was so severely injured when shot down during his services with the Republicans in Spain as pilot, that it took two years to make him fit for life again … He was brought to Warth Mill from a South East camp, and the long transport in the hot train (they were not allowed to open the windows, and had very little to eat) affected him so much, that he suddenly collapsed, and fell on his head, which caused a severe concussion of the brain, affecting his so painfully regained health. Every night there were brought old people up who could not stand any more the conditions in the common rooms.[23]

The conditions at Warth Mills made the largest of all transit camps, an unfinished housing estate near Liverpool called Huyton, seem luxurious by comparison. Given its proximity to the Liverpool docks, Huyton was the place from which a great number of male internees left to embark on their journey to more permanent camps on the Isle of Man. Much like the other temporary camps, there were not enough rooms to sleep all those interned there and so tents were erected in the gardens. Those in the tents lacked washing facilities and those in the houses were often overcrowded.[24] The biggest problem for those interned at Huyton was inactivity and restlessness.[25] For a very small number of internees, Huyton was the only camp they knew as they were released within weeks of arrest and before they could be transported to Douglas.[26]

The Isle of Man

For the majority of those interned, the Isle of Man was their final destination until release. The first camp created was Mooragh, in the north of the island in the town of Ramsey. Boarding-house owners were given no more than seven days' notice to vacate their properties, and instructed to leave all 'furniture, bedding, linen, cutlery, crockery and utensils in the house', though they were allowed to remove some personal effects.[27] Valuations were carried out by government officials so that a rent could be agreed for the items left in the house, as well as the rental of hot and cold water.[28] This caused much hardship for the majority of boarding-house owners, forced to rent alternative accommodation and deprived of their regular income. The situation was significantly less painful for those in the women's camp in Port Erin and Port St. Mary in the south of the island. Those owners were able to remain in their houses and received the women and children as guests paid for by the Manx government.[29] The use of boarding houses guaranteed that the quality of accommodation available to the internees was of a much higher standard than the previous locations where the internees had been accommodated. Houses had bathrooms and many rooms had their own washbasins.[30] Every man or woman had a proper mattress on which to sleep, even if they initially had to share it with a stranger.[31] The random billeting sometimes resulted in Jewish refugees being forced to share with pro-Nazis, but this was the exception rather than the rule.[32] While the mattresses were appreciated, the blankets were not, as they were usually filthy and caused many a case of eczema when they came into contact with the skin.[33] Further into internment, as people were moved between camps, complaints were made about the fact that vacated houses had been stripped of all things useful by the time of their next occupation, leaving 'dilapidated, dirty, drafty and cold, stripped of all furnishings, old boarding houses'.[34] This was particularly hard for those moved from camps that closed as their population dwindled, such as the inmates of Central Camp who found themselves transferred to Onchan. As the population decreased, most of the internees had single rooms in Central Camp, but found themselves forced back into sharing in 'filthy and poorly equipped' houses as 'everything that could be removed had been', with limited washing facilities. It was at times like these that internees 'really felt like prisoners'.[35] Perhaps the greatest improvement to morale was the fact that cooking was done in the kitchen of each house and therefore internees once again had some control over their diet. This was of particular significance to the Orthodox Jews, who had struggled to maintain a kosher diet since their arrest, though some Jews had found that it was possible to get better food in the transit camps if they professed Orthodoxy.[36] Results of this freedom to cook varied greatly, as 'much depend[ed] upon the cleverness of the cook what [was] made of [the] provisions'.[37] In general, the food available on the Isle of Man was better than what could be found on the mainland, but internees could still find themselves going hungry on the rations with which they were provided. When canteens came into existence, internees with money were able to buy snacks or fruit to alleviate hunger and improve their diet.[38] Requests for food parcels were also commonplace, especially for cakes and cured sausages.[39] When people complained about the perceived 'superior' quality of the food in the camps, a local vicar explained that a large number of cooks had been interned and therefore were better prepared for dealing with rations than the general population.[40] Certainly, the camp cafes that sprang up and served selections of Viennese pastries and cakes were well received by both the internees and their guards.[41]

The British government did not wish the internment camps to be run as prison camps, but rather wanted to give the internees some control over their daily activities and minimal responsibilities. The camps were managed by Camp Commandants, and their outlook on the refugee situation informed the general atmosphere of the camp. The overall commander of the Isle of Man camps in 1940, Lieutenant-Colonel S. W. Slatter, penned the following notice that was displayed for all new arrivals to the camps to read in both English and German:

> It is my wish that every man who enters internment on this Island shall be assured that nothing avoidable will be done that might add to his discomfort or unhappiness. It must be obvious to you all that uniform code of discipline is essential if a community of men are to live together successfully. That code will

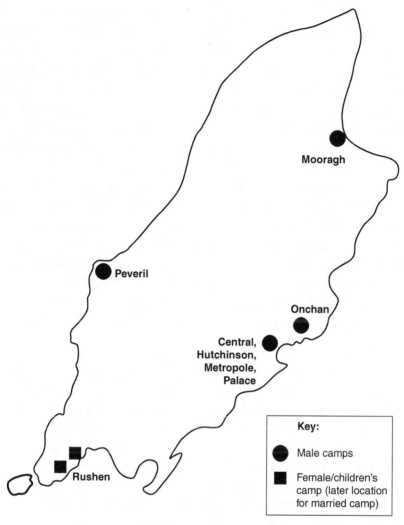

Figure 2.1 Location of internment camps on the Isle of Man.

be mine and will be obeyed. There is, however, a good reason for every order, and there will be no aggression. The Officers and troops who are given charge of you are men of understanding … My duty is concerned with your security and discipline, but my interest goes beyond this. With the help of my Camp Commanders and their Staffs I wish every permissible measure to be taken that can relieve your internment of its irksomeness. This can only be done with your own co-operation – your own goodwill and orderly conduct … There are amongst you men of widely divergent political views and religious beliefs. You will neither find favour nor encounter prejudice from us on this account.[42]

Most of the Camp Commandants got along well with their charges and did everything in their power to assist the internees. The most notable exception to this was Dame Joanna Cruickshank. One internee described her encounter with Dame Joanna early on in internment: 'I drew up a long list and took them to the camp authorities. And I was apparently unlucky because the lady to whom I started to read my queries became very irate and banged the table and said: "Stop telling us what we ought to do."'[43] Dame Joanna continued to cause problems for the female internees until her replacement, Detective Inspector Cyril Cuthbert, was appointed at the end of May 1941.

The male camps soon instituted a system pioneered at Huyton. Each house elected a 'house father' who reported to the 'street father', who in turn reported to the 'camp father', who relayed information to the Commandant. The 'house fathers' were chosen by the internees themselves, but the 'street' and 'camp fathers', while selected by the internees, had to be approved by the Commandant. The 'camp father' was the representative of all those interned and received his information from the 'street fathers', who met regularly with the 'house fathers'.[44] The onerous task of the 'camp father' was described by one such individual as follows:

> The work of the Camp-Father is neither easy nor enjoyable. He has to deal with men who feel themselves treated unjustly and whose nerves are not at their best. Nor are the inmates of the Camp a homogenous body. Amongst them are men of different classes, creeds, professions and opinions, not to mention the extreme individualists … Even a god would not be able to conform to all the wishes of all these men. The Camp-father whoever he may be can only try to make the best of his job and try to facilitate and ameliorate the life of his co-internees, the Camp-father working together with the Housefathers and departmental managers.[45]

It was the responsibility of the 'house father' to make sure the general duties for the house were assigned to the men living there, and also to ensure attendance at roll call.[46] 'Street fathers' were responsible for forwarding grievances and requests to the 'camp father' and ensuring the houses on their street were kept in order. The men therefore took very little time to organize themselves into working units. The female internees, by contrast, were not given the same level of autonomy as the men. Dame Joanna, Commandant of Rushen, 'kept the reins firmly in her own hands'.[47] Unlike the male camps, women were placed into boarding houses where the landlords and ladies were still residing, and therefore had a structure from the very beginning, though rotas were drawn up in the women's camp for basic chores such as cleaning, cooking, and washing.[48]

The women's camp also had the additional complication of family arrangements for those women interned with their children.

Arrangements were made in camps early on for the practise of religion. Reverend Harry Johnson, for example, organized services and midweek discussion groups for the women interned at Rushen Camp, as well as scripture classes for the children.[49] Visits were made to the camps regularly by men of the cloth to check on the spiritual welfare of the internees.[50] Bible classes were held at many of the camps, often with assistance from the reverend in charge of the diocese under which the boundaries of the camp fell.[51] Commandants were reminded to be respectful of religious observances and inspections were not to be conducted on Saturdays or Sundays in order to allow religious observances.[52] In general, the internees found that the British '[had] great understanding for anything concerning religion'.[53] The biggest problem that required immediate attention was what the internees were to do with the time on their hands. They were permitted to write two letters a week of no more than twenty-four lines on official notepaper. The contents of the letters were to 'be confined to private affairs and to business matters in which the writer has a personal interest' though did not have to be written in English so long as the language was marked clearly on the outside of the envelope.[54] The only exception to this was for the 114 Japanese internees, who were permitted to write only in English.[55] Delays of a fortnight were commonplace, particularly in the early days of internment. Perhaps the most frustrating aspect of all this was that letters between husbands and wives who were both interned had to pass through Liverpool, and so it could take several weeks for a letter to arrive in Port Erin having been posted in Douglas.[56] The frustration of knowing a partner was so close and yet so far added to the stress of the environment.

With the exception of letter writing and morning and evening roll calls, there was much time to be filled by the restless internees, who needed distractions from worrying about the fate of their families. A great number of intellectuals, artists, and musicians were interned. For those with a creative bent the primary issue was finding suitable materials with which to sketch, paint, or sculpt. In Hutchinson Camp, the windows that had been painted a 'poisonous blue' because of blackout regulations and cast a gloom on all inhabitants became the focal point for artistic endeavour with etchings created showing scenes from the Talmud, mythology, and female nudes.[57] Pens and pencils were easier to come by, although sometimes paper was in short supply.[58] Spare pieces of linoleum and furniture stored in attics or cellars were often looted in order that lino cuttings and wood carvings could be made. Wood was also used to make buttons, toys, and, in the women's camp, for children's creative play along with scraps of cardboard and discarded boxes.[59] Stair rods at one house were used to make buttons that were given as gifts and sold by the internees, as well as pillow stuffing used in making stuffed toys for the children.[60] Internees were mostly free to draw and create what they wished within the confines of the camp.[61] Sculptors found it trickier to procure materials. Kurt Schwitters, for example, used porridge as a plaster of Paris substitute, much to the consternation of his housemates who had to put up with the smell as the porridge putrefied.[62] Exhibitions were arranged in the different camps to demonstrate the fact that even behind barbed wire, man's creativity could not be tamed. As the newspaper of Hutchinson Camp explained:

> The human being is not content to live and vegetate only. The tendency to produce, to create and to build up whatever it may be is deeper rooted in our conscience than many of us believe. To keep this spirit even under the most difficult circumstances, not to loose [*sic*] heart under hard conditions and to secure progress wherever we are, is more than our duty, it is our fate … [An] exhibition is more than a mere collection of drawings, paintings, sculptures and so forth. It is a sign, a signal and a challenge to everybody here: Go on with your work as well as you can; and if you cannot do anything in your old line, try a new one.[63]

The female internees used their creativity for particularly practical needs. When the internees had been arrested it had been in the warmer months of the year. The harsh winters on the Isle of Man resulted in wool stocks being bought up by female internees as knitting became a popular hobby.[64]

Highly renowned academics were to be found in all the camps, and this led to the creation of camp 'universities' in the male camps, where individuals could attend lectures.[65] The 'universities' provided the opportunity for individuals from a broad sociocultural background to mix with others with whom they would not usually associate. It was a place where 'new interests were kindled', and created an atmosphere conducive to the free exchange of ideas, one 'learned something, met people worth knowing, people one would not have met normally'.[66] Developing out of the trend for education as a form of protection against stagnation within the camp, libraries and reading rooms became commonplace as internment progressed.[67] Each camp also established its own newspaper. In the early days, these were mainly intended to fill the void created by the ban on newspapers from outside the camp, which was a huge sap to morale. Without reliable news, rumour was rife and 'despair, unhappiness and insecurity dominated'.[68] Loudspeakers were introduced to the camps in late 1940 so that radio as well as messages from the Camp Commandant could be broadcast.[69] Hutchinson Camp even developed a 'technical school' at which to train members of the camp in vocational skills. The attitude was summed up in their promotional advertisement in the camp newspaper: 'Teaching and learning, training and working, are far better for your release and for your future existence than any grumbling and complaining. DON'T YOU SHARE THIS ATTITUDE? Then why don't you join the Technical School!'[70] The subject matter of lectures and classes varied greatly: from experts on nutrition and doctors discussing human physiology, to those teaching French and English classes.[71] Schools also had to be provided for the children interned in Rushen Camp, though these took several months to come into being, which caused problems for many who worried about their children falling behind their peers.[72] One school was established at the Strand Cafe in Port Erin and later a second school was created under the leadership of respected educationalist Minna Specht.[73] The aim of the schools was not only to occupy the children, but also to help prepare them for rejoining English schools upon release. Such was the demand for places that children could only attend one class per day, either in the morning or the afternoon.[74] Many of the children resented what they considered to be 'playing at school' with their sometimes untrained teachers.[75] When Port St Mary became the Married Camp in 1941, children had to travel under escort to Port Erin for classes until October that year. There was, however, a kindergarten available at both Port St Mary and Port Erin. Adult classes in music and art were also popular, particularly in Rushen Camp.[76] Unlike in the male camps, women were prevented by Dame Joanna from lecturing in any subject in which they were not academically qualified. In the early stages of Rushen the women therefore turned their frustration into a practical approach to the problems of obtaining items in camp and created a 'Skills Service Exchange Scheme' where skills were exchanged for tokens that could be used to purchase food in the canteen or for access to communal services such as the library or camp entertainments.[77] The Skills Service Exchange was unique to the women's camp, and can be seen as a creative solution to the frustrations and problems of camp life, particularly under the early leadership of Dame Joanna.[78] Lectures and classes provided the opportunity to relieve some of the tedium of internment as well as train individuals in new skills that would hopefully assist them in their post-internment careers. Physical exercise was a way of physically expressing the frustrations of incarceration and each camp soon created their own football teams and had inter-camp competitions.[79] Internees also played card games and for the Japanese *shogi*, or Japanese chess, also served as a distraction.[80]

Cabaret was a popular form of entertainment in both the male and female camps. The number of talented individuals interned meant that performances were usually of an exceptionally high standard, even with the limitations of having only male actors in the male camps.[81] In both the male and female camps, comment was often made about how unnatural the circumstances were that they were isolated in their pools of gender.[82] Hutchinson, widely recognized as the most intellectual of all the camps due to the high number of professionals within its confines, offered entertainment at the highest level. Captain Daniels, the Commandant, upon learning that one-half of the popular piano duet act Rawicz and Landauer was in his camp, hired two high quality pianos and arranged for a concert, reuniting the two.[83] 'The thrill and charm of beautiful music' had the power to banish thoughts of war from the minds of internees on a temporary basis.[84] Theatre performances were also popular, and later into internment weekly trips to the cinema were arranged, which were 'the chief distraction in [the internee's] monotonous life'.[85] As Alfred Lomnitz remembered, 'Everybody seemed busy at some occupation of escape from the depression that never relaxed its relentless siege'.[86]

Married Camp

Internment placed a great strain on the internees, especially family members inside and outside the camps. Initially, all those interned were placed in single-sex camps, and therefore many married couples found themselves trapped on the same island but unable to communicate with each other with any great regularity. As previously mentioned, mail between the women's camp in the south of the island and the men's camps in the north of the island could take several weeks due to the necessity of passing the letters via the postal censorship office in Liverpool.[87] The British government therefore ruled that in cases where a decision needed to be taken by both parties, married visits should take place once a month.[88] Initially such visits were organized primarily with the intent of encouraging couples to consider the options of transport abroad, rather than for the internees' emotional welfare.[89] The married visits also served to showcase the lack of accurate records kept regarding internment. On the first visit many women waited expectantly for their husbands to arrive, only to discover that their men had, in fact, already been sent overseas.[90] There was much upset caused by this oversight as the sea was a much more dangerous place than the Isle of Man. For those who were fortunate enough to see their partners, the visits formed a 'joy and consolation to last until the next time', though the visits were never long enough to greatly ease the distress of separation, nor the uncertainty of just how long incarceration would last.[91] Eventually, as the numbers of individuals released increased and the number of camps decreased, the decision was made to turn Port St. Mary into the 'married persons' camp in 1941. In the first edition of the Married Camp newspaper, the *Camp Tribune*, the editor took the opportunity to express his and his fellow internees' 'gratitude for having been transferred to this camp and re-united with our families and for the most satisfactory living conditions as far as the billeting, freedom of movement, food etc. goes'.[92] Even though the couples in the Married Camp still yearned for release, they were able to enjoy a much better standard of living than had been possible before. For the mothers, being reunited with their husbands enabled them to share some of the burdens of childcare. Johanna Rieger, for example, had travelled to the Isle of Man alone with her three children and given birth to her fourth child while interned. Support from her husband, Hannes, was therefore greatly appreciated.[93] Life in the Married Camp assumed greater regularity than was possible in the single-sex camps, and certainly for many children life 'proceeded happily and peacefully. It was really like a family holiday without an end'.[94] Additional benefits included the allocation of allotments on which many husbands set to work cultivating fruit and vegetables to share within the camp.[95] The Married Camp therefore helped families return to some semblance of normality while they awaited their release.

Christmas 1940 and 1941

Although many hoped to be released before Christmas, due to the complexity of the release system, they were often still behind barbed wire as the festive season drew near. Determined to make the best of their situation, every effort was made to make December 1940 as enjoyable as possible. This was easier for those in Rushen Camp as the landlords and landladies of their houses were often keen to help the internees plan festive activities. Christmas in the male camps was a more subdued affair. Some internees in Onchan Camp invited their local minister to visit with them on Christmas Eve and share a cake, which had been baked from all the internees pooling their rations in the house.[96] As one internee in Hutchinson Camp noted, 'We ... men who remained decided "to try to make the best of it". Not to talk about Christmas, but to be together and to try to bear it together and to hope for better things for the New Year.'[97] Some of the Italians decided to brave the chilling Irish Sea on Christmas Day in order to disrupt the guards' celebrations and give them an opportunity to leave the confines of camp.[98]

The contrast between the celebrations in the men's camp and the women's camp can be explained by the presence of children in the latter. When the Married Camp was created in 1941, those who were still interned for a second Christmas found the children entertained, their curfews extended, and an attempt to vary the food. The men who were still interned further north on the island organized a variety show in order to enter into the festive spirit.[99] In Australia, Bauhaus-trained artist Ludwig Hirschfeld-Mack made a woodcutting that was used to create a Christmas card. The scene comprised 'a figure stand[ing] behind barbed wire, beneath the brightly-shining Southern Cross and Pointer stars. The words "MERRY CHRISTMAS 1941" frame[d] this bleak scene. The print juxtaposes an internee's solitude and the annual festival, when many internees' thoughts would have turned to their families, so far away'.[100]

Transport abroad

What became the most controversial aspect of internment was the government's decision to transport internees abroad. Britain was in danger of invasion and wanted to remove enemy aliens from a position where they could potentially assist the enemy. To this end, several governments in the British Dominion were contacted and asked to accommodate some of these 'dangerous' individuals. After some hesitation, the Canadian and Australian governments consented. Canada agreed to take a defined number of internees, whereas Australia left the offer open ended. The terms were made clear – the Dominion governments were only required to provide the camps, guards, and provisions, and the British government would retain responsibility for both transportation and release.[101] Thus the transports began, a mere three weeks after the scheme was first proposed. The intention was for the British government to only transport those who posed the highest risk to security, that is, those categorized as 'A' by the internment tribunals, captured prisoners of war, and merchant seamen. The *Duchess of York* set sail for Canada first, on 21 June 1940, with approximately 2,100 German and Austrian 'A' class internees, and 523 prisoners of war (POWs). The second ship to depart on 30 June 1940, the *Arandora Star*, had around 1,564 men on board, also en route to Canada. Of these, approximately 734 were Italians, and the rest were a combination of Germans and Austrians, as well as the ship crew and the British soldiers guarding the internees.[102] The Italians had no classification, seeing as the tribunals had been mostly disbanded by June. However, as the Italians had only recently been arrested, there were a large number of internees who had not yet been transported to the Isle of Man and were therefore considered 'convenient' for sending overseas. There was no effort to actually adhere to the principle of transporting only those who were perceived to be the greatest security risk. With tight departure schedules and poor records regarding the internees, the easiest option was taken, for which the Italian community paid the ultimate price. The *Arandora Star* was torpedoed and sunk early 2 July 1940, with the loss of over 650 lives. Approximately 60 per cent of the Italians on board perished, a much higher percentage than any other nationality due to the poor quality accommodation they were offered on the lowest decks, in contrast to the cabins on the upper decks provided to Germans and Austrians.[103] Despite this tragedy, the *Ettrick* sailed for Canada the next day, 3 July 1940, with 1,307 Category 'B' and 'C' internees, 407 'young single' Italians, and 880 POWs. The following day, on 4 July, the *Sobieski* also departed for Canada, with 983 'B' and 'C' internees, as well as 545 POWs. The survivors of the *Arandora Star* had meanwhile been rescued and taken to Scotland, where 444 individuals were deemed fit to endure the further ordeal of another boat journey, this time on the *Dunera* along with a further 2,288 'B' and 'C' category Germans, who departed for Australia on 10 July 1940.[104]

The internees on the *Duchess of York* enjoyed great freedom, with tragic results that resulted in much harsher conditions on later ships. Because the guards on board the *Duchess of York* were vastly outnumbered, a disturbance on deck ended with a German POW shot and killed.[105] Subsequent transports were more closely guarded. The quality of accommodation on each ship varied dramatically. One internee described how on board the *Ettrick* the lowest four decks of the ship were filled with internees on one side and German POWs on the other, with only airshafts connecting them with the upper decks. The experience of being separated 'by a thin strand of wire from hundreds of highly trained, effective, and obviously fanatic Nazis for almost ten days was distinctly unnerving'.[106] One thing in common on all the ships was the lack of adequate sleeping quarters and sanitary arrangements for the internees, who were crammed into spaces designed for a much smaller number of passengers.[107] Queues for the latrines were commonplace, as was seasickness and diarrhoea. The following scene was not uncommon:

> I have a ghastly and unforgettable memory of an elderly man, lined up at least one deck away from the heads and clearly convinced that he would not reach them in time, grabbing the nearest suitcase (clearly not his own) and relieving himself into it. All the time he remained in the line, doubtlessly on the assumption that he would be in need again by the time he eventually reached the heads.[108]

The conditions on the *Dunera* were widely acknowledged to be the worst of all the transports. From the moment of embarkation, the internees knew they were in for an unpleasant journey. The hostile guards pilfered anything of value from their passengers including 1,200 watches and hundreds of gold wedding rings.[109] Internees were only allowed on deck for one hour per day in order to exercise, guarded by soldiers bearing rifles fixed with bayonets, though this was an improvement over the *Ettrick*, where there was no sight of the upper deck for the duration of the journey. On the *Dunera*, however, one man was able to break through the barbed wire in order to commit suicide by jumping from the ship during the journey.[110] The true tragedy, however, was the *Arandora Star*, which was torpedoed and sunk in the early hours of 2 July 1940, with the loss of over 650 lives. None of the transport ships were marked as carrying POWs. Instead they sailed unaccompanied, equipped with anti-submarine guns, and employed a zigzag pattern in their movements, making the ships obvious targets for German U-boats; as one individual described it, the boats were 'sinister like … veritable coffin[s]'.[111] Like her sister ships that went before and after her, the *Arandora Star* underwent several changes in appearance for her new cargo:

> All portholes were boarded up shutting out all daylight and the ship was armed. The boarded up promenade decks were separated from the other parts of the ship by double fences of barbed wire reaching from floor to ceiling. The only means of communication between the aft and forepart and to the boat-decks was through the lower cabin gangways which were closely guarded by sentries.[112]

The boat had fourteen lifeboats, with a maximum capacity far short of the number of passengers aboard.[113] No drill was given as to what to do in the event of an emergency. Had some safety precautions been taken, it is possible that many more individuals would have survived. As it was, 'many people, especially sick and older ones, and those from the lower part of the ship could not reach the open decks', and therefore had no chance of survival, even had the lifeboats been functional.[114] One Italian described his brother-in-law's ordeal:

> [He went] under with the ship. Whoosh! And it sucks all his clothes off him. The next he knows, he comes up, bumps his head and he grabs and is holding onto a raft. He is absolutely naked holding onto this raft. And there's about half a dozen other men holding onto the raft as well! And the water is full of oil … He says this oil saved him because the sea was frozen but the oil, you know, took the cold out of the water. He considered that saved him. He was hanging on and every now and again, a man 'Oh!' he lost his thread and he went down to his death … But my brother-in-law was lucky. He was able to hold on for a few hours.[115]

The survivors were picked up by a Canadian destroyer and deposited at Greenock, Scotland, where those who were not severely injured were placed upon the *Dunera* and transported to Australia.[116] That the internees had just survived a tremendous ordeal seemed of no importance to those managing the transportation of 'dangerous' prisoners.

Only males were transported abroad, despite promises that families would be reunited in Australia or Canada if married men volunteered for the transport.[117] The majority of the men transported had no choice in the matter and so it was not uncommon for their wives to only find out their husbands were abroad some time after their husband's journey.[118] Sadly this was also true in the case of notifying the next of kin after the sinking of the *Arandora Star* as there was no accurate list of who had actually boarded the ship. The Canadian and Australian governments had been prepared to accept some of Britain's most dangerous POWs. The reception the survivors received upon their arrival in their host country was therefore far from welcoming. The internees who disembarked in Canada and Australia were met by soldiers bearing rifles and filtered off to their respective camps, which were surrounded by barbed wire and watchtowers. The mislabelling of internees as POWs led to 'a profound identity crisis'.[119] One internee remembered that 'throughout our stay in Canada, that POW delusion was never cleared up, nor was the public amazement that so motley a crowd could ever have had any military impact – the conquest of France, no less!'[120] Whereas the Canadians never overcame the misunderstanding, the Australians soon entered into a more casual attitude with their charges, quickly realizing they were not the 'Nazi parachutists whom they had been led to expect'.[121] The overall feeling of internment in Canada was that it was 'not a bad experience, but rather boring!'[122] Initially pro-Nazis were not separated from genuine refugees, which led to several unpleasant incidents.[123] The internee experience in Canada was also rather cold, with POW uniforms given to the internees in an effort to help them stay warm, although this was in many ways an indignity.[124]

Extremes of weather were common to those in both Canada and Australia. The Australian outback was a forbidding environment, with great variation of temperatures, when the wind 'turned from dry desert oven heat to blasts from the Antarctic, bringing cold rain; temperature drops of 50–60F within the hour'.[125] It took a little time to separate the pro-Nazis from the refugees, but once that had been arranged, camp life took on its own momentum. In both Canada and Australia conditions were primitive and it took some time to get provisions beyond the basic needs of daily meals.[126] Something the internees were extremely thankful for, despite the climatic issues of their new homes, was the quality of the food available. After some of the food problems from the previous camps and the lack of edible food available on board their transport ships, the internees could not believe that they could receive 'fresh butter, milk, sugar, fresh vegetables, and fruit, marmalade, jam, eggs, [and] fresh meat' as part of their rations.[127] Fresh fruit and vegetables were available in abundance once the internees created their own market gardens with which to supplement their standard rations. In fact, many more opportunities for farming and animal husbandry were available in Australia than in Britain for the internees, and soon arrangements were also made for Orthodox Jews so that they might observe the Sabbath and prepare kosher food.[128] Much like the camps on the Isle of Man, the internees worked hard to create their own artistic and musical entertainments, as well as forming essential services such as administrations, hospitals, and canteens.[129]

Evacuation in the United States

As has been noted in the previous chapter, the first step towards restricting the movement of enemy aliens on the West Coast was the introduction of prohibited zones where enemy aliens were forbidden from residing. This included not only the Japanese, but also Germans, Austrians, and Italians. However, the treatment of Germans, Austrians, and Italians should be seen in a different light to the internment of those of Japanese ancestry. Germans, Austrians, and Italians were considered on an individual basis, a policy motivated by multiple factors, including the fact that European enemy aliens had been able to naturalize before the war and therefore assimilate into American society, an option not available to those of Japanese ancestry. This in no way lessens the seriousness of internment suffered by Europeans, but their cases can be seen in the context of selective internment, rather than the exclusion of an entire people group based on their ethnicity. Enemy aliens on the West Coast were advised that they could 'voluntarily' relocate from Military Area No. 1 to Military Area No. 2, or even further inland. This was not only impractical for many, but when time ran out for voluntary relocation in June, those who had relocated to Military Area No. 2 found that their relocation did not protect them from internment.[130] However, when it came to evacuation, those of Japanese ancestry were afforded the dubious accolade of being the only racial group forced to 'relocate' en masse, and this was accomplished in two stages, beginning in June 1941. As General DeWitt, head of the Western Defence Command, said: 'You needn't worry about the

Italians at all except in certain cases. Also, the same for the Germans except in individual cases. But we must worry about the Japanese all the time until he is wiped off the map.'[131]

Hawaii

The situation in Hawaii was in stark contrast to that of the US mainland. Arguably, there was a better case for internment on Hawaii than on the mainland as Hawaii had actually been attacked by the Japanese. However, the decision was taken to declare martial law on the islands instead of pursuing a policy of mass internment. This was partly due to the fact that whereas on the mainland the Japanese constituted 2 per cent of the population, in Hawaii that figure was closer to 33 per cent.[132] Internment would therefore have paralysed the islands with the loss of a third of the workforce. Instead, around 1,500 Germans, Italians, and individuals of Japanese ancestry were interned in Hawaii at a variety of camps including Wailuku, Maui, Honouliuli, and Sand Island, a former quarantine station at the entrance to Honouliuli, Harbour. After the attack on Pearl Harbor, Supreme Court Justice Owen Roberts was appointed to report on the disaster. Privately, Roberts believed that the Japanese American population on Hawaii, perhaps more so than the Japanese Americans on the mainland, was untrustworthy. However, he reported publicly that there was little evidence to substantiate the claim that those of Japanese ancestry posed a direct threat to security in Hawaii. He also said that the lack of evidence did not prove the loyalty of the Japanese.[133] Secretary of the Navy Frank Knox, along with President Roosevelt, pressured the Hawaiian Department to evacuate those considered the most dangerous enemy aliens to the US mainland, but the Hawaiian authorities preferred to 'treat the Japanese in Hawaii as citizens of an occupied country'.[134] The introduction of martial law on Hawaii caused problems for all those resident on the islands. Enemy aliens could be arrested, as elsewhere, on spurious grounds. Doris Berg Nye, herself a child at the time of the Second World War, recalled the trauma of both her parents and elder sister being arrested on the word of an unscrupulous guest in their nursing home. Doris and her sister were left alone, as minors, with no one to care for them, and no regard for their plight given by the authorities.[135] For six months, the internees lived in tents with no floorboards until barracks were completed in May 1942.[136] As the camp at Sand Island became more established, loudspeakers were installed in every barracks. However, the loudspeakers not only broadcast music, they also contained receivers so that the conversations of the internees could be monitored.[137] Sand

Island internment camp existed until 1943, when remaining internees who had not already been transferred to the US mainland joined their contemporaries in the Relocation Centers or were transferred to Camp Honouliuli, which earned the nickname of 'Hell Valley', in the Waianae Mountains.[138]

Department of Justice camps

Germans, Austrians, Italians, and Japanese who were arrested in the immediate aftermath of Pearl Harbor were not taken to Assembly Centers. After their arrest and confinement in local police stations and holding camps, suspect enemy aliens were taken to camps managed by the Immigration and Naturalisation Service (INS), on behalf of the Department of Justice (DoJ). The INS managed these camps until May 1943, when control was returned to the DoJ, and many of these camps only existed for a few months before the internees were moved to other locations.[139] According to *Fortune Magazine*, only the DoJ camps could be termed 'true internment camps'.[140] Approximately 11,500 individuals of German ancestry and around 3,000 of Italian ancestry were held in DoJ camps.[141] Run as military camps, discipline was strict and communication with the outside world severely restricted. Different nationalities had their own barracks, but would sometimes come together for sporting activities.[142] Family members from outside the DoJ camps sent their husbands and fathers letters and care packages that were stripped to ensure no secret communications were contained within sweet wrappers, for example.[143] Conditions were basic and the housing often consisted, at least initially, of tents with no floorboards, until barracks were constructed.[144] Much like the other Relocation Centers, internees provided many of their own services, and the camp facilities, particularly in the early days, were limited.

As time progressed, some of the Japanese internees in the DoJ camps were reunited with their families in Relocation Centers, while those who remained could request to have their families transferred to Seagoville or Crystal City, both in Texas. The DoJ converted facilities into family camps, where wives and children – regardless of whether or not they were themselves internees – could live as a family unit.[145] Crystal City was not where any of the internees wanted their families to be, but it was preferable to continued separation. Many of the children who lived in these family camps struggled to adjust to the environment, especially as they had enjoyed 'prewar Americanization and acculturation', and life in the camps was full of 'chaos [and] uncertainty'.[146] Seagoville and Crystal City, alongside other camps, were also the destination of many of those arrested and deported from South America.[147] The United States believed

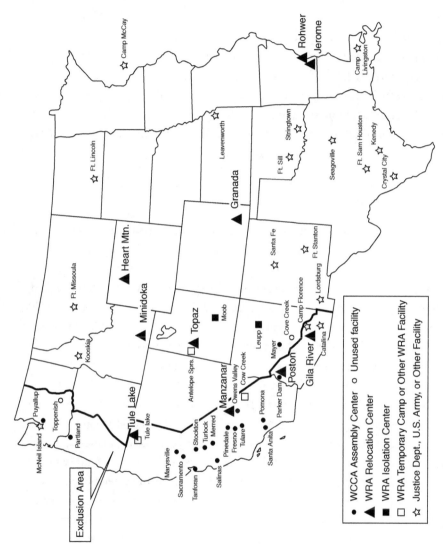

Figure 2.2 Camps and holding facilities for those of Japanese ancestry in western United States. Courtesy National Park Service.

in the importance of hemispheral security, and pressured Latin American governments to detain and deport enemy aliens to the United States for internment. Approximately 3,000 residents of Latin America were deported because they were viewed as potential threats to national security, but also because the United States wanted enemy aliens who they could exchange for American citizens held by the Axis powers. Over two-thirds of those deported were Japanese nationals, and the vast majority were from Peru.[148] The INS, who were in charge of these internees, labelled them as having entered the country illegally, thereby rendering them liable to forcible repatriation. As a result of the way these enemy aliens were brought into the country, and the nebulous legality concerning their incarceration, these internees suffered a much longer internment than those who were resident in the United States at the outbreak of war.

Assembly Centers

Before mass evacuation occurred, notices were displayed in prominent places in Japanese neighbourhoods.[149] Every area was treated differently, and so it was possible for as little as twenty-four hours' notice to be given in some areas, while were given up to ten days to prepare for their departure.[150] As one internee asked, 'How can we clear out in ten days a house we've lived in for fifteen years?'[151] Evacuation caused many practical issues for the Japanese. Anti-alien land laws prevented the Issei from owning property. Some property had been placed in the name of Nisei children, enabling their Issei parents to manage the property. However, if the entire Japanese population on the West Coast was to be interned for the foreseeable future, then suitable custodians for not only the properties but also possessions had to be found. Evacuation orders stipulated that only as much as could be carried be taken to the Assembly Centers. Those of Japanese ancestry felt forced to sell as many of their possessions as possible. The involuntary sale of possessions 'was very difficult ... because most of the people, neighbors, and so forth, knew that we had to leave. So, the longer they waited, the better bargains they [got]'.[152] Some Caucasian members of the West Coast Community were sympathetic to the plight of their Japanese neighbours and offered to store their goods or let their houses on their behalf while they were away. Such arrangements varied in success between the safe storage and return of all goods and property to their rightful owners after the war and unscrupulous 'friends' who sold of property and pocketed the profits in the internees' absence.[153] The federal government was slow to institute safeguards for the evacuees, creating an 'interval of golden opportunity to swindlers and tricksters who had a terrified group of people at their mercy'.[154] No government agency wished to take the initiative to protect the interests of the internees, and so by the time any policy was formulated it was too late to protect the interests of the vast majority of those of Japanese ancestry. Eventually the War Relocation Authority (WRA) assumed responsibility, but the organization encountered constant problems with the law enforcement agencies on the West Coast, who showed 'a considerable indifference to vandalism and even to arson committed upon evacuee property and ... put up effective passive resistance to requests to conduct investigations which might lead to arrest and prosecution of offenders'.[155]

The evacuation notices listed the Civil Control Centers where the internees were to assemble at on the day of their departure. Failure to report to a Center was considered a felony, as Gordon Hirabayashi demonstrated by his refusal to obey the evacuation order. Charged both with violating the curfew and failing to report, he was found guilty.[156] Hirabayashi, a peace-loving Quaker from Seattle, was hardly likely to be a threat to national security and yet his conviction was upheld in the Supreme Court in 1943. Fred Korematsu did not initially set out to challenge the legal system; he had surgery to make him look less Japanese so that he could remain living in California. However, the surgery was not as successful as he hoped and so he was arrested and charged with failure to report to an Assembly Center. Korematsu was found guilty, and again the constitutionality of the order to report was avoided in favour of focusing on the issue of obeying a military order.[157] Like Hirabayashi and Yasui his conviction was upheld in the Supreme Court. The Supreme Court had decided that 'the identification and exclusion of a single racial group was allowable through the war powers of Congress and the president'.[158] The only test case in which a favourable verdict was reached was that of Mitsuye Endo, who was handpicked as a prime example of a loyal Nisei who obeyed the evacuation order in full. The Supreme Court eventually ruled that no 'loyal American citizen could ... be held in a relocation camp against [their] will', but even this was a hollow victory as the case was delayed so that the ruling was made after it became possible for loyal Nisei to leave the camps under their own volition.[159] Apart from a few individuals who breached the evacuation order, all other individuals of Japanese ancestry reported to their assigned Assembly Center unless given special permission to report at a later date. Each family was assigned a number and a tag with that number was to be attached to every family member, as well as to their bags.[160] The numbering of internees was a dehumanizing experience: one's identity was hidden behind an impersonal and imposed form of identification. As Hatsuye Egami explained,

> Since yesterday, we Pasadena Japanese have ceased to be human beings – we are now simply numbers or things. We are no longer 'Egamis' but the number 23324. A tag with that number is on every suitcase and bag. Even on our breasts are tied large tags with this same number – 23324! Again, a sad and tragic feeling grips my heart![161]

Once assembled, the internees were loaded onto buses and driven to temporary Assembly Centers. While travelling the window blinds were pulled down, allegedly for the safety of the internees, but this only proved to make the journey more unpleasant and disorienting for the internees.

Assembly Centers were often constructed at race tracks or fairgrounds where there were some structures that could be adapted into facilities for the internees, and also space to construct additional accommodation. Internees usually spent several months at these locations before the Relocation Centers were completed. Conditions at the Assembly Centers were primitive, and construction was usually still under way when the first groups of internees arrived. For those who were sent to race tracks the stables had been converted into two-room 'apartments', deemed suitable for housing one family in each. The rear room often had no windows and the walls, which were thin and full of knotholes, and had horse hair and other detritus painted onto them during the whitewashing process. Miné Okubo described the accommodation at Tanforan as follows:

> A swinging half-door divided the 20 by 9 ft. stall into two rooms. The roof sloped down from a height of twelve feet in the rear room to seven feet in the front room; below the rafters an open space extended the full length of the stable. The rear room had housed the horse and the front room the fodder. Both rooms showed signs of a hurried whitewashing. Spider webs, horse hair, and hay had been whitewashed with the walls. Huge spikes and nails stuck out all over the walls. A two-inch layer of dust covered the floor, but on removing it we discovered that linoleum the color of redwood had been placed over the rough manure-covered boards.[162]

Bathroom facilities consisted of wash blocks where there were normally no partitions between toilets or showers, or if there were, there were no doors to offer privacy.[163] This made daily ablutions particularly unpleasant for both genders. Hatsuye Egami wrote about her first trip to the latrines with her two daughters:

> Guided by a neighbor, all of us go to the latrine, which is about a block away. As soon as we enter, my daughters shriek. I could not help become wobbly and stare before me. I indeed felt sorry for my daughters. In the latrine the cloak of

modesty must be shed and we must return to the state of nakedness in which we were born. Polished civilized taste and fine sensitivity seem to have become worthless here.[164]

As Minoru Kiyota recalled about his time in camp,

I don't believe anyone, no matter how thick-skinned, would find it easy to use a toilet that is just one long plank of plywood with holes in it – with no semblance of privacy and with maggots swimming in the tank below. Adjusting to this novel way of going to the bathroom was our initiation rite into communal living, a rite that took most of us a good long time to pass.[165]

Makeshift screens were constructed out of cardboard, which women would carry with them to the latrines. Many Issei were also unaccustomed to the use of showers and would therefore bring buckets and barrels into the showers in order that they might attempt to bathe. Mothers also worried about their children falling in to the toilet when using the facilities.[166] Incomplete drainage meant there was often an unpleasant odour emanating from the area of the latrines, and there was also a constant shortage of hot water. The internees slept on army cots in their 'apartments'. Any food that required cooking was banned from the camp as all food was to be eaten communally in mess halls. Some internees brought with them hot plates so that they might heat their baby's milk in their apartment. However, due to fears regarding electricity surges and fire risks, hot plates were branded as contraband and confiscated.[167] Initially the quality of the food in the mess halls was of a very low standard, and throughout the Assembly Centers' existence the standard varied immensely. A letter from an early inhabitant of Merced Assembly Center described lunch as 'a horrid affair – 1 frankfurter, a mess of overboiled cabbage, white bread, pasty rice, and canned cherries [but] One consolation is that we don't have to wash dishes yet'.[168] Certainly in the early days there was a preponderance of starch in the form of bread, potatoes, and rice, and a lack of fresh fruit and vegetables.[169] Internees were required to stand in line in shifts outside the mess halls in order to obtain their meals, which they ate at long tables and benches. Internees would sometimes write to Caucasian friends requesting foodstuffs to supplement their diet.[170] However, as time wore on, the standard and variety of food offered improved.

As the initial shock of the conditions at the Assembly Centers began to lessen, attention turned to the need for some sort of timetable for daily activities. Some structure was unavoidable, such as daily roll call, which was compulsory for all internees. One child at Tanforan described his reaction to the early morning roll call: 'When the siren ring I get so scared that I sometime scream ... we run home as fast as I could then we wait about 5 minutes then the inspectors come to check that we are all home … After the camp roll call finish the siren rings again … I hate roll call because it scares you to [*sic*] much.'[171] However, despite roll calls and mealtimes, there were many hours to be filled, and 'until recreational activities got under way, the internees had plenty of time and no place to go'.[172] An immediate need was the creation of activities for the children so that they would not run riot within the confines of the camps. Nursery schools and sports clubs were created for the children. There were also English-language classes for those who wanted to improve their linguistic skills. Requests were made to religious and charitable organizations for basic school supplies so that classrooms could be established in grandstands and auditoriums. Some of the college age women and older teenagers volunteered to help in the nursery, and Japanese American schoolteachers assumed responsibility for taking at least one class per day. The volume of students was so great and the times that the grandstands and auditoriums could be used so limited that teaching sometimes went into the evening. The Nikkei attempted to adjust to their confinement and were able to receive visitors during certain hours.[173] The visitors often had to queue for several hours and there was no guarantee they would get to see their friends. However, the evacuees were unable to adjust to the continued invasion of privacy that they suffered whenever the FBI decided to conduct raids for so-called contraband. The effect of such raids, when stalls could be turned upside down in the quest for radios, hot plates, and anything else deemed suspect, was to lower morale throughout the camps.[174] Reports that 'supposedly harmless objects as scissors, nail files, buckets, tubs, geta (wooden clogs), saws, chisels, files, electric razors, knitting needles, crochet hooks, and even cash were being confiscated' spread through the camps, creating a dangerously charged atmosphere.[175] In Santa Anita, this resentment resulted in a riot one Tuesday in August 1942, and martial law was imposed on the camp for several days until Colonel Karl Bendetsen offered to return non-contraband items to their owners.[176] While the immediate crisis was contained, the seeds for further discontent remained and parents feared for the safety of their children.

Relocation Centers

The majority of internees spent between a week and several months in the Assembly Centers before being moved to semi-permanent accommodation at the Relocation Centers.[177] Evacuees were transported to the Centers in crowded and overheated trains.[178] Upon arrival internees underwent interviews and physical examinations before seeing their accommodation. The ten Relocation Centers were located in the western states, with the exception of two camps in Arkansas. There was much debate over what could be considered suitable semi-permanent sites for the camps. The land chosen had to fulfil the dual criteria of being both government owned and isolated. Some of the camps were constructed on Native American reservations, such as Gila River, and Poston, while others were situated on land acquired for non-payment of taxes or forced purchase, such as Jerome, Topaz, and Granada. When each site was considered various data was obtained to assist in the decision regarding suitability. This included noting seasonal highs and lows of temperature, but only in relation to how it would affect agricultural production, as opposed to how hospitable the habitat would be for the evacuees.[179] Unlike the Assembly Centers, there were no preexisting buildings to be modified into accommodation for the internees, with the notable exception of Manzanar. Instead it was necessary to construct the camps from scratch, an activity that the US Army Corps of Engineers supervised along with volunteer internees.[180] Construction followed a standard pattern of barracks built in blocks contained within a barbed wire fence. Terrain influenced the exact layout of each camp but the principles remained the same. Each block usually consisted of twelve barracks, a mess hall, and a recreation hall. There was a wash house for the men, one for the women – this time with partitions between stalls – and also laundry facilities in a separate building.[181] The barracks at Granada and Gila River had solid concrete foundations and walls constructed from fibre board, which offered slightly more protection against the elements. In all the other camps, barracks were constructed out of green wood covered in tar paper. The use of unseasoned wood meant that as the buildings aged the wood shrank, creating gaps between the wall and floorboards. Gila River was unusual in that it was built as a showcase Relocation Center, where the roofs were double tiled in order to protect the internees from the excessive heat, a luxury denied to other camp inhabitants, though Gila had its own issues.[182] In the other camps the roofs were tarred.[183] Each of the residential barracks was subdivided into one-room apartments in which a family dwelt, the smallest of which measured twenty by sixteen feet.[184] The partitions between each apartment did not reach the ceiling, and so privacy was all but impossible.

Each apartment was furnished with an army cot for each member of the family and internees were given sacks to fill with straw for mattresses upon their arrival. Internees were also issued with blankets, as well as a heater for each apartment, though fuel was not always immediately available.[185] The arrival at Manzanar was described by Harry Ueno as follows:

[There was] hardly no privacy ... I ... put the nail between and pull own sheets for privacy ... We could hear all the talking and everything ... we got ... five steel cots ... They give us one sack for mattress. Go to the laundry room and fill in with straw. So we did that. I take about – almost midnight before we get all the mattress ready and they give us two or three blankets each ... but that was very cold. They have an oil stove but no oil there. So we can hardly sleep night-time. The straw makes a lot of noise and my small kid was only five years old. You put the straw too thin; the steel cot hurt your back. So we put a little more. He roll out on the floor ... Then our mess hall is not open, so we have to eat in Block 16.[186]

Nothing in the camps was finished in the early days. Gaps in the floorboards of wooden barracks meant that everything inside was covered with a fine layer of dust, much like the outside.[187] Most of the internees had lived at sea level prior to their evacuation and the altitude at many of the Relocation Centers required some adjustment.[188] The terrain was also a shock to many a system. One Caucasian visitor from the YWCA explained the reaction to her host family's arrival at Minidoka: 'They thought they had been uncomfortable in their horse stall in the fairgrounds, but they wished they were back. At least they had had cool water and green grass ... when they saw how barren the Idaho desert was, they were just sick. Most of them had never lived anyplace but along the coast. The contrast was very depressing.'[189] The inhospitable climates at the camps created many practical issues. In the camps situated in desert terrain internees had to be provided with salt tablets to prevent dehydration.[190] Rattlesnakes and scorpions had enjoyed the natural habitat of the camps long before the arrival of the internees, and indeed continued to do so, requiring stock of various antivenoms in camp hospitals.[191] Mosquitoes and mites were an additional problem in the swamps of Arkansas.[192]

One of the reasons for the interviews upon arrival at the Relocation Centers was to ascertain which skills internees had that could be used to the Center's advantage. This was particularly the case where cooks and carpenters were concerned. Feeding a multitude of people required an army of cooks and mess hall workers. Some of those who had risen to the challenge in the Assembly Centers volunteered their services again in the Relocation Centers. Even so, it was only after a few weeks that all mess halls within any given camp were fully opened. Again, like the Assembly Centers, meals were served in shifts and the same problems regarding sourcing fresh fruit and vegetables were frequent in the Centers' early days. Forty-five cents was the amount allocated per day for each internee's food, in direct contrast to the extravagant claims made in the press that the internees were 'among the best-fed civilians in the world', receiving large amounts rationed foods that were diverted from the general population.[193] In reality, rationing affected the life of those in the camps at least as much, if not more, than the rest of the American population. In times of shortage, only small children, nursing or expectant mothers, and those with special dietary needs had access to a milk ration, for example.[194] The WRA and notable officials involved in the internment process were constantly rebutting claims regarding luxury. Indeed, the First Lady herself felt it necessary to make her opinions clear on the matter to the West Coast, when she stated to the press that '[the internees] are living in conditions which certainly are not luxurious, as some report. Neither can it be said that they are not decent, although I would not like to live that way'.[195] The practicalities of camp living meant that, as in the Assembly Centers, there were no facilities for mothers to heat their babies' milk in their apartment. Selected mess halls provided a 'baby food service' for the heating of milk, which although inconvenient, fulfilled the need.[196] The seating arrangements in the mess halls also created problems when it came to family eating. Seating consisted of benches, sometimes connected to the table that made the feeding of toddlers and small children awkward.[197] As time progressed, the practice of eating together as a family unit disintegrated as the Nisei discovered the freedom they could enjoy by eating in groups with their peers instead of with their parents.[198] Years of family tradition were being eroded through the unnatural circumstances in which Japanese families found themselves.

Because the Relocation Centers were intended to be in existence for several years, ambitious agricultural schemes were developed in order that the internees might provide some of their own food. The 1943 target for Topaz was to create half a million dollars' worth of foodstuffs, for example.[199] However, desert climes were not the most hospitable environments for farming, despite the government's best intentions. Topaz was so barren that even though thousands of trees of various ages were planted in the camp, 'the dust eliminated the trees'.[200] This, however, did not prevent the internees from achieving some impressive results. In fact, before the war, several Japanese Americans suggested to the US government that their skills might be best used during the war in establishing cooperative farms away from strategic areas.[201] At some camps there was already cultivated land available such as at Granada, Tule Lake, and Gila River.[202] In 1942 at Tule Lake, 450 evacuee labourers harvested 837 acres of barley, 570 acres of potatoes, 208 acres of potatoes, 208 acres of onions, 145 acres of carrots, 152 acres of rutabagas, and other vegetables.[203] Poultry and livestock were also raised by the internees in an attempt to make the Relocation Centers as self-sufficient as possible.[204] Internees were also hired out to farms around the Relocation Centers where they were used as cheap labour, suffering varying levels of abuse.[205] However, despite the problems of being outsourced as workers, many internees at least appreciated the freedom of being outside the barbed wire fence.[206]

Each camp had its own Caucasian Director, supported by an all-Caucasian staff, which was in overall charge of the camps. The existence of the Caucasian staff was a bone of contention because the administrators were paid a competitive wage for their work. Payment for the internees, in comparison, was on a scale varying between $12 and $19 per month, though the majority of internees were paid $16 or $19.[207] The Caucasian staff were also housed in far more luxurious surroundings. As the internees of Poston noted: 'The administration live in cheery white frame houses, the walls are lined and sealed in contrast to the bare tar-papered barracks of the evacuees. The staff has maid service and towels are changed daily. The food is better and more plentiful. It is served in an administrative dining room by young Japanese American girls.'[208] The desire of the WRA was that the internees should be involved in their governance as much as possible. To this end the role of block manager was created. Block managers could not be elected by their peers; instead they were selected by and reported to the administration. Their duties were manifold:

> [To] act as liaisons between the resident and the administration. They requisition and distribute government equipment and supplies and are responsible for non-expendable government property. They disseminate information concerning facilities and administrative regulations. They keep a record of the residents of the block council and distribute mail, report emergencies to health, fire, and police departments. They assist in settling grievances within the block.[209]

The internees were allowed, however, to elect their own councils and council members, who could represent their views and wishes to the camp administration. Through the Camp Councils, committees were formed to advise on every aspect of the Centers' functions, including education and general welfare.[210] The US government was keen to make a distinction between Issei and Nisei, and wanted the Nisei to play a major part in the running of the camp. The reasoning behind this was that the Nisei were American citizens and were, therefore, trusted slightly more than their Japanese parents. This policy naturally created tensions within the Centers as the Issei, by reason of age, had traditionally been the natural leaders. The arrest of so many Issei in the weeks following Pearl Harbor left a power vacuum in the Japanese community, and as the Nisei filled this vacuum, it became very hard for those Issei who had been arrested and were eventually reunited with their families in the Relocation Centers to adjust to their new reduced status. Popular positions for the Issei were as block managers, as their age often gave them respect from their fellow internees. Issei could also find positions on the Camp Councils, but were unable to assume any positions that worked directly for the camp administration. Once again, government policy undermined the family structure by encouraging the younger generation to supplant their elders.

Attempts at organizing schools began at the Assembly Centers but the process was formalized in the Relocation Centers. Despite the fact there were no allocated facilities, schools were established from the earliest days in camp. It was believed that 'inadequate schools ... were better than unsupervised leisure for so many children without space to play and living in one room with their families'.[211] The Issei had always invested greatly in their children's education as it was a means for them to elevate their position in society. One interned student expressed a common Nisei sentiment: 'since I am sure that American education is the best means of mingling again with my Caucasian friends, I shall not neglect study'.[212] Even as late as November 1943, schoolrooms were heavily overcrowded and inadequately lit.[213] During the first winter in the camps school sometimes had to be cancelled due to a lack of heating, and sometimes in summer the heat was too intense for effective study.[214] Schools were staffed by a mixture of Caucasian and Japanese American teachers, which led to some conflict as, like all other roles in camp, the Japanese workers were paid significantly less than their white counterparts.[215] Despite the children's lack of freedom, they were still expected to pledge their allegiance to the American flag each day. The high school at Topaz had the motto 'On the Youth of Today Rests the Democracy of Tomorrow',[216] which was particularly poignant given the denial of constitutional rights to the Nisei. Outside of the schoolroom there were many other educational and social activities. Sports clubs, ikebana (flower arranging), sewing, and art classes abounded.[217] Wives and mothers had more free time than they had enjoyed prior to the war and were no longer expected to cook for their families. Women were therefore particularly amenable to learning new skills and hobbies. Rose Honda remembered: 'My mother was always interested in sewing. She kept busy with embroidery. She would order embroidery kits and make pillowcases, or pictures to be framed. She also did a lot of crocheting. We were seemingly always ordering things through Sears and Montgomery Wards for her crochet threads and embroidery thread.'[218] In Rohwer 'the women with no houses to keep or meals to cook had leisure to enjoy. Many of them, a waiting line of them, enjoyed it in weaving useful objects and materials on the twenty-two hand looms furnished by WRA.[219] Indeed, some of the traditional gender roles were altered in camp life. Hatsuye Egami commented in her evacuation diary of how arduous trips to the laundry were and how many Issei men were recruited to assist in the traditionally female enterprise of washing.[220]

Social activities strengthened the community, acted as a distraction to the deprivations of camp life, and also were opportunities to fundraise for the benefit of the community. In Rohwer, for example, federal spending on community activities never exceeded $500 per annum. However, through carnivals, talent shows, and movie screenings, the residents were able to raise thousands of additional dollars to reinvest back into the community.[221] There were numerous festivals organized by the internees during their time in camp, and these served as opportunities to unite communities and mix Japanese and American culture. Traditional practices such as *kabuki*, classical Japanese dance-drama, and *Noh* theatre were 'radically intercultural, bringing together immigrant Issei and more-assimilated Nisei, Japanese speakers and English speakers'.[222] Indeed, at Tule Lake, a group of visiting *kabuki* artists from Japan had been trapped in America at the outbreak of war and put on regular performances in camp, as well as giving lessons to fellow internees.[223] Performances were not only instigated by the internees themselves – often the high quality of internee performance was seen as an opportunity by the camp administration to involve the local community and show the camps as 'normal' communities.[224] This sort of event served to turn internment into a 'spectacle' for the white audience, effectively reinforcing the idea that these were 'Japs who think they are American'.[225] Therefore, though performances were popular in camp, this way of being perceived by outsiders through performance has perhaps influenced the fact that in the years following the camp closures, the numerous theatre performances of the time are largely forgotten by the Japanese community.[226] Performance was of particular significance in Tule Lake, where traditional Japanese performances were combined with modern American artistry to celebrate fundamentally American celebrations such as the Fourth of July after Tule Lake became a Segregation Center. This knitting together of two sets of pastimes 'neither asserted "disloyalty" to America nor admitted an overriding allegiance to Japan and its culture. Rather, the suturing together of national pastimes and cultural performances from both nations asserted the transnational community of these Japanese Americans and their performative statement that this intercultural identity entitled them to partake in U.S. Independence

Day'.[227] Thus, performance could be used to register traditions of both nations, melding together the 'best of both', and showing how there was much from Japanese culture that could be beneficial to America. Much better remembered are the communal gardens created for recreational use. Aesthetically there was little pleasing about any of the Relocation Centers, although some were situated near imposing mountain ranges. The internees therefore set about creating water and vegetable gardens, which provided not only physical activity, but also visual inspiration in the wilderness.[228] Each camp instituted its own periodical through which camp news was disseminated and that also offered employment opportunities to those with journalistic or artistic leanings. The *Topaz Times*, *Heart Mountain Sentinel*, *Minidoka Irrigator*, and *Gila News Courier* were initially published twice a week, the *Manzanar Free Press* thrice weekly, while the *Tulean Dispatch* and *Poston Press Bulletin* were produced daily.[229] There were limitations on what could be published in each paper and negative reporting was actively discouraged. Sections of each newspaper were written in Japanese for the benefit of the Issei but the majority of the paper was expected to be published in English as the camp authorities were highly suspicious of what might be coded into Japanese writing.

As the majority of those interned were in family units this meant that births, deaths, and marriages continued as they would in any society. Many couples who were engaged or had been considering engagement rushed their plans to ensure that legally they could not be separated.[230] The primitive hospital arrangements meant that giving birth in camp, particularly in the early days, was high risk.[231] Each camp had its own cemetery, several of which are still in existence, though family members were often reluctant for the remains of their loved ones to be permanently linked with their enforced incarceration.[232] Some of the deaths were caused by a lack of medical provision, but not all of the deaths were as a result of health problems. There were several accidents in the camps that caused the death of internees.[233] The death that caused the most controversy, however, was that of James Hatsuki Wakasa at Topaz in April 1943. Wakasa, an elderly internee, was walking close to the perimeter fence when he was shot. The soldier who shot him claimed Wakasa had been trying to escape and that he had shouted a warning twice before firing a fatal shot into Wakasa's back.[234] Despite promises of a court martial for the sentry, in reality the soldier was reprimanded and then transferred elsewhere.[235] The news of the killing rapidly spread, adding to the unrest fomenting within the Relocation Centers. The poor quality of accommodation, food, and paltry pay did nothing to improve the morale in the camps. The often high-handed approach of the Caucasian administration led to many demonstrations of unrest, of which one of the most significant was at Manzanar in 1942. Harry Ueno, an internee who had led the way in investigating sugar shortages in camp, as well as unionizing the mess hall workers, was arrested 5 December 1942 for the assault of Fred Tayama, a leader in the Japanese American Citizens League (JACL). Ueno was never charged for the assault, which had been carried out by masked attackers, but was held without trial because of his stand against the corruption of certain camp officials. Internees were not allowed to organize mass meetings, but hundreds of individuals gathered to demand the release of Ueno. The crowd refused to disperse unless something was done about Ueno's arrest, at which time tear gas was lobbed into the crowd by the MPs and several shots were fired, wounding ten internees – two fatally.[236] For several days Manzanar was under military control and the internees were reluctant to leave their barracks, especially if they had children. Unrest was not limited to Manzanar. JACL leaders found themselves targets of aggression from pro-Axis supporters who were angry with the rights denied them by the American government. The camps may have been full of a people of shared ancestry, but their views, like of any group of people forced together, ranged across the political and religious spectrum. To expect the internees to live together in harmony because of a shared ethnicity was naïve at best. As time went on the pro-Axis supporters radicalized and it became increasingly dangerous for anyone to be seen to support the US government in any way.[237] Members of the JACL, as a result of its stance to cooperate without hesitation with the government's requests, found themselves the victims of violence. The president of the JACL, for example, had the door of his barracks torn off, his wife and children were terrorized, and he himself was beaten severely because the JACL was blamed for the camps.[238] In protest of poor camp conditions and the lack of heed paid to internee concerns, strikes were also called in multiple camps, as it was seen as the only way to gain the attention of camp administrations.[239]

Segregation

One of the most controversial aspects of internment was the creation and distribution of what became known as the 'Loyalty Questionnaire'. Every internee over the age of seventeen was required to complete the questionnaire, which the US government hoped to use to ascertain how many of the internees were loyal to America. As J. Edgar Hoover, director of the FBI, noted in 1942:

I remarked that there had not been the weeding out of the Japanese because in the Western Defense Command they had all been placed in camps, both good and bad, whereas over the rest of the country the bad Germans and Italians had been drawn away from the good ones. Therefore, for the reason that we do not have extensive records on most of these Japanese undesirables, any record check made with us would not be all-conclusive.[240]

As a result of such concerns, the Loyalty Questionnaire was instituted. Questions 27 and 28 were the most divisive: Question 27 asked if an individual was willing to serve in the American Armed Forces, while Question 28 asked the individual to swear unqualified allegiance to the United States of America and, most controversially of all, forswear any form of allegiance to the Japanese emperor or any other foreign government, power, or organization. For the Issei, denied the right to naturalize and become American citizens, forswearing their Japanese citizenship effectively made them stateless. A refusal to answer 'Yes' to both questions was seen as a declaration of disloyalty to the United States of America. Leaving the answers blank was also seen as a declaration of disloyalty, as was writing anything in addition to the words 'Yes' or 'No'. For Nisei, American citizens by birth, Question 28 appeared a trick, requiring them to prove the American authorities right when they had claimed before internment that the Nisei were loyal to the emperor because Japanese blood flowed through their veins. Those deemed disloyal were subject to hearings before a Board of Review. If, after a board appearance, an internee was still considered to harbour pro-Japan views, he or she was to be segregated.[241] It was believed that no matter which rights were denied to those of Japanese ancestry, those who were loyal would remain loyal despite their experiences, and would also still be willing to take up arms for their country.[242] After sacrificing their freedom, the Issei were being asked to sacrifice their children in the war effort.

Information given to the internees by camp administrations varied tremendously, leading to a great disparity between the level of 'No' answers given. Rumours were rife because no one knew what the consequences would be if loyalty was not sworn to America.[243] The WRA also failed to appreciate the strains that such questions could put on an individual or family. If an Issei still had family in Japan, they worried that answering 'Yes' to Question 27 could cause problems for their Japanese relatives. If an Issei answered 'No' and was dependent on his or her children for support, his or her children knew that if they answered 'Yes', the family unit would be separated. There were also bands of pro-Axis Japanese who threatened those who they thought had answered 'Yes' on the Loyalty Questionnaire. Intimidation prevented many families from registering at all, which left them categorized as disloyal.[244] Not all Nisei wanted to join the armed forces, especially with the knowledge it would do nothing to speed the release of their families.[245] For those Nisei that did want to fight, the only option was to be in a segregated unit, unlike those of German and Italian ancestry who were able to fight in standard regiments.[246] This segregation of units, as Emily Roxworthy has noted, 'bore an uncomfortable resemblance to the ideology of racial purity that underwrote fascism'.[247] There was, therefore, nothing straight-forward about the questionnaire and much hostility arose in camp because of it. The true irony of the situation is captured in the following quotation:

> In retrospect, the entire registration program appears to have been a sopho-moric and half-baked idea, if not indeed a stupid and costly blunder. In the long run, nothing could have been more certain or more simple than this: If there had been any actual Japanese agents or spies in the Relocation Centers, in February, 1943, they would have been the very first to profess their loyalty on paper, so that they could carry on their work.[248]

This flawed test of loyalty resulted in a policy of segregation. Those who had requested repatriation or expatriation prior to 1 July 1943 were immediately moved to Tule Lake.[249] A Board of Review was formed for individuals who had not answered Questions 27 and 28 'satisfactorily' to determine where their true loyalty lay. If their loyalty was not considered to lie with America, the individual and any dependants were also moved to Tule Lake.[250] Minoru Kiyota, a Kibei, recalled his interrogation at the hands of the FBI:

> 'You dirty Jap! [he shouted] Liar! You were a member of the Butoku-kai [Martial Arts Association], were you not?'
>
> 'I just took some kendo lessons. I guess the San Francisco Kendo Club was affiliated with the Butoku-kai, but I never knowingly became a member of that.'
>
> 'I am not asking you what you knowingly did. I am telling you that the Butoku-kai is a reactionary organization. What kind of training did they give you? What sort of orders did you have when you came into this camp? ... Why do you lie? The head of the Butoku-kai is General Araki Sadao. What orders did Araki give you? Orders to commit sabotage, right? You speak Japanese – you're a perfect candidate for sabotage. You're a kibei, and a member of the Butoku-kai. You are a dangerous individual! And you are not getting out of this camp!'[251]

Such treatment created enemies out of internees who decided they would not yield to such an 'oppressive force'.[252] To say that all 'segregees' were disloyal, then, oversimplifies the composition of the camp. It has been estimated that approximately 70 per cent of those relocated to Tule Lake post-segregation were

American citizens.[253] Many of these Nisei were transferred as a result of their parents' decision and had never visited Japan. This situation put extreme psychological pressure on the youngsters, who faced the possibility of being removed from the only way of life they had ever known.

A large number of the American citizens in Tule Lake were Kibei, children of the Issei who were sent to Japan for their education before returning to America. The situation of the Kibei was unique – neither considering themselves wholly Japanese, like their Issei parents, nor wholly American, like the Nisei. Often Kibei were sent to Japan for their formative years because of financial problems in the family. When the Kibei returned, they found themselves trapped between two worlds which they were expected to bridge.[254] The Kibei had to deal with feelings of rejection by their parents, and adjust to life in families where they hardly knew their siblings who had grown up in America. The Kibei were also hampered by the fact that they did not speak English as fluently as the Nisei, and spoke whatever English they knew in a Japanese accent, which immediately marked them out as distinct from their contemporaries.[255] The Kibei were, therefore, forced into a very difficult situation; 'emotionally, the Kibei were Japanese, but their complicated situation made their relationship with parents, siblings, and … Nisei, as well as their lives in the United States, difficult'.[256] Nisei often distrusted the Kibei, and due to the Nisei's superior command of the English language, Kibei were more often than not relegated to more lowly positions in camp.[257]

There were many factions in the camp – some more violent than others. 'Strong arm squads' patrolled the camps, trying to make the camps more 'Japanese'.[258] The more antagonistic Kibei broke up Nisei gatherings, only allowing Japanese activities to continue.[259] The WRA had also hired some members of the camp to act as informants, who reported the goings on in camp. Suspicion and malice towards such informants ran high, leading to many a violent incident were one to be suspected of informing.[260] Unrest developed in Tule Lake as internees agitated for improved conditions and greater freedom.[261] In November 1943, control of the camp was temporarily transferred to the US Army as a result of protests due to the death of a farmworker and the serious injury of four others when the truck in which they were travelling overturned due to the inexperience of the driver.[262] The mass protests could have been avoided had the administration not handled the matter in such a high-handed way, rejecting all suggestions for improvements made by the internees.[263] Further proof of the negative way the internees were viewed by the military can be seen in the shooting of a Nisei on his return from work assignment. The guard was disciplined for wasting a bullet, rather than wasting a life.[264] This heaped fuel on the fire of the deep burning resentment, and Tule Lake continued to get more and more violent as it was, in effect, an unpoliced community. Those not members of pro-Japanese organizations lived in daily fear for their safety, and that of their families. It 'was like all abnormal, oppressive societies where individuals grasp any little vestige of power they can get hold of, just so they can throw their weight around and make other peoples' lives miserable'.[265] It was significant then, that Tule Lake was the only camp to have a stockade.[266] The government, however, refused to acknowledge that there was indeed a prison within the camp, leaving the Tule Lake Military Police free to conduct any 'discipline' they deemed necessary.[267] This did nothing to improve the behaviour in camp and strikes led to shortages of food and fuel, adversely affecting the health of the young and the elderly. The jailhouse remained in existence for as long as Tule Lake itself, and beatings were commonplace. The conditions in the stockade led to several hunger strikes by inmates, particularly as it regularly housed three times as many people as it was designed for. It was no wonder that 'dissatisfaction and antipathy toward the government escalated further' under such inhumane conditions, and the stockade is remembered with horror to this day.[268]

Conclusion

Despite the efforts to accurately classify whether enemy aliens might be a threat to national security in Great Britain, ultimately all men over the age of sixteen were interned, as were several hundred women and children who had been categorized as either 'A' or 'B'. In America, there was no such distinction in the internment of the Nikkei, and children with even a fraction of Japanese blood were removed from their homes. Children and babies were never a threat to national security, further reinforcing the fact that evacuation in America was done for purely racial reasons, as opposed to taking measures against the threat of an imminent invasion. Britain's proximity to Europe made an invasion a much greater risk than Japanese landings on the West Coast of America. More likely, perhaps, would have been an invasion of Hawaii, given its proximity to Japan. However, economic concerns outweighed the perceived threat to national security and there was no mass relocation. Instead there was only selective internment of a few thousand males of Japanese descent and martial law was imposed. These inconsistencies in policy fuelled feelings of anger, frustration, and disenfranchisement in the American camps. The Issei, accustomed to prejudice and discrimination 'in conversation and demeanor … seemed far more patient than the Nisei' in camp.[269] The Nisei, by contrast, had been betrayed by the country of their birth and had a maelstrom of emotions with which to deal. Conversely, in Britain, many of the younger generation viewed internment with a mix of trepidation and excitement as a sort of adventure.[270] As Renate Scholem, a teenager at the time of her internment on the Isle of Man, wrote in 1941, 'I learnt to love the rocks and the sunsets and storms while I was there.'[271] For the older generation who were fully aware of the gravity of the situation, being interned was, as Hellmuth Weissenborn explained, 'something that which is beyond my endurance … even fighting to me is less horrifying to me than being in prison'.[272] The age of the internees therefore played a major role in how internment was experienced. Gender also affected the experience. In Britain, women and children were initially interned separately to their husbands, though the later creation of the Married Camp did much to alleviate some of the stresses of single parenthood. In America, families were interned in units, with the exception of men arrested in the initial round up who were held in separate DoJ camps. Ironically, despite the hardships of camp life, many women were in some ways liberated from their daily routines and able to engage in more leisure activities.

On a practical level, the rival approaches to internment led to differences in the construction of the camps. In Britain, nothing new was built as the camps were intended to be temporary. In many transit camps tents were erected, but there was nothing more permanent with the exception of the camps in Canada and Australia. In America, however, even in the transit camps semi-permanent structures were created, and entire camps were created from scratch in the desert and swamps of the American interior. This semi-permanence and involvement of the internees in the work of construction, combined with the fact that the majority of those interned were American citizens, lent the camps a different atmosphere to those in Britain. However, the camps in both countries still shared many common traits. For those interned in America and those transported to Australia and Canada, the climatic extremes required adjustment. Education became the focus of the majority of internees regardless of where they were interned as a means for improvement, to alleviate boredom for all ages, and to create some form of normality for the children. Internees also engaged in artistic ventures in order to protect themselves from the potentially stifling environment of the camps.

The forced proximity of so many strangers led to various tensions in the camps, despite the attempts of the military to involve internees in the internal running of the camps. Riots erupted in several American camps including

Santa Anita, Manzanar, and Tule Lake. There was never the same level of unrest in the British camps, though there was also never the same level as provocation as the Loyalty Questionnaire. However, there were tragedies involved in internment in both countries – the shooting of James Hatsuki Wakasa at Topaz, accidents in several American camps, and the sinking of the *Arandora Star* as it transported several hundred Italian internees and German POWs and internees to Canada. Ultimately though, despite many common themes running through both countries, there were as many different experiences as there were internees, and while looking for commonalities the historian must be careful not to underplay the trauma that individuals suffered during this period.

Endings and Aftermath

Release from the Isle of Man and Dominions

From the very moment of internment, efforts were made by sympathetic members of Parliament (MPs) to expedite the release of the refugees. As Major Cazalet said to the House of Commons in early July 1940:

> I fear that the authorities in this matter have been somewhat stampeded, even against their own better judgment. Alas, all unwittingly, they have given some material to the German broadcasters as regards conditions in this country and the fact that we are now starting to pursue the Nazi policy of interning every Jew in the country. I think it is understandable, and up to a point excusable, but what is not excusable is delay in sorting the cases and in keeping large numbers of people for a long period in internment, when they ought to be released and when there can be no possible shadow of complaint against them.[1]

Cazalet, Eleanor Rathbone, Colonel Josiah Wedgwood, and numerous other MPs were vociferous in their calls for improvements to the treatment of internees as well as for the release of individuals who would be of greater benefit to Britain at liberty than behind barbed wire.[2] As the Association of Jewish Refugees (AJR) remembered on Eleanor Rathbone's passing, 'It wasn't merely that she gave to every single case the most careful consideration: it was that she never ceased to *think* "How can I best help these people? How can I carry the work a stage further? What is the *next* thing to do?"'[3] As a result of these politicians' valiant efforts, the release of internees from the internment camps on the Isle of Man became possible through White Papers concerning 'Categories of Persons Eligible for Release from Internment and Procedures to be Followed in Applying for Release'. The first White Paper was released in July 1940 and contained eighteen categories. However, despite the number of categories, the number of refugees who could apply for release was limited.[4] There was initially little help offered to political refugees, artists or scientists, or students. Those who could assist in an obvious way in the war effort, such as engineers, dentists, doctors, and agricultural workers, had fewer problems when applying for release.[5] For the remainder it seemed that unless they were fit, able, and willing to join the Pioneer Corps there was no hope of freedom or being reunited with their families. The categories were expanded in a second release of the White Paper at the end of August, as a result of press criticism of the first White Paper and suggestions made by the Asquith Committee. Significantly, this included Category 19, which covered people 'who by their writings or political activity had over a period of years taken a prominent part in opposition to the Nazi system and who were actively friendly towards the Allied cause'.[6] This additional category enabled many more internees to apply for release and ultimately 1,502 gained freedom through it, though approximately 1,900 internees had their applications rejected as their cases were not considered appropriate for Category 19.[7] Finally, the categories were increased to twenty-two in the White Paper of November 1940. The delays in the process caused anxiety, frustration, and ultimately obsession with the categories for release. The situation was parodied in the camp journals. In one such article in *The Camp*, the Hutchinson periodical, a fictional character pondered why he had yet to be released:

> Wasn't he under 16 years of age if one took the mental age? Wasn't he more than 65 years if one considered the ages he had lived through? Hadn't his constant longing for freedom developed some acute disease? Was he not a research-worker exploring the depth of his own patience? Wasn't it skilled hardship to live under the same roof with ten Austrians? Wasn't the fact that he never had been a member of any of the 46 German parties a convincing proof of his political eminence?[8]

Reclassification of internees

Before any internee could be released he or she first had to attend a tribunal. This followed a similar procedure to the pre-internment classification tribunals. Only those who possessed a classification of 'C' were considered suitable for release. This meant that any internee classified as 'B' had to be reclassified by the tribunal before their freedom could be assured.[9] This was a time-consuming process, and priority was given to the young and those who might be useful to the war effort. The initial of one's surname also determined the speed at which one might appear before the tribunal. Early on the tribunals were ordered alphabetically. The order was then reversed over a fear that those at the end of the alphabet would be disadvantaged. As a result, if one's surname began with a letter in the middle of the alphabet a longer wait was guaranteed.[10] Mr. Peake, the Undersecretary of State for the Home Office, attempted to quell some of the fears surrounding the process by publicly stating that

> under the scheme which involves scrutiny of each case individually some persons necessarily obtain their release earlier than others, and the fact that one internee is released before another does not imply that he is more loyal or reliable than the man whose release is deferred. Except in the case of persons detained on security grounds personal to themselves, internees not yet released have no reason to fear that their reputation or future will be prejudiced by their continued internment.[11]

For those transported to the Dominions the problem of release was aggravated by their distance from Britain. Internees who wished to immigrate to another country, such as the United States of America, experienced multiple problems. Visas could only be granted to free persons, and while in Britain internees could be transported to London and then freed following notification from the US Consulate, Canada and Australia were reluctant to allow similar liberties.[12] This matter was further complicated for internees in Canada because proof was required that immigrants had paid their own way across the Atlantic, which the internees clearly had not. In order for those internees in Canada, therefore, to have a chance of emigrating to America, they first had to secure transportation back to Britain, almost as perilous a journey as they had endured en route the first time to North America. Ships for transport were naturally prioritized for use in the war effort, making return almost impossible unless one was to enlist in the Pioneer Corps. For those who chose to enlist transport was provided.[13] Transport was also provided to the Isle of Man for the small number of internees in Canada who were granted release on other grounds. For many internees their transport back to Great Britain was luxurious in comparison with their original journey, though also fraught with danger from enemy U-boats. By the spring of 1942, only a few hundred internees were left in Canadian camps, by which time the Canadian government's attitude had mellowed, allowing release to those who wished to remain in the country.[14] Some of those who remained went on to achieve great success, such as Eric Koch, who became an internationally recognized author, broadcaster, and professor.[15] In Australia there were fewer ships with capacity to transport internees back to Britain. When berths became available, priority was granted to those who had signed up for the Pioneer Corps.[16] Australia, like Canada, was initially reluctant to allow the internees leave to remain in the country. Eventually, in 1941, the

Australian government started the process of recruiting internees who could be useful to the Australian war effort, finally creating the Australian Labour Corps for interned refugees.[17] The number of internees who remained in Australia was similar to those who remained in Canada, and as former internee and historian Ronald Stent notes: 'The men who stayed in Canada and Australia probably found it simpler to integrate and become wholly accepted than those who returned and settled in Britain because it is much easier to do so in new and evolving societies than in old established and relatively closed ones.'[18] There were several incidences of poor record keeping that led to confusion during the release process. Internees who were transported to Australia or Canada had sometimes swapped with fellow internees. One such transportee, Mark Lynton, was believed to have been on the ill-fated *Arandora Star*, and was therefore informed that no monies had been allocated to bring him back to Britain as he was believed to be dead. As there was no financial assistance available to Lynton or his friends, they were offered the train fare to Halifax from where the group offered themselves as crew on boats sailing to Liverpool.[19] For youngsters such as Lynton, who had been a student at the University of Cambridge prior to internment, this formed part of the adventure of the experience.[20] It was not such a positive experience for those who were older or wished to be speedily reunited with other family members. Nor was it always possible to return to Britain safely, as many former internees tragically perished on their return journey from Australia when the boats on which they were travelling were torpedoed and sunk.

By the end of August 1940, only 616 people had been released from internment camps, and as the process was refined, this number increased to 2,516 by mid-September. By mid-October, the number of releases had doubled, and by mid-February 1941 this had increased to 10,112.[21] As more internees were released, the number of camps decreased, until finally the only camps in existence were Peveril and Rushen Camps. The majority of the internees left in Peveril were enemy aliens with pro-Nazi beliefs, political refugees, and those who had been detained under 18B.[22] Some of these detainees attempted to gain release through their own methods. On their return from a concert just outside of Peveril Camp in Peel, three internees with Nazi sympathies slipped away from the main group and stole a boat in Castletown Harbour. Under wartime regulations, all boats were immobilized when left moored. With no motor the escapees used two stolen oars and attempted to row across the Irish Sea to neutral Ireland. Two days after their escape they were apprehended seven miles off the Calf of Man and returned to Peveril.[23] Less than two weeks later, an even more audacious escape bid was discovered – a tunnel had been dug from within the camp to a narrow path running between the barbed wire and the outside guardroom on the other side of the fence.[24] It should be noted that the only rioting and genuine escape attempts on the Isle of Man were undertaken by British 18B detainees. Not once did any refugee internee attempt a similar feat.

After internment

The internment experience heightened the desire to assimilate into British culture and therefore led to many cases of name changes. These took place either to mask Jewish origins, such as the case of Manfred Moses who became Steven Vajda, or to Anglicize a Germanic name, such as the case of Ronald Stentsch, better known as Ronald Stent. This was particularly important when internees joined the British military and needed to have Anglicized names in case of capture.[25] When refugees arrived in Great Britain the refugee associations had encouraged those seeking asylum to blend in as much as possible, as well as to disperse themselves around the country. Ultimately, it was internment that led to both of these things occurring. Many of the areas in which the internees had dwelt prior to internment were designated 'Protected Areas', and therefore return was impossible. The Dalheim family, for example, had lived in Hull but were unable to return and moved to Leeds instead.[26] Anna Bill-Jentzsch, a student nurse based in the South-East prior to internment, moved to Bolton post-release in order to take a job as a staff nurse.[27] Sometimes these moves were only temporary, as in the case of Orazio Caira, who moved between Pitlochry and Nairn on his release because they were not Protected Areas, before ultimately returning to Ladybank, where his business was based.[28] Those who had either been in Britain long enough to establish themselves, or had lived outside a Protected Area, were free to return to their previous location.[29] In the Italian community many of the businesses had continued to run through the hard work and determination of the Italian women. Only second-generation women were allowed to remain, and these women therefore took on 'the burden of familial responsibilities at a very young age, running shops and cafes and attempting to keep businesses operating as viable concerns, at a time when many premises had been severely damaged during the riots'.[30] British women who had married Italian men and forfeited their citizenship often had to rely on private charity following the internment of their husbands, as well as manage family businesses sometimes from afar, because of the prohibitions surrounding the Protected Areas.[31] For those of Italian ancestry who had lived in Great Britain for decades, even if they were not interned, there was still suffering. As Wendy Ugolini, in her studies of the Scots-Italian community, has noted: 'For second-generation women ... who remained in protected areas to run businesses and who witnessed the anti-Italian riots at first hand, these incredibly disorienting events served to fatally undermine their sense of belonging within their local communities.'[32] The return of the internees was therefore welcomed, especially because of the losses sustained by the Italian community because of the *Arandora Star*.[33]

One of the biggest effects of internment for the former internees was on their careers. In some cases, this involved a 'war' occupation, followed by a recommence of studies or plans made pre-conflict. During the war, for example, Max Sussman worked for a firm of furriers who manufactured fur-lined tunics for pilots. After the war, he recommenced his studies and ultimately achieved a PhD from the University of Leeds before pursuing a career in academia.[34] The war interrupted plans and delayed eventual professional qualifications for everyone, not just those who were interned. Hans Sturm began his training to become a first mate in 1939, only achieving this eight years later in 1947.[35] Eva Wittenberg had to delay taking her school-leaving certificate as a result of internment. However, when she did go on to further education she was able to take up a career in microbiology, ultimately working at the Royal Marsden Hospital.[36] Wolfgang Nelki was forced out of his legal studies in 1933 and worked as a dental technician before coming to Britain in 1939. It took another twenty-two years before he qualified as a dentist at the Royal Dental Hospital in London.[37] Margot Pottlitzer would have embarked on a career in the BBC had it not been for her offer of employment arriving at a previous wartime residence. As a result, she instead worked for a group of German businessmen who wished to have an alternative form of representation from Bloomsbury House.[38] Individuals and families were often forced to take any work they could get in order to support themselves and their loved ones, regardless of any qualifications they may have held. Some turned the challenges of internment into opportunity. Three of the four members of the Amadeus Quartet, for example, met in the internment camps.[39] Fred Uhlman, a 'provincial lawyer in a provincial town' before the war, was able to use his creativity during his captivity to change careers and become first a painter and then a writer. He painted a vast amount of work while in Hutchinson Camp and his exhibitions were well received in the 1940s and 1950s.[40] Sir Ken Adam, the only known German to serve as a fighter pilot in the Royal Air Force, had an impressive career in the film industry, working as a production designer on some of the best-known films of the 1960s and 1970s. He was awarded both an OBE and a knighthood not only for his work for the film industry, but also for his services to relations between Britain and Germany.[41] These individuals, and many more, made the most of every opportunity available to them, in spite of what happened to them during the war. Personal plans were also placed on hold during internment. While some rushed into marriage prior to arrest in order to minimize the likelihood of separation, others were forced to wait until after one or other of the couple had been released. Joseph Pia married his girlfriend, who had visited him several times in camp, six months after his release.[42] Some even had to wait until many years after hostilities had ceased. Elisabeth Bickel, for example, escaped to Bedford from Germany in 1937 while her fiancé, Emil Rueb, fled to the United States the following year. Bickel, who was interned on the Isle of Man, returned to London and her job as a governess upon release, before ultimately being reunited with Rueb in 1946 when they married in New York.[43]

Serving in the Pioneer Corps

The alternative to obtaining release through the White Papers was enlistment in the Auxiliary Military Pioneer Corps (AMPC). Captain Davidson travelled from London to the camps on the Isle of Man to encourage internees to sign up, even though he was viewed by some as 'insensitive' to the needs of the internees.[44] As one internee noted, 'It was so illogical to put people into the Army, who were interned, to release them if they agreed to it, thus to trust them again, but not if they did not join.'[45] Another internee remembers explaining to a soldier why he was against enlisting:

> I've been put into prison and that sort of thing. All my friends might think I'm a … criminal or a spy or a traitor or something. I've done nothing at all! So, release me. Let me be like any other fellow. Let me volunteer for any regiment. I'm quite willing to join the Royal Scots, the HLI, any regiment you like just like any other fellow. But not just the Pioneer Corps.[46]

Some of the relatives of those interned had tried to volunteer for the Army or for Defence roles, only to be turned down because of the nationality of their father. Then conscripted, they highlighted the irony of the situation where their family members were interned, yet they were expected to fight for their country, when previously they had been discounted as dual nationals.[47] One of the sons of those lost on the *Arandora Star* asked his MP in 1940 'whether his experience [could] help to fight for this country?' when he had been turned down for military service due to his father's nationality, his father was missing presumed drowned, and he was soon to be conscripted.[48] For the Italians, the issue of serving in the military was doubly complicated, therefore, given how the majority of those interned had families who had long resided in Britain.

The AMPC was created in October 1939 as a mainly unarmed corps, with the intention to 'absorb into this corps those men whom the normal fighting units and the corps of the army did not want on account of asocial behaviour, mental disabilities or criminal tendencies, or for other reasons, which made them less desirable than others. It was to be organised into "Q" (queer) and "C" (criminal) companies'.[49] Later this was extended to include 'A' (alien) companies, though the history of the regiment explains the reason why many internees felt it an insult to be restricted to the Pioneer Corps. The AMPC, later abbreviated to the Pioneer Corps, became the only part of His Majesty's Armed Forces where an enemy alien with no special qualifications could serve.[50] The original badge of the corps contained a rifle, pick, and shovel with the motto of 'Work conquers all', further reinforcing the idea that the Pioneers were solely a labouring unit.[51] The majority of those who served in 'A' companies prior to internment had originated from Kitchener Camp in Kent. By 1942, however, approximately 4,500 Germans, Austrians, Italians, and Czechoslovakians were serving in the Pioneer Corps.[52] Those foreigners who did serve in the Armed Forces were understood to be at a greater risk than the standard British soldier were they to be caught. The British Army was aware from the beginning of 1940 that there was a risk that reprisals could be made against the families of foreign-born fighters, and it was also understood that none of the foreign-born soldiers wanted to fight their friends or relatives on the continent. The Italians, for example, ended up with their own company based in Slough from 1941 to 1946.[53] When joining the army, internees were escorted by armed guard to their training base, but as soon as the uniforms had been collected the internees were 'free' to serve in the Armed Forces. One internee, Walter Horst Nessler, commented on the irony of the situation, noting that 'in a matter of minutes, we were transformed from being dangerous or at least doubtful characters into soldiers of His Majesty the King'.[54] Initially women were denied the option of signing up for military service and therefore could not use that as a reason for release, even if a woman's husband joined the Pioneer Corps. Eventually women were given the opportunity to assist in the war effort through organizations such as the Auxiliary Territorial Service.[55] In many cases, these women's skills and knowledge was not utilized, although a minority were transferred to Bletchley Park and other secret listening stations.[56]

The former internees served in many roles in the Armed Forces. It had been hoped to use some of the Italians recruited into the Pioneer Corps for sabotage missions run by the Special Operations Executive (SOE), but it was found that because the vast majority had lived or been born in Britain, their Italian was not fluent enough for recruitment.[57] SOE were able, though, to find many suitable candidates for their work who were German or Austrian. Many of the Germans and Austrians who had recently fled the continent were also recruited to serve in Military Intelligence and the Interpreters Corps, providing essential translation for the interrogation of German prisoners of war and other intelligence-related tasks.[58] The vast majority of those who served in the Pioneers spent two to three years doing essential non-combative work, such as building Nissen huts, constructing coastal defences, forestry, and so on. The first transfers out of the Pioneers started in 1942, when Small Scale Raiding Forces (SSRFs) were sent on secret missions into North Africa, Norway, and Normandy for extremely hazardous reconnaissance behind enemy lines. In 1943, members of the Pioneers were finally given the opportunity to transfer into all regiments of the British forces. Horst Adolf Herzberg, for example, joined the Royal Navy, and his motivation reflected that of so many of the Germans and Austrians who served in the British military: 'Having been in Germany and lived through what was happening, every fibre of my body suggested that I had to do something. The regime was so evil. I was aware of the plight of the Jewish people and I considered it unquestionably my duty to fight at the highest level.'[59] Those who fought in Europe were at a high risk of being discovered and considered as traitors. The fact that so many of the former internees were willing to fight on the side of Britain and volunteer for dangerous missions behind enemy lines testifies to their resilience and determination in the most trying of times. As the conflict drew to a close, most enemy aliens were transferred out of their regular units and into the Intelligence Corps or the Interpreters' Pool in Germany, where they were involved with essential work that greatly assisted the rebuilding of Europe.[60] Once their service came to an end, there was still the question of what would happen to these valiant aliens. In light of their service, the British government allowed former fighters to apply for British citizenship, and these former foreigners helped each other in setting up small businesses. Despite starting out from virtually nothing, these former soldiers went on to build highly successful enterprises and endeavours.

Compensation

There was a lot of transience in the population in general, which naturally translated into transience in the refugee community. It was, therefore, not only internment that changed the fortunes of the internees, but the war itself. Internment was one more hurdle to be overcome. Some attempts at compensation for the internees were made during the Second World War and in the years immediately following. There were numerous instances of internees receiving payment for suitcases damaged en route between Huyton and the Isle of Man, and also compensation for items lost on both the *Dunera* and the *Ettrick*.[61] Claim forms were issued to internees in Australia but it was hard for the internees to provide all the information required, such as receipts.[62] There was also some remuneration given to the individuals on the Isle of Man whose houses had been requisitioned, though the monies paid did not adequately represent either the loss of furnishings or income.[63] No attempts were made by the former internees in the years following the war to claim reparations. This can in large part be attributed to feelings of mostly gratitude from refugees who survived the war, though it can also be seen as a result of continuing latent anti-alienism in British society.[64] After the war, many former internees had to contend with the knowledge that family members who had been unable escape from the continent had perished at the hands of the Nazis.[65] Internees were grateful that they had been given the opportunity to survive and forge new lives in Britain and in other Allied nations. Perhaps as a result of internment, many former internees became naturalized at the earliest opportunity, though this was sometimes delayed by the post-war bureaucracy.[66] For those who had lived in Britain for many years prior to the war, the internment experience encouraged them to claim British citizenship so that they could avoid a repetition of such an event in the future.[67] The group who undoubtedly suffered the most financially and emotionally were the family members of those internees lost on the *Arandora Star*, a large number of them of Italian descent who had lived in Britain for a great many years. If anyone had a case for reparation, it would be these, but their voices went largely unheeded in the eagerness of Britain to put the experiences of war behind it. Little sympathy could be found from the general population as the country was still suffering from the effects of the conflict well into the 1950s.

The closing of the American camps

From the moment those of Japanese ancestry entered the internment camps the American government intended them to be able to apply for release, or 'leave clearance' as it was known in camp. The War Relocation Authority (WRA) wished to encourage 'loyal' Issei and Nisei to disperse to areas of the United States that were away from the West Coast. The poorly constructed 'Loyalty Questionnaire', as discussed in the previous chapter, was the main way for the WRA to ascertain whether an individual was suitable or not for release. For those not joining the military, obtaining clearance was a bureaucratic process that usually took several months from the point of application to the day of release. The problems the process created were summed up by frustrated internees in Tule Lake:

> We are ... handicapped because of the seeming bottle-neck in Washington in getting clearance for applicants for private employment that we have requested. Most of these opportunities require fast action and by the time we get a clearance the job opportunity is gone. I see no hope for this plan of getting people out unless some method is worked out whereby we can obtain faster clearance than we now have.[68]

The process proved a bone of contention in all camps. As Greg Robinson has noted, 'Even Interior Secretary Harold Ickes was forced to wait for some eight months during 1942–43 before he could obtain release and transportation for a pair of Japanese American laborers for his farm.'[69] The interned artist Miné Okubo noticed there was much 'red tape', and that 'jobs were checked by the War Relocation offices and even the place of destination was investigated before an evacuee left'.[70] Students were in the best position to apply for leave as there were several organizations established to assist with finding college places for internees. Between 1942 and 1946 the National Japanese American Student Relocation Council helped 4,084 Nisei leave the camps and continue their studies.[71] This was not without its own problems as many universities limited the number of Nisei they would accept in order not to 'upset' their other students.[72] Relocated Nisei were encouraged to write back to their still interned colleagues and offer guidance on how to 'behave' when released. Lillian Ota reported from Wellesley College:

> It is scarcely necessary to point out that those who have probably never seen a [N]isei before will get their impression of the [N]isei as a whole from the relocated students. It won't do you or your family and friends much good to dwell on what you consider injustices when you are questioned about evacuation. Rather, stress the contributions of [our] people to the nation's war effort.[73]

From the University of Texas another student wrote:

> What a big change it is to live in a city of over 90,000 in which there are only 8 Japanese, having lived in a city like the one I left in which the whole town of 8,000 is Japanese. The transition may be very difficult for many and you had better warn applicants of it. In fact, it may be wisest if you would even try to discourage

some, in order to impress on them that life out here isn't a bed of roses. Remind them of the difficulties our parents had when they first came to America, for I believe in many instances the same sort of predicament may arise.[74]

The students who relocated often gave the first pictures of life outside the camps and how those of Japanese ancestry could expect to be treated on their release. Treatment of the relocated internees varied from acceptance to the type of hostility experienced by the Issei on their arrival in the United States several decades previously.

If an individual wanted to leave a camp and undertake paid employment, he or she mostly had to look east of the Rockies. Regardless of an individual's educational ability, he or she would, more often than not, be recommended for a position as a gardener, domestic, or factory worker.[75] Many state governors were keen not to have an influx of Japanese or Japanese Americans move into their towns, cities, or agricultural land. When Roy Uyehata went in search of farmland for his parents after internment he found that '[in] San Juan Bautista [they] had a big sign at the cattle ranch owned by Congressman Anderson, which said, "Japs keep out." Every other post had [a] sign: "Japs keep out." So I said, "Gee, this is a heck of a place for trying to find a home."'[76] Ralph L. Carr, the governor of Colorado, was in the minority when he expressed a desire to support the former internees.[77] As a result of his pro-Japanese American stance, a number of internees relocated within his state and reported 'no animosity, or fear, or anything ... Japanese were good workers, good farmers, so [we] were respected'.[78] Other popular locations included Chicago and New York. Some of the larger manufacturers instituted a pro-internee hiring policy, such as the Ford Motor Company and the Chrysler Corporation.[79]

The draft and serving in the US Armed Forces

For Nisei males of the age for military service who answered 'Yes' to Question 27 of the Loyalty Questionnaire, their exiting of the camps was expedited when they were counted as volunteers for the US military. The War Department had hoped that up to 3,000 Nisei would be recruited out of the 10,000 eligible males, but in reality the number was only 1,208.[80] Volunteering led to its own complications such as violence and social exclusion within the camps.[81] Some Issei felt so strongly about the possibility of their sons fighting against Japan that they threatened disownment. When the recruiters from intelligence units tried to interview Nisei volunteers inside internment camps they were forced to do so at night, in order to offer some protection to the Nisei.[82] In contrast, in Hawaii, where no substantial exclusion or detention was enforced, almost 10,000 Nisei volunteered.[83] To plug the hole in recruitment for the armed services a draft was instituted. Debates raged in the camps as to the legality of the draft and how it would affect families. The Nisei, like African Americans, were only permitted to serve in segregated units. The Issei and Nisei were well aware of the high casualty rates being sustained by the 442nd Regimental Combat Team and 100th Infantry Battalion in Italy during 1943 and 1944.[84] In light of all the arguments above, many young men, in acts of defiance against the decision of the US government to restore one constitutional right while withholding another, refused to acknowledge their draft notices and failed to report for their physical examinations. In the majority of cases such action was taken by isolated individuals. However, in one Relocation Center draft resistance became a movement. The Heart Mountain Draft Resisters asked 'if we are loyal enough to serve in the army, what are we doing behind barbed wire?'[85] The federal response to draft resistance was, in all but one case, to avoid the legality of the issue and instead sentence the resisters to up to five years' hard labour.[86] The draft resisters took a brave stand, knowing that they would end up convicted felons if they continued in their defiance, as well as suffer discrimination from certain parts of the Japanese community.[87] Thousands of Nisei did join the Armed Forces, however, and they defended both their country and the honour of their families with great valour, be it in Europe, in the Military Intelligence Service as translators, or in the Women's Army Corps.[88] The Nisei were not the first minority group in America to serve in the hope of obtaining recognition and citizenship. However, as the experience of the Issei showed, even when an individual served in the American military, it was no guarantee of future protection. Many Issei men had fought for America during the First World War. Granted naturalization in 1935 by Congress in return for their sacrifice, this failed to protect them from incarceration, nor from being labelled disloyal enemy aliens.[89]

The almost completely Nisei 442nd Regimental Combat Team, which incorporated the 100th Infantry Battalion, was the most decorated regiment in the US Army, living by the motto 'Go for broke' and becoming known as the 'Purple Heart Battalion'.[90] The 100th Infantry Battalion was primarily made up of those from Hawaii, whereas the 442nd was constituted of mainland Japanese Americans. There were many cultural differences between the two units, and initially the two units failed to mix well. The Hawaiians thought the continental Nisei were too quiet and reserved, while the continental Nisei thought the Hawaiians were too cocky and quick to fight. The Hawaiians had not had the same war experiences as the continental Nisei, and after a trip to a Relocation

Center was arranged, the two units got along much better.[91] It was this bond that served to unite them through the hardships encountered during the severe fighting in European theatres. The 442nd was deployed to Europe, as it was considered too dangerous to send them to fight the war in the Pacific where they might be forced to fight family members or friends. They became known as an incredibly brave fighting force, known particularly for their daring rescue of the 'Lost Battalion' in Italy in 1944. In order to rescue some 200 trapped fighters, the 442nd sacrificed over 800 men.[92]

While the 442nd is the best known of the Nisei regiments, Nisei served in many areas of the military, not least in intelligence. There were many individuals able to speak European languages in America who were recruited in order to help intercept and interpret enemy messages and interrogate prisoners of war (POWs). It soon became obvious, though, that there were not enough Caucasians in America who could fluently speak Japanese. Equally, many of the Nisei were not fluent in Japanese, nor were any familiar with Japanese military terms. The individuals best qualified to work in military intelligence, therefore, were the Kibei, especially as some of them had undergone Japanese military training before their return to the United States. However, the option of using the Kibei was not without problem – while some of the Nisei were disqualified from intelligence roles because their Japanese was not good enough, some of the Kibei were unsuitable due to their lack of fluency in English.[93] There were also fears that the Kibei might not be loyal to the United States, having spent their formative years in Japan. It was with great difficulty, therefore, that individuals were found to fill positions in the intelligence division, and many of those who were chosen had to take intensive courses in Japanese to be brought up to an acceptable level of fluency. The Nisei women were often more fluent in Japanese than their male counterparts, and they would have been a huge asset to the American war effort had they been allowed to enlist. One recruiter from Military Intelligence offered the entrance exam to several interned women, and found that they 'were better qualified for this school than many of the boys we accepted'.[94] Unfortunately for the military instructors, the authorities at Camp Savage were unwilling to accept women as either instructors or students, and it was not until 1945 that the first recruits were trained. Nor was it only the military who discouraged women from enlisting – many Nisei women were prevented from joining the army by their family members. It was too much for the Issei to sacrifice their daughters in addition to their sons.[95] Those Nisei and Kibei who served in Military Intelligence were posted across the United States, as well as in the Pacific and Aleutian Islands. They were often viewed with suspicion by their Caucasian comrades until they were considered to have proved themselves. The work of the Nisei in handling POWs, translating, and numerous other tasks that required a knowledge of Japanese were invaluable to the war effort. Their knowledge of the Japanese culture was put to good use not just for gaining intelligence, but also for serving in a humanitarian sense when, following the surrender of Japan, Nisei linguists prevented Japanese POWs from committing mass suicide.[96] After the war was over, the Nisei and Kibei were invaluable in assisting with the rebuilding of Japan, serving with the Allied occupying forces in a variety of roles into the 1950s.[97] Even when serving in the American military, however, Nisei were still not exempted from experiencing racism. Only permitted to serve in segregated units unless working as translators, Nisei soldiers had to serve under Caucasian commanding officers. When President Roosevelt visited military bases and defence installations during April 1943, Nisei soldiers were kept out of sight, ordered to remain confined to their barracks.[98] In Minnesota, where many of the Nisei trained at Camp Savage, some were refused service at bars as they were mistaken for Native Americans.[99] Despite their bravery, there was still no fundamental re-evaluation of the treatment of those of Japanese ancestry living in America. The sacrifices Japanese Americans made for freedom abroad were particularly poignant when the flags and medals commemorating their deaths were displayed by their still interned parents in their one-room barrack apartments. America had demanded the ultimate sacrifice from American sons without offering any reward to their families, despite the fact that, as one leading authority in the American military admitted, the war might well have lasted two extra years without the dedication of the Nisei linguists.[100]

Life outside of camp

In some ways, internment offered new opportunities to women as when they relocated they found opportunities as clerical workers, particularly in cities. The Second World War was in fact a turning point for Japanese American women. By 1950, 47 per cent of employed Japanese American women could be found in clerical and sales jobs, and a mere 10 per cent remained in domestic service, which was a marked difference from the jobs their Issei mothers had endured.[101] However, in the immediate years following release, those who returned to the West Coast found that the employment opportunities for women were similar to before the war. Rose Honda, for example, was initially employed as a domestic before securing a job in childcare, while her mother picked vegetables.[102] Domestic work usually provided the former internee with accommodation, which was another reason why it was urged onto the internees. As Gerda Isenberg, involved in assisting relocation from the camps, wrote to one family: 'Is [your daughter] not able to do domestic work? This is the only way that you could re-settle in California at the present time.'[103] Hostels and boarding houses were the accommodation of necessity for many upon their immediate release. Sometimes through the contacts made in these crowded places, employment offers would be made by those sympathetic to the plight of the Japanese community.[104] The government provided $25 to each internee in addition to rail fare to their chosen destination.[105] The majority of the internees had come from farming or fishing industries. The jobs they were able to obtain post-internment were mostly in cities and in industry, which were lower paying and lower status jobs.[106] As a result of the cap on pay in the camps the internees had very little on which to subsist outside of camp. This situation was compounded by the fact that most Americans had prospered during the war, further increasing the gap between internees and other Americans. In such an economic situation, the former internees had to take what they could get in terms of accommodation and employment, causing additional stresses on individuals and families.[107] Many families had been separated at the beginning of internment, were reunited in camp, and then were separated again upon release. It was common for one member of the family to secure a job and accommodation before sending for other relatives. Joe Yoshioka, for example, arrived alone in Chicago in 1943 and found a one-room apartment with a gas plate. He then sent for his wife and baby, born at Santa Anita, who travelled up from Poston.[108] Commonly, the husband or adult children would be the first to relocate. The necessity of providing for families that had lost so much financially as a result of the internment experience demanded the postponement of personal ambitions. Two of the adult daughters of the Suzuki family relocated to Chicago and obtained jobs in a factory where they cut bra straps. One of the daughters, Shibby, wanted to become a cosmetologist but had to delay applying for beauty school until the rest of the family were more financially secure.[109] There was, however, no guarantee that families would be fully reunited outside of camp. In the Honda family the youngest sister relocated to Chicago while her mother, father, and other siblings returned to Los Angeles.[110] The government had succeeded in its aim to dislocate the family unit.

As time progressed, some former internees started their own businesses. Dry cleaning stores were seen as a 'safe' option for both Issei and Nisei.[111] In Los Angeles, stores were reopened in Little Tokyo, but generally by those who had not lived in the area prior to internment, such as former fishermen from the San Pedro region.[112] Those who had previously owned shops in Little Tokyo often did not restart their businesses, partly because of age, but also because of the painful emotions associated with what had happened during the war.[113] By the end of the war, however, the employment situation had improved dramatically, with Nisei in a variety of skilled and sales jobs such as dental lab technicians, social workers, and the civil service.[114] White collar positions, however, were still out of reach for most unless they were serving the needs of the Japanese community, such as in healthcare.[115] It took several decades for the Nisei to push through the formidable barriers of internment and racism in order to enter the professions, and this was in part made easier due to the relocation of the former internees away from the West Coast.

The closing of the camps

Relocation altered the course of thousands of lives, and as more internees departed from the camps the number of camps decreased, until only Tule Lake remained. Those left in the camps by the time they were closed tended to be the elderly or the infirm, or, in the case of Tule Lake, were 'segregees'. Age was a major problem for the Issei: financially crippled as a result of internment, some were too old to find employment upon release and support themselves. The costs of supporting elderly Issei naturally fell to other family members.[116] Other reasons for remaining in camp included the difficulty of providing for large families on the sort of wages offered in the jobs the internees were offered outside the camp, as well as a considerable fear factor.[117] Stories had been told and retold of racist attacks on former internees after relocation.[118] Even when not the victims of physical abuse, former internees often found themselves victims of more subtle forms of racism, such as when in search of accommodation: 'Wherever there was sleeping room, I rang the bell and said, "I'd like to rent a room." But in practically all cases, they would just tell you that the room was rented already. And you ask them: "Gee, the sign is still in the window." And they said, "Oh, I forgot to take the sign off."[119] The problem of rehousing internees was acute, particularly on the West Coast, where there was a significant shortage of housing in general.[120] It was much more likely for an internee to find accommodation at a place where Issei or Nisei had lived previously and those of Japanese ancestry were considered good tenants. Families could therefore expect to continue living in overcrowded conditions after leaving the camps.

Some of the friends with whom the internees had entrusted their property were faithful custodians and not only looked after the internees' property and possessions, but also returned them after the war. Sadly, for many, the opposite was the case. So-called friends absconded with the proceeds from selling the internees' possessions and land. Haruko Hurt (neé Sugi) remembered her family's good fortune with their friend, Miss Hudson:

> She took care of our house, had it rented out, because it would be very bad to have it vacant. It could get vandalized. That happened to some other people's homes. So she rented it out, paid the property tax and insurance, and whatever costs out of the rent proceeds ... So when the war ended and my parents were coming back, they notified her, and she had the renter move out, and had all the furniture that belonged to us which she had stored, moved back in place. She even had all of the utilities re-connected in my father's name – the water, gas, electricity, and some basic foods in the refrigerator. My mother was (chuckles) so surprised ... She was just flabbergasted. But this is in contrast to many, many other families that lost everything.[121]

By contrast, Hisako Koike's (neé Inamure) family 'rented [our house] out to a Caucasian family. For rent – but of course after the first month, my parents never received any monies for the house'.[122] Despite this theft of monies, however, the Inamure family were fortunate in that they were able to resume living in their house post-release, and their 1929 Pontiac was still in 'tip-top condition'.[123] Others were not so fortunate, told 'I'm so sorry. Somebody broke in and took everything, and the house is gone now. All your things are gone', or sometimes that their possessions had been destroyed by fire or vandalism.[124] Ben Chikaraishi's family ran a hotel prior to internment and entrusted the running of the business to a friend:

> We were leasing the hotel. But all the equipment there, all the supplies like the beds and the mattresses and whatever you had were all ours. And what we did was, we had a friend. 'Friend' – with quotes on – who said, 'They'll be happy to take care of it for you.' And they'll pay us a certain amount of the money that's collected from the weekly rents and things like that. And so we said, 'Oh, that's fine. That'll be nice.' And so he took over our possessions ... It was all right for maybe about three or four months as he sent some money. And then it stopped. And that was the end of it ... This is typical of what happened. And we had no course of action to be able to collect the money outside of legal action. But nobody had money for legal action and being so far away, too.[125]

Despite WRA Property Officers documenting these cases and collecting evidence, they were 'almost helpless when it came to placing the blame and obtaining reparation'.[126] As the WRA noted in 1946, 'Whether the evacuees will receive remuneration for losses depends upon the will of Congress to acknowledge Federal responsibility for losses sustained.'[127]

Restitution

The first move towards restitution took place in 1948, when the Japanese American Evacuation Claims Act was signed with the intention of offering former internees some compensation for the loss of possessions. The 1948 Act was largely the result of a campaign launched by the reconstituted Japanese American Citizens' League (JACL) in the post-war years. After the war the JACL continued with its platform of Americanization, but the experiences while in camp had convinced JACL leadership that building political coalitions with other minority groups was the way forward.[128] The links formed with groups such as NAACP led to an agenda of challenging white supremacy, and demands that some attempt at remuneration be made for the substantial financial losses caused by the evacuation policy. The rate of reimbursement was minimal – approximately ten cents on the dollar – and the paperwork formidable. In order to make a claim, the claimant had to be in possession of receipts of purchase. Given the nature of the roundup for internment, and the small quantities of items the internees were able to transport, the likelihood of receipts surviving was exceptionally low. Many Issei were, therefore, unable to take advantage of the Act or receive compensation.[129] Those who made successful claims were in the minority, but were still unable to regain much of what had been lost. The Act resulted in a government payment of $37 million in response to claims of $148 million. The Federal Reserve Bank estimated that Japanese Americans lost over $400 million in property, excluding losses of earnings or profits.[130] Many of the Issei wanted to put the experience behind them, not that they had much of a choice, as there was little public sympathy for what the former internees had endured. The findings of the test cases brought by Yasui, Hirabayashi, Korematsu, and to a lesser extent Endo further cemented the understanding that the US government was not interested in discussing or apologizing for its actions during or immediately following the war. Out of necessity then, few mentions were made regarding internment after the 1948 Act.

It was not until the 1970s that the campaign for reparations gained momentum. The Emergency Detention Act, Title II of the Internal Security Act of 1950 was repealed in 1971, directly as a result of campaigns launched by the JACL. The fact that Title II was on the statute books meant that further detentions of 'disloyal citizens' continued to be legal, and indeed holding camps were created in Arizona, California, Florida, Oklahoma, and Pennsylvania in order to hold communists and other government undesirables.[131] The JACL believed that 'the American Japanese, as the historic victims, [had] a public duty to prevent a revival of these camps', and the repeal of Title II became a priority.[132] The revocation of Title II proved to be the first step in the reparations movement and served to free the former internees from their quarter of a century silence. One Nisei, Daniel Okimoto, wrote in his autobiography also published in 1971:

> For much of my life, I had struggled with the conviction that I was an American in disguise, a creature part of, yet somehow detached from, the mainstream of American society. This sense of alienation had been a fact of my life from its very beginning, as I was born, the last son of immigrant parents, in the stables of a racetrack in Southern California designated as a transfer point for those Japanese on the West Coast who were being herded into wartime internment camps.[133]

The legal fight enabled many Nisei to begin to come to terms with their experiences, spurred on by their more radical children, the Sansei. The Sansei lived through the campaigns for civil rights in the 1960s, which gave them an impetus for combatting social and racial injustice. Some of the African American leaders had suggested slavery reparations during the campaign for civil rights, and the Japanese American community certainly had an obvious case for financial claims against the US government. Therefore, spurred on by the success of the battle against Title II, three parallel programmes were launched that contributed to the overall redress movement: the California redress for state employees; the judicial battle of the National Council for Japanese American Redress (NCJAR); and three *coram nobis* legal cases.[134] Between December 1941 and May 1942, all Nisei employed by the Californian civil service were dismissed without receiving pay or severance on a collective charge of 'treason'. In 1981, a sponsor for a redress bill for the former members of the Californian civil service was finally found, and Assembly Bill 4087 became law on 24 August 1988. The bill 'provided state income tax exemption for the national redress payments and the right of surviving spouses to receive the state redress payments if the original state employee was deceased'.[135] It thus served as a dress rehearsal for more extensive federal reparative legislation, and demonstrated how long it might take for words to be turned into action – eight years in this instance. Simultaneously, the NCJAR pursued redress from a different angle. The decision to pursue a lawsuit so long after the wartime injustices was a risky business and many expected it to fail. This did not stop over 3,500 individuals subscribing to the NCJAR and donating over \$400,000 towards the legal fight.[136] By 1983, the leaders of the NCJAR felt ready to challenge the Supreme Court's rulings in Korematsu, Yasui, Hirabayashi, and Endo in order to have the exclusion and curfew decisions reversed. While ultimately unsuccessful, without the copious levels of archival research undertaken it would not have been possible to push forward with the *coram nobis* cases. The NCJAR case also served to highlight the historical injustices to the public and served as a means of education, thereby preparing the way for what was to come.

Finally, between 1983 and 1988, a series of legal cases set to address a fundamental error made in the Supreme Court's rulings on the test cases of Korematsu, Hirabayashi, and Yasui. Korematsu, Hirabayashi, and Yasui filed petitions to have their cases reopened under the rarely used legal mechanism of writ of *coram nobis*, 'which is used when a decision is believed to be fundamentally unjust and the defendant has been convicted and already served a sentence'.[137] The government had wilfully withheld information from the Supreme Court, and as a result of the archival research of the earlier NCJAR case, evidence had been uncovered to prove that fact. Ultimately the decision in the Korematsu case was found to have been based in error and the Hirabayashi case was reversed. A similar outcome would no doubt have been the case in the Yasui case had he not sadly passed away before a decision had been made. The judiciary played a very clever game with the way it handled the overturning of the Korematsu and Hirabayashi verdicts, as it essentially absolved itself of any wrongdoing, and failed to take responsibility for the part it had played in the process. The emphasis of the *coram nobis* cases was to lay the blame with the War and Justice departments, who wilfully misled the court. However, this fails to take account of the fact that the Supreme Court intentionally segmented the original cases when they came before the court in the 1940s, because they did not want to rule on the legality of internment.[138] As Jerry Kang has noted, 'The Court demonstrated no sense of either the ironic or the absurd. It also took no special responsibility for the fact that, in coordination with state judiciaries, it itself had sanctioned the very curtailment of fundamental rights in the past, which justified further continued oppression.'[139] Nonetheless, the efforts of all of these cases

> continued and expanded the educational focus to expose the unfairness of the exclusion and imprisonment and explain the enormous toll in human suffering and other losses. Thus, the disclosure of evidence attacking the underlying legal bases which upheld the exclusion and detention coincided perfectly with the redress efforts seeking to persuade the public and Congress that no legal, moral, or factual basis existed for the mass imprisonment.[140]

Yet even though the ground had been prepared and redress seemed a possibility, the final result still depended on the actions of Congress. In response to the growing cries for redress Congress created the Commission on Wartime Relocation and Internment of Civilians (CWRIC), which reported its findings in 1983. The CWRIC was given three objectives: to review the facts and circumstances of Executive Order 9066 which authorized the detention of American citizens; to review directives of the US military forces requiring relocation and detention of American citizens including those from the Aleutian and Pribilof Islands; and also to recommend appropriate remedies.[141] The CWRIC Commissioners held twenty days of public hearings between July and December 1981 in ten locations where testimony from over 750 witnesses was heard.[142] Extensive archival research was also used to create a comprehensive account of every injustice that occurred as a result of Executive Order 9066. The Commission reported that 'the promulgation of Executive Order 9066 was not justified by military necessity, and the decisions which followed from it – detention, ending detention and ending exclusion – were not driven by analysis of military conditions. The broad historical causes which shaped these decisions were race prejudice, war hysteria and a failure of political leadership'.[143] There could, therefore, be no other option than to apologize for the actions during the Second World War which hinged on the spurious motives of Executive Order 9066. After several years of congressional debates and multiple attempts at writing and rewriting a bill, named for the all Japanese American 442nd Regimental Combat Team, the question remained as to whether President Reagan would sign it. The year 1988 was an election year and both the major presidential candidates, Vice President George Bush and Governor Michael Dukakis of Massachusetts, endorsed the redress legislation. Bush released a statement describing the forced relocation as 'an unfortunate chapter in our nation's history ... During times of war, it is often difficult to resist succumbing to hysteria. However, we should always try to remember our basic purpose – to defend freedom and civil rights for all'.[144] When Reagan finally put pen to paper he admitted the historical error of the American government, based largely on the findings of the CWRIC. He noted: 'We gather here today to right a grave wrong ... More than forty years ago ... 120,000 persons of Japanese ancestry living in the United States were forcibly removed from their homes and placed in makeshift internment camps. This action was taken without trial, without jury. It was based solely on race.'[145] The redress movement culminated in the Civil Liberties Act of 1988, which offered an official apology and individual reparations of $20,000 to the approximately 60,000 survivors. The act had taken over forty years to come to fruition, and it came about a further twelve years after President Ford had publicly declared that 'we know now what we should have known then – not only was that evacuation wrong, but Japanese Americans were and are loyal Americans'.[146] As one Nisei said, 'The Isseis are the ones who really, really should have benefited. Most of them, I'd say 80 percent of them were gone by then, especially my mother, who would have been so happy'.[147] Another Nisei captured the mixed emotions involved in the eventual reparation payment with apology:

> Well going back to the feeling of hurt and injury, and trying to get over it, [this] really had nothing to do, in my mind, with a monetary payment or reparation. I think the harm had been done. And it certainly was a strong gesture, because money speaks a lot in this country, for the apology and for the payment.[148]

The overall feeling, however, was relief that finally the internment of Japanese Americans during the Second World War was recognized as wrong on every level.[149] The Civil Liberties Act was a watershed in American history, declaring that historical injustices should be amended, and this is a theme that other racial minorities who have suffered discrimination in the United States have attempted to use in their separate claims for justice.[150] Just as the movement for reparations was, in many ways, inspired by the fight for civil rights, African Americans have gained hope for redress from the experiences of Japanese Americans. In this case, the Act was specifically designed with those of Japanese ancestry in mind and excluded those of Japanese ancestry who had been removed from Latin America, as well as those of German or Italian ancestry regardless of their citizenship status.[151] For those individuals of German or Italian ancestry who suffered alongside those of Japanese ancestry, this unwillingness to apologize or admit to the mistakes of the war remains unacceptable. At the time restitution was made for those of Japanese ancestry, Senator Inouye presented a private relief bill to Congress to ask that Bertha Berg, an American citizen of German ancestry arrested in Hawaii, receive the same amount of restitution as those of Japanese ancestry. The bill was rejected, demonstrating how there is still an unwillingness to treat all former internees equally.[152] This inequality in reparation claims can also be seen in the African American community, where redress has only been achieved in certain specific cases, such as in the case of the Tuskegee 'medical' experiments from 1930 to 1970 where African American men were told they were receiving treatment for syphilis, but in fact were denied medical attention in order to see how untreated syphilis would progress; the events in Rosewood, Florida, in 1923 that led to blacks being burned out of their homes and murdered; and the 1921 race riot that took place in Tulsa, Oklahoma. In the

1990s, after the success of the movement for redress in the Japanese community, campaigners for the Tuskegee men, and surviving descendants of the Rosewood and Tulsa riots were successful in achieving financial compensation, either in the form of money directly to family members, memorials, or scholarships for the community.[153] The decision to 'atone' for various individual acts of historical transgression has continued since, and led to increasing pressure in the campaign for slavery reparations, particularly in America. Since these watershed decisions in the 1990s, further acts of apology have been made to the former internees, such as in 2000, when President Bill Clinton awarded the highest military honour, the Medal of Honor, to twenty Japanese American veterans for acts of heroism during the Second World War. During the ceremony Clinton noted,

> Rarely has a nation been so well-served by a people it has so ill-treated. For their numbers and length of service, the Japanese Americans of the 442nd Regimental Combat Team, including the 100th Infantry Battalion, became the most decorated unit in American military history. By the end of the war, America's military leaders in Europe all wanted these men under their command.[154]

It had been a long fight, but finally recognition was won for many, but not all, survivors of the war, and other ethnic minorities in America have used this as a foundation within their campaigns for addressing historical wrongdoing. The significance of the Japanese American redress movement, therefore, cannot be overstated in the effect it has had on American society as a whole.

Conclusion

In America, the Nikkei had dealt with prejudice for decades, and internment was merely another manifestation of this evil. In Britain, many of those interned had experienced concentration camps in Europe and were therefore relieved to be treated better in British internment camps, yet were also consumed with anguish over the fates of their family members and the possibility of German invasion. In Britain, release became a possibility very early on, thus minimizing the duration of internment for the majority of internees. Those who had to wait the longest were often the internees who had been transported to the Dominions and awaited return transport to the British Isles in order to formalize their freedom. Eventually, both Canada and Australia relented on their refusal to admit the castaways from Britain, and many internees resettled successfully in these countries. In America, it took a lot longer for leave clearance offices to be established, thus prolonging the internment experience. While there were limitations to where internees could relocate in both America and Britain, this had less of an impact on the British internees as fewer of them had well-established roots in a particular area. It was harder for the primarily West Coast population of the American camps to consider new lives East of the Rockies – particularly among the elderly – who felt forced to wait out the war in the hope then they could return home. Many internees secured their release by serving in the military, though this was not always through choice. In Britain, internees were only able to serve as logistical support in the Pioneers until 1943, when they were able to disperse throughout the Armed Forces. In America, serving in a segregated unit was the only option, and even the choice to serve was taken away by the introduction of the draft. Some valiant men protested the outrageous demands placed on them by the US government and were sent to prison for resisting, while other valiant men lived by the 'Go for Broke!' motto of the 442nd Regiment. Men or women, whether fighting on the front lines, working as translators, or assisting on the home front, all sacrificed greatly for either their country of birth or their adopted country of refuge.

All internees, regardless of camp location, lost something in the experience. For many this was in a material form of land, houses, or possessions. Those who had arrived in Britain shortly before the outbreak of war had mostly lost their possessions in their country of birth; however, what few possessions they had managed to hold on to often were of significant sentimental value. This makes the actions of the soldiers on board the transport ships to Canada and Australia all the more reprehensible. Loss, however, was also tangible in the loss of childhood innocence and faith in one's nation of birth – be that America as a direct consequence of internment, or Germany, Austria, or Italy as a result of the war in general. The greatest loss sustained, however, was of life on the *Arandora Star*. Furthermore, their loved ones suffered and were forced to continue without them. Only after a long and hard-fought battle did the Nikkei finally receive an apology for the injustices they had endured. The apology came too late for many, but was a welcome gesture to the survivors, many of whom donated their redress payments into education to prevent the same persecution happening in modern times. There has never been a similar movement in Britain, although undoubtedly the family members of those lost on the *Arandora Star* would have a case.

4

Memory

Memory in Britain

Internment in Great Britain for the majority was over within a year to eighteen months. However, the legacy of the internment experience lived on even after the former internees had reconstructed their lives, and indeed continues to this day. For many, gratitude at being offered refuge in Britain meant that memories of internment focused on the frustration at being delayed in assisting in the fight against Nazism. As Margot Hodge expressed her feelings: 'I had been in Port Erin 13 months. I have never been bitter about having been unjustly interned – only sorry that so much time had been wasted, when I could have been so much more useful pursuing my proper nurse training.'[1] Margot was not unusual in her magnanimity towards internment. Gerd Brent, who changed his name after the war to Bern and moved to Canberra, said that in retrospect

> I think I'm very lucky to have been interned and sent to Australia … my enforced stay behind barbed wire for 16 months, together with hundreds of people of all ages and backgrounds I would not otherwise have had the chance to meet, enabled me to upgrade my general education, taught me much about Homo Sapiens that helped me in later life, and took me to this splendid country in the antipodes to which, at that time, living in wartime Britain as I did, I would not have gone voluntarily.[2]

Eric Koch reflected some forty years after internment that

> we quietly accepted the injustice that was being done to us. As refugees, we were grateful to England for having given us a haven at a time when other countries were making every effort to keep us out. Besides, we felt it was infinitely better to sit behind British barbed wire than to be exposed to mortal danger in Nazi Europe. After all, refugees usually don't tell their hosts how to behave in times of extreme peril.[3]

This attitude was particularly common in the young, who mostly viewed their time in internment as a prolonged holiday with or without other family members. Renate Steinert, interned at the age of six, remembered her time on the Isle of Man as a 'bittersweet experience', both pleasant but also an anxious time.[4] She wrote many decades later:

> I do understand why we were interned. It was totally ridiculous, it was grossly misjudged, and it was entirely understandable ... When you ask, 'Is it still a thorn in your side?' well it doesn't even rate, doesn't even score on the register. There was no question that we wouldn't be returned in good condition as far as the British were concerned. It does sometimes surprise people that one can be so charitable about it. But you have to see it in the context of what else was happening at that time.[5]

However, some young people who were interned without other family members found the experience isolating. One such former internee, taken to the Isle of Man at the age of sixteen, alone because her parents had secured Costa Rican citizenship, never got over her sense of abandonment and this affected her relations with her family for the rest of her life.[6]

The policy of internment did very little to make Britain a safer country – in the vast majority of cases those who posed a real threat to national security were British citizens, German prisoners of war, or members of the German merchant navy. The only way internment could in any way be qualified as a success was that it quelled the fears of those who worried Britain had already been overrun by a Fifth Column of saboteurs. Internment was a negative experience for the refugees, who had fled to safety only to be placed behind barbed wire, not always for the first time. While the refugees retained their belief in the overall sense of British fair play and expected to be released, what troubled them was the anxiety of not knowing which way the war would turn. Had Britain been invaded, the internees would have been unable to escape, trapped as they were on the Isle of Man. This mixture of good and bad aspects of the British treatment of the refugees has led to a certain ambivalence in the memory of the camps that has altered over the passage of time. As Helmuth Weissenborn summed up his experience, 'I can't remember a more depressing time but I don't blame anyone for that.'[7] While internees mostly did not enjoy the experience there was, and continues to be, a sentiment that Britain did what was necessary in a time of war. That is not to say that the shock and trauma of the experience did not last for some time after the events of the Second World War. The separation from one's family was the hardest burden to bear, and even after families were reunited the memories still lingered. Camillo D'Allesandro wrote that 'the initial shock of being suddenly and without warning removed from family and daily life. It lasted some time … We were not ill-treated, however. This is one of the chapters in my life, with sorrow and a new experience helping me to feel more that of others'.[8] D'Allesandro's words temper the shock of internment with a positive attitude towards things that were learnt in camp. In his case it was empathy, in other cases it was of an intellectual nature. Herbert Loebl remembered of his time in the camps that 'I found the time I spent in internment not without interest'.[9] However, his father, Robert Loebl, 'was very bitter about being interned at all'.[10] This difference in memory between family members cannot be attributed just to factors such as age. Elisabeth Bickel's mother, for example, while anxious during her time in camp remembered it generously, focusing on the positives such as being warm enough, having enough food, and being away from the bombing on the mainland. In contrast, Elisabeth described internment as something that 'will always be a black spot in history'.[11] The most common reaction to internment, however, was to attempt to suppress the memories and simply not mention it. David Brand recalled how his stepfather, Dr Angelo Lauria, seldom spoke of his experiences.[12] Certainly the author's own grandfather never recalled his experiences of internment to his children, the only references being made to the fact that his girlfriend, who later became his wife, used to send him textbooks so that he could continue his studies in engineering while interned. Some former internees have chosen to revisit this period of their lives and have returned to the Isle of Man and the streets once encircled in barbed wire. Return visits often provoke mixed emotions – children who were interned remember the holiday-like feel of the camp, coupled with the added memories of stories from older family members who understood the gravity of the situation.[13] The majority of those who were interned during the Second World War have never returned to the Isle of Man. There are no regular reunions and there are no indications as you walk the streets of the former internment camps. For the few internees who have revisited the Isle of Man trips have been undertaken with younger family members. Fritz Lustig, for example, returned to the Isle of Man during the summer of 2014, seventy-four years after his time in Peveril Camp, with his son Robin. Fritz found the return visit gave him an 'odd feeling' as he was able to see the town in a way he had never been able as an internee: 'Peel is quite an attractive small town – of course we never saw it as internees, as we were allowed to leave the barbed-wire-enclosure of the Camp only on the few occasions when we were permitted to bathe in the sea, and were taken to the neighbouring beach.'[14] For those interned on the Isle of Man there was no ill-treatment, even if the food and living conditions left something to be desired. The most unpleasant memories stem from the initial arrests, time spent in poorly equipped and unsanitary transit camps, and overcrowded and thoroughly unpleasant journeys to the Dominions. Those who remember internment with the most anger and frustration are those affected from the tragedy of the *Arandora Star*. Gaetano Rossi, a young priest involved in informing the next of kin about the sinking of the *Arandora Star*, wrote,

> The whole affair of the internment was a tragedy which does not say much for those who were really responsible and who were able to deal with the matter. Perhaps I am wrong but I do get the impression that this question of internment was a way of taking the attention of the people away from other problems and it was also a kind of scapegoat to explain certain events ... So the Italian emigrants paid the price of the internment and of the Arandora Star for a war which they did not want and towards which they had not contributed in any way.[15]

By far the most traumatic aspect of internment was the loss of so many innocent lives through the British government's unwillingness to mark the transport ships for the protection of the internees or, failing that, to allow them to travel in convoy.[16]

The bodies of the victims from the *Arandora Star* washed ashore across Northern Ireland and Scotland, including the Isle of Colonsay, one of the Inner Hebrides. Although Colonsay was not the only location where bodies washed ashore, the islanders' unwavering 'devotion ... in preserving the memory of these war dead ... [makes] Colonsay ... the symbolic burial place ... for all the unnamed victims'.[17] Memorials commemorating the disaster have been created in England, Scotland, and Wales to remember the Italian losses. An early commemorative plaque was installed in St. Peter's Church, Clerkenwell, in 1960. More recently, Liverpool installed a commemorative plaque on the Mersey dockside in 2008, which was swiftly followed by one in Middlesborough in 2009, and a memorial in Cardiff in 2010 to mark the seventieth anniversary of the disaster. The Cardiff unveiling was also celebrated with an exhibition that travelled Wales, drawing attention to this aspect of internment history.[18] In 2012 a new plaque was unveiled in St. Peter's Church to commemorate the London victims.[19] By far the largest memorial, however, is the St. Andrew's Cathedral Italian Cloister Garden, which provides 'a special place to remember those of our loved ones who have died. It also provides a focus for a forgotten tragedy which has never been appropriately marked'.[20] The St. Peter's Church and Cardiff memorials are full of religious imagery, and it is fitting that in a largely Catholic

Italian society, the largest memorial can be found next to a cathedral – God has been the only source of solace for the families of those who lost loved ones on the *Arandora Star*. The Anglo-, Scots-, and Welsh-Italian communities have never forgotten the devastation caused by the unnecessary loss of their loved ones on the *Arandora Star* and without their dedication the memory of those who perished would be all but forgotten. All the memorials of the tragedy have been installed by the fundraising efforts of the British Italian community, and the lack of a formal government apology despite the passage of time has intensified feelings of frustration and anger.[21] In recent years social media has been used in order to campaign for an official apology as well as encouraging younger generations to keep their family memories alive by posting items related to the tragedy online.[22] The *Arandora Star*, controversial at the time, remains a highly emotive unresolved event, as does the treatment of the British Italian community as a whole. Certainly, for the women who were not interned but were separated from their husbands and fathers and left to assume responsibility for family businesses, often suffering abuse because of their heritage, the trauma is still hard to articulate.[23]

Memory in popular culture

The memory of internment has been preserved in fictional depictions of internment, which began to appear from the 1980s, though only a few works have been written. Alexander Ramati, himself a former internee, wrote a documentary novel in which he attempted to capture his experiences as well as those of his contemporaries. In the mouths of his characters he placed sentiments common to many after internment. The paradox of the variance of experiences was reflected in the husband exclaiming, 'Almost two years ... Interned like enemies', while his wife took the more measured view that 'it wasn't all bad ... From the time we were reunited. Two wasted years. I, too, want to contribute to the allied victory ... I can do my share'.[24] As Ramati emphasizes, the family separation was considered the hardest part of internment. He concluded his novel with the statement that his fictional, but highly plausible, family 'bear no ill feelings. Recalling those times, they and the others who were in a similar situation express the opinion that "all is fair in love and war". For they are profoundly grateful to the British for saving their lives and for helping them to overcome their fears and suspicions with love'.[25] Other fictional representations include Francine Stock's *A Foreign Country*, published in 1999, and David Baddiel's *The Secret Purposes*, published in 2004.[26] Both Stock and Baddiel tell the story of internment mainly from the perspective of British citizens – the female protagonist of *A Foreign Country* is a former War Office employee responsible for interviewing arrested Italians during the Second World War, while the female protagonist of *The Secret Purposes* is a translator from the Ministry of Defence. As such they offer an outsider's view of the internment experience and are heavily influenced by historical research that has taken place in the years since the war. Natasha Solomons's 2010 book, *Mr Rosenblum's List: Or Friendly Guidance for the Aspiring Englishman*, takes inspiration from the guidance offered to refugees on their arrival in Great Britain and touches on internment in her description of the trials and tribulations of a German refugee in his lifelong attempts to Anglicize and gain British acceptance.[27] The inspiration for Baddiel's and Solomons's work lies in family history – Solomons's grandfather was interned, as was Baddiel's father.[28] Baddiel's family connection to internment has also been documented through an episode of BBC1 television series 'Who Do You Think You Are?', first aired in 2004.[29] Stock, however, chose to address the internment experience as a result of a chance reference to the sinking of the *Arandora Star* in a book she was reading, causing her to abandon her original piece of work.[30] Despite focusing on different aspects of the internment experience, a common theme that links these novels is the emphasis on psychological scarring from the experience that ultimately changed the course of the lives of the main characters. The message of these novels is that all those involved in internment, regardless of which side of the barbed wire they were on, suffered emotionally.

Television has also been used as an accessible way of telling the story of the Second World War. The subject of internment has been mentioned in many popular television shows including the David Baddiel and Tamzin Outhwaite episodes of 'Who Do You Think You Are?', as well as 'Great British Railway Journeys', all of which were produced by the BBC.[31] The topic of internment has also been discussed on radio, most notably by David Cesarani in a two-part series called 'Behind the Wire', first aired on BBC Radio 4 in 2000.[32] Only one fictional representation has been made that focuses solely on internment – *The Dunera Boys*, a drama written and directed by Ben Lewin, starring Bob Hoskins, and produced in Australia in 1985. The mini-series followed the adventures of a group of Jewish refugees sent to Australia on the *Dunera*. The series attracted complaints from viewers about the depiction of the behaviour of British soldiers on board the ship. In actual fact, *The Dunera Boys* toned down the mistreatment of the internees by British soldiers as it was feared that if the portrayal were honest the show would be extremely badly received in Britain.[33] *The Dunera Boys* also took artistic liberty with the fact that the internment experience is shown solely as a Jewish experience, despite the fact that Italians and National Socialists were also sent to Australia.[34] Overall, though, *The Dunera Boys* was heralded a success for Australian television and made accessible the subject of internee transports to the wider public imagination. The fictional portrayal of events in the Australian camp and on board the *Dunera* is a double-edged sword, in part to be praised for discussing an oft-forgotten piece of wartime narrative, while also having to sacrifice full historical accuracy in order to maintain audience attention. However, as the only real attempt to engage viewers in a saga where empathy is generated for the main characters it is to be lauded, although more recently the subject of internment was also touched on in an episode of the popular wartime drama *Foyle's War*.[35]

As has been noted in previous chapters a multitude of talented artists were interned on the Isle of Man, and their creativity was hindered, but not suppressed, during their time in camp. Art can be used as a powerful instrument in communicating the subject of internment to the public and keeping its memory alive. Celebrations of interned artists' work have taken place across the country. Kurt Schwitters, perhaps the most famous of the interned artists, has been the subject of several exhibitions in recent years.[36] These include 'Kurt Schwitters, Responses to Place' at the Sayle Gallery in Douglas, Isle of Man, which followed on from the 'Schwitters in Britain' exhibition shown at Tate Britain, both in 2013.[37] The exclusive focus on Schwitters followed the highly successful 'Forced Journeys: Artists in Exile 1933–45' exhibition, also held at the Sayle Gallery in 2010.[38] The significance of these exhibitions lies in the fact that great emphasis was placed on the fact that Schwitters and his contemporaries had fled Nazi Europe and endured internment. An entire room at the Tate exhibition was devoted to Hutchinson camp, bringing thousands of individuals into contact with the subject, and mention of internment was made in reviews of the exhibition in local and national periodicals.[39] Without the work of the many artists interned on the Isle of Man we would have very little record of what the camps actually looked like. Some photographs exist from the time, but there was never a comprehensive attempt made to record camp life. Consumed by boredom, many internees used the materials available to sketch their confinement and these allow the camps to live on in a more publicly accessible way. The ability to visualize the camp and its surroundings is a powerful medium for communication and commemoration. This has further been highlighted by the release from the Isle of Man Post of a special set of stamps celebrating the work of six interned artists named 'Isle of Man Internment Art History' in 2010. An everyday item was thus turned into an instrument for opening new dialogues on internment.

The image on the 55p stamp did not shy away from illustrating barbed wire and therefore hinted at the reality of camp life, even if the other stamps in the collection do not hold obvious links to internment. Indeed, the colour and vigour of the artwork on the stamps makes them eye-catching, without giving too much of an idea of the privations of camp life or the loss of liberty.

Douglas, the Manx capital, is in many ways the centre of commemorative events for internment. The Manx National Archives holds one of the most comprehensive lists of documents regarding internment.[40] Former internees are encouraged to write down their memories or donate personal correspondence so that younger generations can capture a glimpse of what life during the Second World War was like for the internees. In 1994, an exhibition called 'Living with the Wire – Civilian Internment in the Isle of Man during the Two World Wars' was held at the Manx Museum, and the publication linked to the exhibition continues to be one of the most popular books sold by Manx National Heritage.[41] The success of the exhibition can be linked to the decision taken in 2000 to create as comprehensive a list as possible of individuals interned on the Isle of Man between 1940 and 1945, encouraging family members to submit information pertaining to internment, and the creation of a new dialogue with former internees themselves.[42] The interest in the subject has continued to grow in the years since the exhibition. Yvonne Cresswell, curator of social history at Manx National Heritage, has noted that as the collection has grown, 'the rich and varied story of those who lived behind the wire is constantly growing and the pieces of the jigsaw puzzle, which seemed so fragmented in 1994, are slowly coming together'.[43] Douglas is not the only centre for commemoration, as Liverpool forms another natural site for remembering internment. In 2004, an exhibition entitled 'Art behind Barbed Wire' focused exclusively on the art produced by a handful of artists who had been interned in Huyton. The works by Hugo Dachinger and Walter Nessler had been purchased by the Walker Art Gallery five years before and the exhibition was the first time these works had been ever seen in public.[44] Emphasis was placed on contextualizing the pieces of art in the greater narrative of internment and the role that the unfinished housing estate now known as Woolfall Heath Estate played as a transit camp. The exhibition received national recognition, and one reviewer in *The Guardian* noted the paradox of these images from internment:

> Two bitter resonances emanate from and beyond the work. The first is that which makes the pictures additionally unsettling to contemplate: the iconography is exactly that of the Holocaust, which the internees, unknown to them, had

escaped by being in Britain. There is disturbing paradox in the fact that these men had escaped the fate of millions they left behind, but were prisoners.[45]

Internment is also commemorated in Australia. In 1999, the *Dunera* Museum was created, located in Hay Railway Station, New South Wales, acting as a permanent reminder of the presence of the internees sent from Britain during the Second World War. The museum collection includes photographs, stories, and music from the camps, and symbolically, the camp searchlight shines for one hour each night.[46] The Dunera Boys, as the internees sent to Australia are collectively known, have not only inspired the television mini-series mentioned earlier, but also several exhibitions. 'On Board – Behind Wire: The Story of the Dunera Boys', for example, was shown at Sydney Jewish Museum from 2007 to 2008, and 'The Dunera Boys 70 Years On' was at the National Library of Australia in Canberra in 2010.[47] Unlike in Britain, the Dunera Boys, as they still refer to themselves, hold reunions every year and in September 2015 celebrated the seventy-fifth anniversary of the *Dunera*'s arrival. There is even a Facebook group where the family members of Dunera Boys post memories and news.[48] The memory of internment in Australia is therefore still highly active. This is perhaps a reflection of the deeper bonds formed between the internees who were sent abroad. Not only did they survive long and gruelling journeys, those who had initially survived the *Arandora Star* disaster were further bound together by their shared experiences. This, coupled with the fact that those interned in Australia and Canada often had their release delayed as a result of their distance from Great Britain, meant that reunions tend only to be organized by those sent abroad.[49]

The memory of internment in Britain has in many ways lain dormant in the public sphere, although not in the private sphere, for many decades. It is in the past twenty-five years that the subject has begun to re-enter public consciousness and only in the past five years that exhibitions have become widespread, opening the history of the camps to a much wider audience across multiple continents. The resurgence of interest can be linked to a general upsurge of interest in stories related to refugee experiences from the Second World War that gained momentum in the 1980s. The *Kindertransport*, for example, became the focus of media attention through the television show 'That's Life' on BBC1 in 1988, and has not left public memory since. The 1973 series 'The World at War' sparked this resurgence in some ways, because during the research for the programme numerous interviews were conducted with individuals who survived the war. As more anniversaries have come and gone, it has become more obvious that in order to capture the memories of survivors, significant work has had to be done, for example, the recording of interviews undertaken by the Imperial War Museum. The depth of research carried out from the 1970s has led to a reassessment of many aspects of the Second World War and the public perception of the conflict. Many former soldiers had experienced internment, and therefore the subject began to re-emerge into public consciousness as their stories were told. Since then, through television, fiction, and art, the public imagination has been sparked into life. However, the coverage given, while a vast improvement on previous years, is still somewhat limited and there is more that can be done to bring this area to the masses. The surviving family members of those lost on the *Arandora Star* are attempting to draw on the resurgence of interest in internment to bolster their appeal to the British government to apologize for the terrible tragedy. Certainly, the memory of the *Arandora Star* and the consequences of internment have never left the memory of the British Italian community.

Memory in America

Internment in the United States of America lasted for between eighteen months and three years for the majority of the internees, although there were significant variations on the duration depending on whether a family was segregated in Tule Lake or were otherwise unable to leave until the camps were closed. The upheaval of entire family groups caused multiple problems that lasted long after the last camp was closed. By turning Tule Lake into a Segregation Center for 'disloyal' internees, the most damaging psychological aspect of internment was set in motion. Families who had argued over their answers to the Loyalty Questionnaire were split up depending on the answers given by the head of the household. When these answers differed from those of their adult children, separation sometimes took place. In one particularly striking example, Mabel Imai Tomita, an infant of internment, was raised by her paternal grandparents. Imai Tomita's mother's family answered 'No-No' to the Loyalty Questionnaire and were ultimately repatriated to Japan, while Imai Tomita's father's family answered 'Yes-Yes' and several family members joined the army. Both of her parents remarried and created new lives and families while she grew up not knowing the full story until the age of thirty-six.[50] The stress caused by answering the Loyalty Questionnaire led to many family separations, rifts, and estrangement. So many aspects of internment were designed to wrest apart family bonds – from eating meals in mess halls, to asking families to decide in which country they placed their allegiance. While some of the anger and frustration of the former internees was tempered by cultural traditions that had been ingrained into the Nisei from an early age *on*, such as the lifelong obligation of every citizen to one's government and to one's parents, and *giri*, the obligation to the dignity of one's name, this did not mean that the psychological scars of the time did not remain.[51]

Internment in popular culture

During the time that the camps were open, War Relocation Authority (WRA) ethnographers and approved journalists created images of camp life in words and pictures that reinforced the view that internment was not a departure from the American ideal. Ethnographers who evaluated the behaviour of the internees, for instance, concluded that 'far from being an ugly irrational racist enterprise, relocation was fair and democratic'.[52] This view has since been challenged, as we will soon see, but this portrayal is still deeply rooted in American memory. Photographs that were taken inside the camp were also used selectively in order to reinforce this narrative as authorized camp photographers were limited as to what they were allowed to document. Photographers such as Ansel Adams, however, did their best to challenge this view. Adams, perhaps best known for his stunning photographs of Yosemite National Park, was a friend of Ralph Meritt, who invited him to Manzanar in 1943 to create a photographic record of internment. In his introduction to the publication of his photographs in *Born Free and Equal* Adams wrote,

> I believe that the arid splendour of the desert, ringed with towering mountains, has strengthened the spirit of the people of Manzanar. I do not say all are conscious of this influence, but I am sure most have responded, in one way or another, to the resonances of their environment ... Out of the jostling, dusty confusion of the first bleak days in raw barracks they have modulated to a democratic internal society and a praiseworthy personal adjustment to conditions beyond their control.[53]

Adams felt the injustice of the situation and respected the internees' attempts to improve their environment. Despite orders that prohibited photographing the guard towers or barbed wire, Adams was still able to incorporate them into some of his photographs, and the words that accompanied his photographs in *Born Free and Equal* led to copies being burned in protest in 1944.[54] Adams used his images to subvert the popular view of the Japanese at the time, particularly with his photographs of interned schoolgirls, dressed as any young American girl might be, which 'thwarts the possibility for a visual memory of Pearl Harbor that the specter of Japanese American schoolboys potentially embodies'.[55] After the unsuccessful publication of his photographs during the war, Adams gave his negatives to the Library of Congress with the hope that his photographs would be published in a more objective time.[56] It was not until 1988 that the works were once again released, by which time a formal apology had finally been made to the survivors of internment. Adams was not alone in documenting the camps, or in failing to see his work gain public approval. Dorothea Lange, famous for the documentary photographs she took during the Great Depression, travelled around various sites associated with internment. Lange's work was commissioned by the federal government, and also suppressed by them for the duration of the Second World War. The first time any significant portion of the photographs was published was in 1972, and no 'coherent selection' was published or exhibited until 2006.[57] Lange was an avid supporter of Franklin Delano Roosevelt and when hired by the WRA to photograph the internment program it was anticipated that her work would support the work of the WRA. However, the honesty of Lange's photograph failed to show internment in a light favourable to the WRA, and hence the suppression of her work. Lange persevered, even when hounded by Military Police and restricted in her movements around the camp, as she believed that 'a true record of the evacuation would be valuable in the future'.[58] Lange's work has been invaluable to the preservation of accurate depictions of the camps and has been used in countless exhibitions and publications, presenting internment in an accessible yet thought-provoking way. A third photographer maintained a record of the camps, but his background could not have been more different than that of Adams and Lange. Toyo Miyatake was a professional photographer interned in Manzanar. In defiance of the law that forbade those of Japanese ancestry to own a camera, Miyatake smuggled a lens and shutter into the camp. Using pieces of scrap lumber he was able to create a wooden box camera with which he documented life in the camps.[59] When Ralph Merritt discovered the illegal camera, instead of confiscating it he allowed Miyatake to continue his work, and without his photographs we would have a much more limited pictorial record of life inside the camps. Miyatake's work offers an 'insider' view of internment, itself a counterpoint to the 'official' history of the camps eschewed by government agencies and other photographers. His work is not the only 'insider' view of camp life, however. Remarkably, Dave Tatsuno, a home movie enthusiast, smuggled a shoebox-sized cine camera into Topaz and clandestinely filmed various aspects of camp life between 1942 and 1945. Tatsuno's documentary film, *Topaz*, was released in 1945 and remains one of only two amateur films to be included in the National Film Registry.[60] His work gives an unprecedented view of camp life and is a powerful medium for visualizing the daily realities of life in camp.

Art has also been used to perpetuate the memory of the camps. Miné Okubo, for example, created a series of sketches of camp life that have been widely published.[61] The internees were given greater flexibility in expressing themselves through art, which was mostly uncensored, and these images where they survive are powerfully emotive.[62] In 2010, an exhibition entitled 'The Art of Gaman: Arts and Crafts from the Japanese American Internment Camps, 1942–1946' ran for almost a year at the Smithsonian American Art Museum.[63] *Gaman* is a Japanese term for 'bearing seemingly unbearable with dignity and patience', which makes an apt title for the diversity of artwork on display, from paintings to sculpture.[64] The exhibition has since toured Japan but returned to America in 2014 where it is being hosted at the Bellevue Arts Museum in Washington State.[65] The intricacies of the designs on display are all the more remarkable considering the limited resources available to the internees in camp. Once again, through their creativity, the former internees transformed the most humble of circumstances and objects into things of beauty, items that can be considered small acts of defiance in the face of oppression.

As in Britain, internment was not fictionalized until the 1980s. Gene Oishi, a former internee, wrote *In Search of Hiroshi* in order to preserve the memory of children's experiences in the camps. In Oishi's introduction he discusses his research of the time he spent in Poston and the continued effects of internment several decades later: 'As I struggled to capture Hiroshi in fiction, and as I talked to other Japanese Americans, I began to see that the war and the internment had affected not only me but my entire generation more profoundly than I had realized. We were not simply scarred; we were crippled in ways that are becoming apparent only today.'[66] Since the 1990s there has been an upsurge in publications written by Japanese Americans and others to perpetuate the memory of this provocative period of history. *Snow Falling on Cedars* is perhaps the most famous of these novels, having also been turned into a film.[67] Set on the fictional island of San Piedro, off the coast of Washington State, the plot focuses on a murder trial where a Japanese fisherman is accused of murdering a Caucasian fisherman who fell overboard and drowned. The trial brings simmering tensions in the fishing community to a head, with multiple recollections of events related to internment. *Snow Falling on Cedars* won multiple awards and comparisons with another great American classic, *To Kill a Mockingbird*.[68] Both books share many similarities in their stories, as the struggles of racial minorities in America bear many of the same hallmarks. In a different genre, Danielle Steel, the prolific writer of romantic fiction published *Silent Honour* in 1997, a story in which internment is the backdrop to emotionally charged interactions and relationships within the Japanese community.[69] While Steel's books tend to revolve around unrealistic characters, the book topped the bestseller chart in America after its publication. An argument can be made that the characters do not realistically reflect the former internees, although the novel did open up new discourses in the public memory. While *Snow Falling on Cedars* and *Silent Honor* were written by those outside the Japanese American community, in 2002, the first publicly acclaimed novel based on family experiences of internment was published by Julie Otsuka. Otsuka's grandfather was arrested by the FBI as a suspected spy for Japan the day after Pearl Harbor was bombed, and her mother, uncle, and grandmother spent three years in Topaz.[70] *When the Emperor Was Divine* tells the story of a family's experiences prior to internment, through the camps, and the attempts to rebuild shattered lives after the war.[71] Significantly, Otsuka's book has 'been assigned to all incoming freshmen at more than 40 colleges and universities,' which will introduce a whole new generation to the subject.[72] The importance of introducing students to the internment story cannot be underestimated, and Otsuka's novel is particularly poignant, based as it is on familial experience. The addition of *When the Emperor Was Divine* to national curriculums demonstrates how far, in some ways, America has come regarding race relations. However, the continuing open hostility to racial minorities in America shows not only how important it is to include books such as these in educational establishments, but also how quickly some of these lessons seem to be forgotten. The interest in the subject has continued to be explored though, most recently by Jamie Ford in 2009. *Hotel on the Corner of Bitter and Sweet* is based on a different racial relationship than the traditional Caucasian/Japanese conflict. Instead, Ford chooses to focus on the relationship between the Chinese and Japanese immigrant populations.[73] The Panama Hotel is the central location in the novel and the discovery of property belonging to former internees brings about reminiscences of a time before the community of Japantown was dispersed. All three books mentioned have been bestsellers, have won awards, and been translated into several languages. Several children's books have also been written in order to engage younger readers. *The Lucky Baseball* is but one example of how the story of internment is being introduced to children.[74] The impact of the historically based novel has been to introduce an extremely wide and varied audience to the topic, and the emotionally charged writing has helped readers to engage deeply with the subject matter. Internment has become a subject that both Caucasian authors and former internees feel comfortable addressing in fiction, and it is certainly a medium which has the potential to influence a great section of the American populace.

Films have also been used to convey the deeply complex issue of internment and interracial relations in America. There have been hundreds of documentaries about the camps.[75] One that has gained particular coverage in recent years has been *The Manzanar Fishing Club*, released in 2012. The film began as a lecture about the story of several avid fishermen who were interned at Manzanar but would sneak out of camp in the dead of night in order to fish for trout in the Sierra Nevada's high altitude lakes and rivers. The acts of defiance made by these men have now been remembered in a feature-length documentary that has toured the United States.[76] In addition there have also been a handful of Hollywood feature films, including the 1951 release *Go for Broke!* that starred many of the veterans from the 442nd Regimental Combat Team, and *Bad Day at Black Rock* released in 1955. Both films were well received at the time and nominated for several Oscars. Reviews of *Bad Day at Black Rock* drew comparisons with another popular movie of the time *High Noon*. While the storyline was recognized as focusing on the treatment of a Japanese family, more was made of the virtues of valour and justice, as these were more acceptable centres of focus.[77] *Go for Broke!*, met with some criticism at the time it was released because war movies declined in popularity in the early 1950s, as well as criticism over the use of veterans with little or no acting experience. However, for some, this was precisely the film's strength. *The New York Times* noted that

it is this quality in the picture – this accomplishment of sincerity and credibility in the Nisei soldiers, many of whom are actually played by veterans and heroes of the 442d – that deserves the highest praise. For in making his Nisei genuine people, with the characteristics of average young men – not fancified little tin heroes – Mr. Pirosh has simply achieved precisely the affection, the understanding and the tolerance for them that they deserve.[78]

More recently *Come See the Paradise* was released in 1990 and *Snow Falling on Cedars*, based on the hugely popular novel, was released in 1999. *Snow Falling on Cedars* starred Ethan Hawke and Max von Sydow, was released by Universal Pictures, and was nominated for an Oscar. *Come See the Paradise*, a much smaller production that reintroduced the subject of internment to the general public, starred Dennis Quaid, was released by 20th Century Fox, and was nominated for a Palme d'Or award at the Cannes Film Festival. The storyline of *Come See the Paradise* focuses on Quaid's character running away from a troubled past, falling in love and marrying a Japanese American woman, and then getting drafted into the US Army while his wife and daughter are interned. Both *Come See the Paradise* and *Snow Falling on Cedars* have many similarities in plot, yet the former was a box office flop whereas the latter met with great success, which can in large part be attributed to the popularity of the novel upon which it was based. With the release of two major films and countless television documentaries, the images of internment have become readily accessible to the American public. This has further been highlighted in the inclusion in many modern television series of a character who suffered internment. In a 1983 episode of 'Magnum P.I.' a civilian guard who killed an internee on Sand Island, Hawaii, is eventually tracked down and murdered by one of the witnesses to his crime.[79] A 'Cold Case' mystery in 2007 told the story of a Japanese American man who was killed in 1945 while trying to get his deceased son's heroic war record recognized.[80] In 2013, the remake of 'Hawaii 5-0' showed a series of camp reminiscences while the team tried to trace the man who murdered an internee in 1943.[81] These three programmes illustrate the fascination that America now has with this part of its history, which it initially rejected in the decades following the war. They have also enabled millions of individuals to learn more about certain aspects of their nation's history through entertainment. While liberties are almost certainly taken, it is remarkable how modern interpretations of internment invariably are mostly historically accurate, making them powerful tools in keeping popular memory of internment alive. In late 2015, the story of internment took to Broadway in George Takei's *Allegiance*, a musical that focuses on Japanese Americans during the Second World War. Takei, himself a former internee, has dedicated his life to raising awareness of internment.[82] *Allegiance: The Musical* debuted in America in 2012 to mixed reviews. The *Los Angeles Times* opened its article by describing the musical as 'a mild story of broken family ties, not a judgment of U.S. mistakes related to the internment of Japanese Americans in the 1940s'.[83] One of the greatest criticisms of the musical has been directed at the fact that all the characters in the play are fictional, with the notable exception of Mike Masaoka, leader of the Japanese American Citizens' League (JACL). Gerald Yamada, in his open letter sent on behalf of the Japanese American Veterans Association, voiced the opinion of many that *Allegiance* 'implies that JACL and Masaoka colluded with the government in shaping various governmental policies'.[84] Significantly, there is little mention of the actions of President Roosevelt or Lieutenant General John DeWitt. Therefore, it is left for the audience to infer that the JACL had a role in shaping governmental policy, which is patently untrue. The writers of *Allegiance* address these criticisms by pointing out the play is only 'inspired' by actual events, and therefore 'need not be held to the standards of strict documentary'.[85] Nonetheless, there has been much controversy in the Japanese community regarding the play, with individuals torn between applause for making the subject accessible to the general public, and criticism for implying that draft-resisters made the 'right' decision and those who served in the 442nd made the 'wrong' choice. The open letter from the Japanese American Veterans Association highlights what is still a highly controversial aspect of internment: 'In hindsight, both groups should recognize that there was more than one way to show one's loyalty. Neither choice was the right one or the wrong one. Today, we should celebrate both groups for following their convictions rather than fueling this hostility by continuing to pit these two groups against each other.'[86] Even the British reviews had their criticisms, *The Guardian* calling the play 'an unexceptional though often affecting new Broadway musical'.[87] The mixed reviews may partly be responsible for the decision to end the show in February 2016 after a comparatively short run, though it has since been shown in selected cinemas. However, what is agreed across all sections of society is that bringing the story of internment to a larger audience is a good idea, but care has to be taken in the execution. *Allegiance* was designed to reach mixed audiences, and hence the injustice of internment is emphasized. Conversely, within the Japanese community itself a revue called *Camp Dance* has been entertaining aging former internees in retirement homes and community centres since 2001. This is an 'unabashedly nostalgic revue' performed by Sansei in Los Angeles's Grateful Crane Ensemble.[88] *Camp Dance* is for those directly affected by internment, and therefore seeks to engage the happier memories of internment. The revue also taps into the fact that many of the former internees who are still alive were children when interned, and therefore did not always fully comprehend the gravity of the situation. Robert Nakamura, a filmmaker interned at the age of five years, explained that 'when I [later] learned about the injustice of it all, I felt guilty for having had a good time in camp, apologetic even. So camp has been fraught with ambivalence, a nostalgia mixed with deep resentment, and a lot of anger'.[89] The memory of internment continues, therefore, to be not only multifaceted, but innately complex depending on the role and age of the internee during the war.

Physical reminders of internment

The former sites of the Relocation Centers are themselves testimony to the enduring memory of internment. To look at aerial photographs of the former

Figure 4.1 The recreated guard tower stands alone in the wilderness that is Manzanar. The same fear is not engendered in the modern-day visitor to the camp as was present when this was but one of the guard towers, manned by armed guards, with a barbed wire fence surrounding the camp.

camps shows permanent scarring on the landscape and very obvious footprints of the distinctive camp layouts. All former Relocation Centers and Department of Justice (DoJ) camps fall under the remit of the National Park Service (NPS). In 1999, an eBook was compiled detailing the geography and history of the former camp locations, along with an inventory of surviving evidence of the camps' existence.[90] *Confinement and Ethnicity* offers a history of the architecture and archaeology of the sites, as well as a wealth of data concerning the number of internees and from where they originated. The NPS are officially responsible for maintaining the former sites, but due to budgetary concerns until now they have only able to invest in the preservation of selected sites. Manzanar, perhaps the best known of all the camps, has experienced the greatest amount of investment and is seen by many as the centre of the internment story, and a well-designed and interactive museum is housed in the old High School auditorium.[91] However, the fact that it is the auditorium is the only surviving building is somewhat ironic. As Emily Roxworthy has noted, 'In a real sense, then, a theatre is the only thing that remains of the internees' habitation at Manzanar', and this in many ways has influenced the way in which the site has been 'interpreted'.[92] The museum includes exhibits from the camp, a partial interior of a barracks apartment, and oral and written testimonies from former internees. As you enter the auditorium you hear, on repeat, the sound of applause. The applause emanates from a recording of President Reagan signing the official apology for internment, giving a 'triumphal soundtrack', which Robert Hayashi calls the NPS's 'mission of retelling a progressive history'.[93] As Hayashi has also pointed out, after the presidential apology, the historic sites of Manzanar et al. lost much of their 'potentially controversial meaning'.[94] Two reconstructed barracks have been created to give a sense of the accommodation in which the internees lived. In 2005, the NPS also rebuilt one of the eight guard towers that stood on the perimeter of the camp. Many aspects of the hard landscaping such as stairs, foundation stones, and paths are still present in the camp. The road system still exists, as does the camp cemetery, which is the focal point of the annual Manzanar pilgrimage, organized by the Manzanar Committee.[95] The rebuilt tower stands testament to the controversial history of this space, but it is important that the NPS continues to ensure the parks do not become 'theme parks' and that the gravity of what occurred at the sites is appropriately communicated.

Tule Lake, the most controversial of all the camps, also has a significant NPS presence, although this is based primarily at the Lava Beds National Monument, which is a short drive from the stockade itself. The Tule Lake site, unlike Manzanar, has in large part been built upon by the town and is on mostly private

Figure 4.2 Excavated water garden foundations at Manzanar. The internees created water gardens to add some beauty to their barren surroundings.

land. The majority of the former barrack buildings were used by residents of Newell after the closing of the Tule Lake camp to create houses that are still very much in evidence to this day. Indeed, the stockade was stripped of all usable materials, such as doorframes, before it was secured by the current landowner. The internees' presence is further felt in the rock promontory opposite the former camp site that houses a cross originally built by the internees when they were allowed out for picnics before Tule Lake became a Segregation Center, and in 1982, the cross was replaced with a steel replica placed by the California Japanese Christian Church Federation, making it a permanent feature of the landscape.[96] Recognition was given to the Tule Lake site in 2008 when President George W. Bush designated the stockade a national monument.[97] This action further legitimized public acknowledgement of internment. Pilgrimage to Tule Lake focuses on the stockade and involves the telling of former internees' stories in the hope that it will assist with the healing process from the wartime experience.[98] This has enabled a much wider audience to come in contact with their preservation work, which is particularly important given the additional controversy surrounding the Tule Lake Segregation Center. The significance of protecting the Tule Lake site could not be greater considering the grave injustices that were perpetuated there, and yet the town seems set on assuming as much of the site as possible for other purposes. All of the numerous preservation organizations concerned are in a constant battle to preserve the integrity of the sites. The Tule Lake Committee, for example, continues to spearhead a campaign to prevent the absorption of the former internment site into Tulelake airport.[99] It is perhaps ironic that the Tulelake community wants to fence in much of the old site, having the effect of keeping the Japanese out of the site instead of confined within. At Camp Amache in Colorado, most of the preservation work is undertaken by the high school students of Granada High School under the supervision of John Hopper, a social studies teacher. A small museum can be found in the centre of Granada and with the cooperation of multiple groups including Denver University the site is slowly being restored. The cemetery was the first area to be restored and is a key location in the annual Amache pilgrimage.[100] The Topaz site was owned by a local farmer who lives on the site in a mobile home that uses the concrete slab of Block 28's mess hall as its foundation. In 1998, the Topaz Museum Board bought 417 acres from the farmer in order to prevent redevelopment of the site.[101] However, the US government has now recognized the importance of preserving these sites and in 2013 pledged $1.4 million for their support, including almost $200,000 for the preservation of the Tule Lake stockade.[102] In 2014, the NPS announced $2.9 million dollars for the preservation and interpretation of Japanese American Confinement Sites from the Second World War. Projects selected for development include

the stabilization of the historic elementary school at the former Poston site in Arizona; an educational training program for 600 teachers across California on the local and national stories about the forced removal and incarceration of Japanese Americans during World War II; and an exhibition exploring the significance of the Congressional Gold Medal awarded to Japanese American veterans of World War II who served in the military while their families lived behind barbed wire.[103]

Since 2006, there has been a tremendous boost to the funding of commemorative activities linked to internment that stem from outside the Japanese American community. Prior to 2006 Japanese Americans found that the majority of work on remembrance came through their efforts. Now the long-term efforts of these organizations have been rewarded with the establishment of the Japanese American Confinement Sites Grant Program which has committed a total of $38 million for the life of the programme, of which $15 million has

Figure 4.3 The Tule Lake Visitor Center is shoe-horned into a limited site down the road from the stockade. In the recreated squat guard tower, a mannequin holding a pretend gun keeps ever present watch on the farm machinery and replica barracks.

been allocated during the past six years.[104] Significantly, on the seventy-third anniversary of the signing of Executive Order 9066, President Barack Obama announced the designation of Hawaii's Honouluili Internment and Prisoner of War Camp as a national historic monument. The camp, on Oahu, was the longest running of all internment camps on Hawaii and was only rediscovered in 2002 by a group of volunteers from the Japanese Cultural Center of Hawaii.[105] There is, therefore, still much to be done to both protect and interpret the sites for future visitors.

It is not only the government grants which provide evidence that the US government now sees internment as an important part of American history – three of the four challengers to the legality of internment have now been awarded the Presidential Medal of Freedom. President Clinton awarded the Medal of Freedom to Fred Korematsu in 1998, and President Obama awarded Gordon Hirabayashi in 2012 and, most recently, Minoru Yasui in 2015. The medal exists to honour 'especially meritorious contributions to the security or national interest of the United States, to world peace, or to cultural or other significant public or private endeavors'.[106] The move to add Yasui to the list of recipients has been popular, but now the calls for making the fourth legal test case individual, Mitsuye Endo, a recipient have increased, and there is hope this omission will soon be rectified, though this will depend on future presidential policy.[107] It is a shame that only Korematsu received the honour in his lifetime, once again demonstrating how slow the cogs of historical memory turn at national level. There are also calls for a set of commemorative stamps, like those released in Britain showing the artwork of internees, to honour the service of Japanese American soldiers. The campaign notes that 'if Elvis, Batman, penguins, Harry Potter, butterflies, and Garfield all have commemorative stamps, then the most decorated military unit in U.S. history certainly meets USPS criteria'.[108] This is a point that will be hard to ignore, especially since in 2014 commemorative stamps were launched by the US Postal Service to celebrate the sacrifices of another segregated unit, the Tuskegee airmen.[109]

Figure 4.4 Inside the Tule Lake Stockade as it stands today. The local residents stripped the jail of all usable resources after the war. The stockade was built by the internees under duress, and was the site of some of the worst abuses of power during internment. The pieces of metal on the wall show where the bunks were layered, three high, on either side of the cells. The jail often held many more individuals than its design would suggest possible.

Figure 4.5 Outside the Tule Lake Stockade as it stands today. The outer canopy is to protect the building from further deterioration.

Small exhibitions exist at or near all of the former Relocation Center sites, and it is hoped it will be possible to expand these over time. At Minidoka, for example, the memorial exhibition is located forty miles from the site at Hagerman Fossil Beds National Monument, and the exhibition for Topaz is fifteen miles away in Delta.[110] The former sites are all marked with plaques to explain the significance of the land, and, in some instances, this was a major battle. Gila River, on the site of the Gila River Indian Reservation, is on Native American sacred land. It took three years to obtain permission to place memorial markers at the Gila River camps and permission was only granted provided the Japanese American community never ask for National Landmark or any other official designation. In an attempt to recoup an infinitesimal part of what the government has taken away from them in the course of American history, Native Americans demand a minimum fee of $100 for a permit to visit the former internment site, although this is usually waived for former internees and their family members.[111] In other camps memorials have been vandalized. The plaque at Topaz, for example, has been defaced with bullet holes, demonstrating the strong emotions that still surround this subject.[112] In many of the camps memorials have been placed

Figure 4.6 The memorial in the cemetery at Manzanar.

by Japanese American organizations in the former cemeteries to stand as permanent reminders and focal points for remembrance.

Further public commemoration can be found in parts of California State Route 99 which have been designated memorial highway. The stretch between Fresno and Modesto, an area that encompasses several former Assembly Centers,

Figure 4.7 The memorial in the cemetery at Camp Amache, Granada.

is dedicated to the 100th Infantry Battalion, and the portion between Salida and Monteca bears plaques to the 442nd Regimental Combat Team.

The recent surges in funding have made a huge difference to the preservation of the sites, but in the years preceding government intervention it was almost solely the work of Japanese American organizations to preserve their experiences of the Second World War, and certainly this continues to be the case. Most recently, the Tanforan Assembly Center Memorial Committee was established to create a memorial to be placed in the shopping centre in San Bruno that stands on the site of the former site of incarceration. As Steve Okamoto, himself a former internee and member of the committee says, 'The memorial we are planning at the site will be a symbol not just to people of Japanese ancestry, but all Americans. We want to make it universal so that something like this can never happen again.'[113] In 1986, Japanese American veterans formed an organization called 'Go for Broke' in order to maintain the legacy of 'rising above prejudice and distrust to serve their country with unparalleled bravery and distinction.'[114] The veterans wished to build a memorial to commemorate the patriotic Japanese American men who served in their segregated units or in military intelligence. Over a decade of fundraising eventually resulted in the formal unveiling in 1998 of the monument that now stands in Little Tokyo, Los Angeles. In 2001, this sentiment was echoed on the other side of America with the creation of the National Japanese American Memorial for Patriotism in World War II in Washington DC.[115] Again, it was only through the efforts of the Japanese community that the heroics of the Nisei have been commemorated. The 'Go for Broke' memorial stands on ground close to the Japanese American National Museum (JANM), which has been at the centre of efforts to preserve the memory of the camps so that America never forgets. Part of the mission statement for the JANM explains the importance of its commemorative work: 'We promote continual exploration of the meaning and value of ethnicity in our country through programs that preserve individual dignity, strengthen our communities, and increase respect among all people. We believe that our work will transform lives, create a more just America and, ultimately, a better world.'[116]

The preservation of the camps is just one aspect of the work in which the JANM is involved, but it is an integral one. The permanent exhibition 'Common Ground: The Heart of Community' focuses on evacuation and includes part of a barracks transported from Heart Mountain.[117] In Sacramento, Northern California, the California Museum also hosts a permanent exhibition on internment: 'Uprooted! Japanese Americans during WWII.'[118] In Pasadena, the American Friends Service Committee (AFSC) hosted a temporary exhibition, '50 Years Later: Remembering the Japanese American Internment, from the files of the American Friends Service Committee', which drew upon artefacts, memories, and memorabilia from Pasadena's Japanese American population.[119] The California Museum offers an education programme every winter led by former internees and the exhibition does not only focus on the time of incarceration

Figure 4.8 A section of memorial highway outside Manzanar. The smaller plaque reads, 'In Honor of Americans of Japanese Ancestry who served in the 100th/442nd Regimental Combat Team and the Military Intelligence Service during World War II.'

Figure 4.9 'Go for Broke' memorial in Los Angeles, commemorating the Japanese Americans who served in the 100th, 442nd, and MIS.

but takes the story up to the 1980s to show how former internees have overcome the hardships imposed upon them. On the West Coast, then, the story of internment continues to be told through a range of museum exhibitions, continuing the necessary legacy of education regarding this turbulent time, and opening public discourses through public facing events. Founded in 1992, the JANM is a community-based organization that has sought to capture the rich oral histories of Japanese American society in tandem with the Japanese American Relocation Digital Archive (JARDA) and Densho. Densho's mission, since its creation in 1996, has been to 'preserve the testimonies of Japanese Americans who were unjustly incarcerated during World War II before their memories are extinguished. We offer these irreplaceable first-hand accounts, coupled with historical images and teacher resources, to explore principles of democracy and promote equal justice for all'.[120] JARDA's aim is similar, providing over 200,000 digitized items to assist in the education of others regarding Second World War internment.[121] Having been rejected by their nation, Japanese Americans have worked hard to ensure that the public learn the danger that can be posed to all American citizens when the government makes decisions in the interests of 'national security'.

Interpretation of the past has been a constant consideration for all organizations involved with preserving the memory of the Relocation Centers, including the JANM's 'Common Ground' exhibition. The significance of all commemorative actions regarding relocation is to 'make sense of World War II and its lasting influence on the United States'.[122] When discussing America's failing in race relations there is always a fine line to tread in order to communicate the facts effectively without alienating the general population. One Japanese American reviewer summed up the exhibition:

> To the Museum's credit, the camps did not serve as a historical foil for an insidious narrative in which internment is seen as a blessing in disguise – an event heralding the assimilation of Japanese Americans. A racially-based framework identifies what former internees have known all along: despite their claim and right to full access as Americans, Nikkei have had to deal with the consequences of racism throughout their history. The exhibit vividly displayed the devastating consequences of American racism ... Remembering what happened to Americans of Japanese ancestry during World War II is not an easy task, for it means coming to terms with a period when democracy failed. Nevertheless, the Asian American and redress movements have indicated the possibility of positive social change and offer a measure of hope for the United States.[123]

Such exhibitions and permanent monuments give expression to the feeling of the former internees themselves. The victory of the redress movement has given the Japanese American community the freedom to express their narrative of the Second World War and give voice to their feelings regarding this tumultuous period of American history. Since the presidential apology, the subject of evacuation has been added to American school and college curricula. Numerous reference books for school age children and college students now exist which break down the subject into accessible portions of history.[124] Former internees, such as Yoshiko Uchida, visit schools and talk to children about the experience. As part of explaining what happened Uchida draws on her memoirs from the time and explains, 'I wrote it … for all Americans, with the hope that through knowledge of the past, they will never allow another group of people in America to be sent into a desert exile ever again.'[125] Never before has the subject been discussed so freely, despite remaining controversial. In the words of one Nisei:

> The more times that I have spoken to people individually, or even in little groups about this experience, I have found that I have eased off a little bit more, and a little bit more. Maybe I'll become more levelheaded about the whole thing. But that doesn't run away in other people minds, even if they're educated and so on. But I have a military friend who says, 'But it had to be done, because you were from the enemy country, although we were not from the enemy country.' And [that] the U.S. had to think of its own safety and protection. I guess whatever other evidence they had as 'military', may have backed up their thought. But I've had more friends and people who feel that it was not the right thing to do to many people who, even though they were of Japanese ancestry, to some portion, had no connection with the enemy country at that time, nor in any other significant way. I believe that some of the people were taken to the prison-type places, camp, may have been rounded-up with as language school teachers, or church leaders, or community leaders, or something that made them stand out more as active people in the Japanese community. But even that, I don't find as a good excuse. I don't. I think it is essential to inform and educate our young people, not just our children and their families, but in the education system, about what happened, and perhaps how our politics and our government could be more thoughtful about such a situation. I really feel that. Our own efforts, to make friends with everybody, were very important.[126]

Decades of perseverance have finally paid off for the Japanese American community, not only directly through the success of the redress movement and the receipt of a presidential apology, but also in the freedom that now exists to recognize this period of American history. Through memorials, museum exhibitions, television and films, books, and education the subject has permeated American society so that the consequences of Executive Order 9066 and how the Constitution was denied to certain American citizens is harder to forget.

The memories of the Nikkei are not happy ones, and the psychological scars from the persecution of their race continue to manifest themselves in society today. The one area that remains silent in American internment history has been regarding the internment of German and Austrian nationals from South America who were forcibly removed to the mainland United States. The lack of official apology to those survivors may well result in further campaigns in the future, modelled on the success of the Japanese American redress movement. The American government eventually accepted the need for an apology to its citizens, time will tell whether non-citizens who were interned will be treated similarly, although this remains unlikely due to the fact it could potentially open a floodgate of claims from America's past. However, the perseverance of the Japanese American community has resulted in their narrative gaining prominence in the historical memory of the Second World War.

Conclusion

In both Britain and the United States, the memory of the camps has never been lost to those who were interned during the Second World War. However, these memories for the sake of necessity were, in large part, repressed as new lives were forged and attempts to put the trauma behind were made. Many former internees were stoic in their appraisal of their wartime experiences. As Sumiko Kobayashi, formerly of Topaz, remembers, 'Being in the camps was a small part of my family history. Traumatic, but a small piece.'[127] Steven Vajda, formerly of Sefton Camp, recalled,

> I could not help but reflect on my arrest in Giessen and subsequent transport to Buchenwald 18 months earlier and the difference between the horror then and the gentlemanly procedure now. I, personally, unlike some others, quite understood the motive for internment but deplored the mindless, ignorant, reaction and lack of knowledge and judgement of officialdom (by depriving the country, inter alia, of valuable skilled labour for the war effort).[128]

This by no means downplays the emotional suffering and loss experienced by the former internees, but rather demonstrates the tenacity and sheer force of character required to move on from these experiences. Certainly, neither the British nor the American general populations wished to dwell on what had happened during the conflict. It was not until the 1970s, therefore, that internment became recognized as part of the American war narrative, initiated by the legal fight for redress that lasted into the 1980s. The official apology in 1988 opened the doors for public engagement with the subject of internment, and this has been embraced to include depictions in fiction, television programmes, films, and even on Broadway. In Britain, by contrast, there was no such legal movement, yet there was renewed interest in the history of the war during the same period. This led to research uncovering previously untold stories from the war such as the *Kindertransport*, which leapt to public prominence in 1988. The 'discovery' of the *Kindertransport* led to further research on the fate of refugees at this time, uncovering the stories of internment. However, despite this resurgence of interest, references to Second World War internment are still minimal in British popular culture, although mention was made in the Prime Minister's Holocaust Commission Report in January 2015.[129]

Internment has become accepted as part of the narrative of the Home Front, and significant developments have been made in how the camps are commemorated. Government grants in America have been promised to help continue the work the Japanese community has done in commemorating the physical sites of internment. No such efforts at site preservation have been made in Britain, though this is in large part due to the fact the sites were temporary and therefore consisted of requisitioned properties. However, in both nations there have been attempts to engage the public with the artefacts of internment, such as paintings, photographs, and items the internees crafted during their incarceration. Exhibitions continue to be displayed in prominent locations such as Tate Britain and the Smithsonian, engaging new audiences with the subject. In Britain, the internment story is part of the greater wartime narrative of European racial persecution and illustrates the resilience of the refugees who left their countries of birth. The greatest trauma surrounds the memory of the *Arandora Star*, and this is perhaps why there are a significant number of memorials commemorating this tragic event. In America, the memory of internment falls into a history of racial prejudice, and again illustrates the resilience and perseverance of the Nikkei. The former internees' collective desire is to ensure that America never forgets what happened during the war, and as a social group they continue to stand up for the rights of fellow American citizens. As those who survived the ordeal grow fewer in number over the years, it becomes the responsibility of the next generation to pick up the baton of historical memory and build on the solid foundation of the work in which their predecessors engaged.

Conclusion

When both Great Britain and the United States of America instituted policies of internment during the Second World War it was a disappointing state of affairs, but not surprising in any real sense. Internment of enemy aliens during times of war is a recognized aspect of international law. There is nothing illegal about locking away citizens of a country with which one is at war; rather it as a recognized form of maintaining security. How internment is conducted, however, varies considerably depending on the values of the interning country. Both Britain and America have some standing in the global community for their moral codes, and therefore high standards were expected. Due to the fact internment happens during times of conflict, countries are often lacking in adequate resources and sympathy to provide for enemy aliens, who may or may not be a threat to the interning country. In times of conflict, the issues affecting internees, such as religious or racial persecution, are not considered in the way that they might during peacetime. No longer seen as individuals, but grouped together in terms of nationality or ancestry, it was no wonder that the internees experienced so many avoidable hardships and, in many cases, tragedy.

Internment in both countries can be seen as a direct continuation of over one hundred years of anti-immigration laws. Great Britain did at least attempt to differentiate between enemy aliens and refugees, but for the most part only before 1940. Once internment was implemented, it mattered little as to initial classification. As in America, the only time a classification of 'friendly to the nation' returned to importance was when opportunities were finally created for release. The United States was more interested in maintaining its quota laws prior to the outbreak of war than pursuing a more humanitarian agenda. For those of Japanese ancestry this was nothing new: the Issei, arriving in America in the late nineteenth and early twentieth centuries, had first landed at Angel Island, where they were temporarily incarcerated before being granted permission to enter the country.[1] The American view of the Asian as inferior and a potential threat to concepts of Americanism was, therefore, very clear from the beginning, and something that those of German, Austrian, or Italian citizenship did not experience on their arrival at Ellis Island, where detention was a rarity. The way that the Japanese were treated during internment, in contrast to European enemy aliens, was thus a continuation of decades of discrimination. That is not to say there was absolutely no equality in treatment between enemy aliens in America. Certainly, the vast majority of Germans, Austrians, Italians, and Japanese arrested following their native country's entry into the war were male, considered influential in their ethnic group, and were transported to Department of Justice (DoJ) camps. The initial roundups were made on the basis of judgements made by the FBI, and those arrested were, to some extent, considered as individuals. Sadly, that is where the similarities end. After the initial roundups of Caucasian men, very few threats of detention were made to European families within the continental United States. It is important to note, however, that those on Hawaii and those taken from South America often endured similar conditions to those of Japanese ancestry in the continental United States: that of complete uprooting and the loss of rights and property.

In both countries, the targets of internment were primarily males between the ages of sixteen and sixty years. In Britain, the elderly or infirm were supposed to be exempt from internment, but this decision was often slow to filter down to the arresting officers, and those in poor health were rounded up along with their healthier compatriots. In America, little concern was given to an individual's medical record before arrest took place. In Britain, some women were considered a threat to the nation's security and were also arrested. In certain cases, children were entered into care, and in others children were interned with their mothers. In America, there were isolated cases of female internment similar to that of Britain. Where the two nations diverged was in the case of the internment of family units en masse. Entire families were interned in Britain only in select instances. In America, anti-alien feeling on the West Coast was stirred up to such an extent that Executive Order 9066 granted the right to uproot all those of Japanese ancestry, regardless of age, or most significantly, citizenship. In Britain, only a small proportion of enemy alien women were ever interned on the Isle of Man, which therefore meant the number of children interned was relatively low. The United States took matters infinitely further, insisting on the internment of *all* Japanese women and *all* of their dependents, which resulted in camp populations with large proportions of minors. In fact, internment was not limited to families – even children in orphanages were transported inland. The removal of infants who had even a portion of Japanese blood in them shows how far America had moved away from the policy of interning for the sake of national security. Thus, the policy of internment was used as a cover in America for a much more worrying policy – the detainment of American citizens for no other reason than the colour of their skin. British citizens were also detained in Britain – just under 2,000 British citizens under Defence Regulation 18B – but these were assessed on a case-by-case basis, and those detained were arrested because they were against, or believed to be against, the British war effort. Clearly, in America, Japanese infants and young children were not actively participating in espionage or sabotage, so the use of Executive Order 9066 cannot be compared to 18B in the way it was used.

In American history, racial discrimination is sadly nothing new; the treatment of African Americans is testament to the lack of rights granted to those who are not white. The similarities between the treatment of those of Japanese ancestry and African Americans cannot be ignored. Concepts of American superiority based on skin-tone affected all aspects of internment with regard to those of Japanese ancestry. In Britain, only a very small number of Japanese were resident during the Second World War, and, therefore, only a few Japanese men were interned. These men were treated no differently from the other internees on the Isle of Man. Segregation, though, did occur in both countries, particularly when it came to giving internees the option to participate in the war effort. In America, Japanese American men were expected to bear arms for the United States, despite their families remaining trapped behind barbed wire. As in the case of African American men, the Nisei were only permitted to serve in a segregated unit, though many also served in the Military Intelligence Service as translators. It is hard to marry the concept of Japanese American and African American men serving in Europe for the freedom of persecuted minorities, against the reality of life in a segregated democracy in America, and yet thousands of men served with great courage and made the ultimate sacrifice. Even when a soldier perished in the line of duty, though, this did not mean his family were treated any differently as regards their freedom. Britain also created a segregated unit – the Pioneer Corps – but this was based largely on the fact that those who were signing up were foreign nationals. While joining the unarmed and largely logistical Pioneer Corps was considered an insult to the refugees wanting to fight against Nazism, ultimately those who enlisted were able to join regular troops. Therefore, while segregated units occurred in both countries, it was only in the United States that citizens were segregated as a result of their skin-tone.

Internment, by its very nature, tends to be a kneejerk reaction to current affairs, and plans are seldom finalized for accommodation before the arrests begin. In both America and Britain, those arrested found themselves in makeshift accommodation at racetracks, amusement grounds, and holiday parks. This use of leisure areas for housing suggested, in many ways, to the native population that internment was not a serious matter with which to concern themselves. The choice of locations that had happy memories for much of the population masked the reality of the harsh living conditions the internees were enduring in overcrowded grandstands and hastily converted stable blocks. In Britain, this misperception continued when internees were transported on a more permanent basis to the Isle of Man, a popular peacetime holiday destination. This gave the impression that internees were effectively enjoying a holiday at the expense of the British taxpayer, thereby diminishing the potential for ordinary British citizens to understand the plight of those trapped behind barbed wire, separated from loved ones and concerned for their personal safety. In America, there was nothing holiday-like about the Relocation Centers or their locations, but it was more a case of 'out of sight, out of mind'. In Britain, the internees were taken to a location impossible to escape from due to its position in the Irish Sea. In America, again escape was unlikely due to the fact the camps were in isolated desert and swamps. Even in Hawaii, where martial law was imposed and only a small proportion of those of Japanese ancestry were interned, camps were located in the most inhospitable of areas. Therefore, it was hard for the general American public to imagine what life was like for the internees, if they were even interested, and their views of the treatment of internees was heavily influenced by reports in the press. Much of the media in America was biased against those of Japanese ancestry, consistently reporting faintly ludicrous stories about internees being pampered and living in the lap of luxury. In Britain, the press coverage swayed between articles that promoted prejudicial views, to those where genuine issues were reported, such as the sinking of the *Arandora Star*. Reports of transport abroad ultimately strengthened the case for ceasing this policy by stirring up public outrage. In America, by contrast, the press reports and photographic documentation of the camps by Dorothea Lange and Ansel Adams were used to justify why internment was acceptable. The camps were either portrayed as microcosms of American society, full of happy individuals doing their part for the American war effort, or ignored and given no or very little press coverage – such as in the case with many of the DoJ camps – if this would reflect negatively on the US government.

Attempts were made in both countries to make the camps as 'normal' as possible. Nonetheless, there is a limit as to how 'normal' life can be when individuals are denied their liberty. Many of the administrative roles within the camps were expected to be carried out by the internees, and even medical and teaching roles were assigned to those interned. In the American camps, this was one of the more controversial aspects of life inside the camps, as internee teachers, nurses, and doctors were paid considerably less than Caucasians carrying out the same roles, which again showed how little the authorities thought of the abilities of their charges because of their race. In Britain, the internees, after the initial roundups, were generally treated with consideration and an understanding of the large numbers of refugees in camp, with the notable exception of camps established in Canada. Refugees were eventually separated from Nazi sympathizers, particularly in camps populated with Germans and Austrians, though this took some time to be enforced. When the Italians were interned, there was considerably less understanding with regard to which Italians were and were not pro-Fascist, leading to incidents of violence in the Italian camps where Fascists intimidated and abused those who were not political or who were anti-Fascist. In America, similar violence occurred between some of the Kibei who were largely anti-American, and any Nisei or Issei who were pro-American. This issue was compounded by the ill-conceived Loyalty Questionnaire, and the transformation of Tule Lake into a Segregation Center. The poorly worded questionnaire tore families apart and increased the levels of tension in camp exponentially. In America, there were riots, whereas in the British camps the closest internees came to rioting was when they were treated as prisoners of war (POWs) in Canada. As riotous behaviour is usually a last resort, this would suggest that the British were, in some ways, more effective at communicating with their charges and negotiating settlements than their American cousins. This is not to say that the British approach was without its problems, as the transport abroad debacle demonstrates. The abuse of the internees on board the transport ships was inexcusable, just like the Loyalty Questionnaire.

The number of deaths directly caused by internment was significantly higher in Britain than America due to the tragic sinking of the *Arandora Star*. It was an avoidable tragedy: had the ship been adequately marked as carrying POWs and civilians or been included in a convoy, it is possible it would not have been targeted. The trauma of the sinking has never truly been resolved. Although the Snell Inquiry was conducted after the disaster, the results were never made public, and there is evidence to suggest that the guards on the *Arandora Star* did not believe everything had been done that could have to avert the tragedy.[2] There has, therefore, never been any closure for the families of those who perished in the icy waters of the Atlantic. Across the coast of Scotland and Ireland, bodies were buried where they washed ashore and memorials have been erected in the midst of the communities that were traumatized by the loss of loved ones. The lack of a formal apology has left the tragedy with no resolution. The British government did attempt to make some amends to those transported abroad on the other ships, offering some compensation for items lost, destroyed, or looted during transit, but the elephant in the room that no one will discuss remains the *Arandora Star*.

In America, by contrast, very few individuals lost their lives as a direct consequence of internment. James Hatsuki Wakasa was an obvious exception to this rule, and the fact he was shot in the back and the guard was never properly disciplined again did nothing to ease tensions between any of the camp administrations and their charges. Three internees were killed by guards firing into the crowds during the Manzanar riot: deaths that were avoidable had the guards chosen to rely on non-lethal methods of crowd control. There were also the deaths of two internees allegedly trying to 'escape' the Lordsburg camp in New Mexico. Internees suffered from a lack of healthcare that led to the ultimate demise of many, either in camp or thereafter, and there were accidents in camps that could have been prevented had better facilities and equipment been available. Physical ailments aside, it is the negative psychological effects of camp life that have endured and caused trauma for the vast majority of internees long after the last camp shut its gates. It was not just those of Japanese ancestry who were affected. As mentioned before, Germans, Austrians, and Italians were also detained, and they too remember the hardships of camp life. Entire families of enemy aliens were deported from South America, and they suffered greatly. The United States went well beyond the actions of other nations when allegedly securing its borders. This heavy-handed approach led, perhaps unsurprisingly, to a move for reparations in the 1970s, following on from the civil rights victories of the 1960s. It took several decades, but the eventual apology and symbolic restitution has marked a watershed in American history, opening the doors to other ethnic minorities to make similar claims. So far, the government has shown willingness to resolve specific instances of wrongdoing where events concern American citizens, and where survivors or descendants of victims are readily identifiable. While this may not appease those campaigning for reparations for slavery, it shows how far America has come in the past seventy-five years.

With the reparations watershed, the memory of the camps has been treated differently. Essentially, in the post-apology era, a large part of the controversy surrounding the former sites of internment has been eradicated. The US government has tried to atone for its mistakes, and this has led to a large amount of investment in the preservation of these sites from monetary sources outside of the Japanese community. Still, the new investments do not come without strings attached, and there is a feeling that the National Park Service, responsible for the upkeep of Relocation Center sites, is sanitizing the history of internment. There is a tendency to focus on the eventual apology and downplay the suffering of the preceding decades. By apologizing, the government has again assumed some control over the image of internment, much as it did during the war through the release of selected photographs and press releases. That does not mean that the significant investments in these sites is negative, as there is much preservation work to be carried out, and the Japanese American community continues to, quite rightly, exercise its voice regarding appropriate projects.

The motivation behind the commemoration in America stems from the fact that the United States perpetuated an unjustifiable action against its own citizens. In Britain, only a comparatively small number of citizens were detained, and so few calls have been made to commemorate, for example, the area in Peel where the 18B detainees were held. Similarly, as internment is a justifiable action during wartime for enemy aliens, there has not been a united movement for commemoration of the other sites on the Isle of Man that housed internees. America cannot afford to forget its actions regarding the internment of Japanese American citizens, whereas Britain has skirted the issue to a certain extent because it used internment selectively. It is perhaps unsurprising, then, that the only significant investment for memorialization has come from the Italian community, with the creation of the St Andrew's Cloister Garden in Glasgow, in addition to other commemorative installations. Essentially the British Italian community is in the same place as the Japanese American community was in the pre-redress movement era. However, it is unlikely that there will ever be any proper closure as, were the British government to apologize and offer reparations, it would open up the floodgates for other claims against the country from its former empire.

There is some parity between Great Britain and the United States in terms of the commitment to remember the past, in the hope that such intolerances do not perpetuate themselves in the future. The emergence in the past few decades of references in popular culture and touring exhibits is ensuring that large audiences are continuing to engage with the subject, and hopefully gaining some understanding as to the mistakes made during the war, and how racial and ethnic groups can be persecuted and misunderstood by their host country. However, with the current rhetoric surrounding the influx of refugees from the Middle East and Africa into Europe and America, one may wonder if anything has been learned. In July 2015, for example, comparisons were made in Britain between a *Daily Mail* article of 1938 about Jewish refugees, and media coverage of the Calais migrant crisis, where talk continues to revolve around the scaremongering idea of 'aliens entering [Britain] through the "back door"'.[3] Many similarities can also be seen in how the internees on the Isle of Man were considered to be on a taxpayer-funded holiday, and how modern-day migrants are viewed; the *Mail on Sunday* leading one of its articles with the poorly written sub-headlines: 'Migrants given hotel room, three cooked meals a day and £35 cash a week'; 'Migrant [*sic*] get a double ensuite room, usually priced at £70 a night'.[4] As historian Tony Kushner has noted, 'The Daily Mail has been an anti-alien newspaper since the 1900s. There's great continuity'.[5] As the crisis in Europe persists, it is likely that these types of headline will continue to be produced, giving a misleading view of the true issues at stake, and continuing to feed on latent societal xenophobia. In the United States, there are many similarities to be drawn between the way Asian immigrants were portrayed in the decades preceding the Second World War, and how modern-day refugees were used as a political football in the most recent presidential election. President Donald Trump believes refugees are a 'Trojan horse', a sentiment that harks back to the concept of a Japanese 'Fifth Column' in the 1930s and 1940s.[6] Much in the same way that Asians were excluded from immigrating to the United States through legislation in the late nineteenth and early twentieth centuries, a rush was made back to the legislature to restrict the immigration of Syrian and Iraqi refugees. In November 2015, a bill was passed that would have 'required that the director of the FBI, the secretary of the Department of Homeland Security and the director of national intelligence confirm that each applicant from Syria and Iraq poses no threat'.[7] While this bill has since been defeated by a procedural vote in the Senate, the fact remains that very little has changed in either Britain or America in the past seventy plus years regarding how the foreign 'enemy other' is viewed and treated by society. There are still many lessons to be learned from Second World War internment that are incredibly relevant to the modern-day situations in which both countries find themselves, and these are lessons that cannot afford to be ignored.

Notes

Introduction

1. Heather Stewart and Rowena Mason, 'Nigel Farage's Anti-migrant Poster Reported to Police', *The Guardian*, 16 June 2016. Available online: http://www.theguardian.com/politics/2016/jun/16/ nigel-farage-defends-ukip-breaking-point-poster-queue-of-migrants
2. 'EU Referendum: Immigration Target "Impossible" in EU, Vote Leave Says', *BBC News*, 20 June 2016. Available online: http://www.bbc.co.uk/news/ uk-politics-eu-referendum-36573220
3. Patrick Sawer, Laura Hughes, Robert Mendick, and Luke Heighton, 'Jo Cox's Sister Calls Her "Perfect" and "Utterly Amazing" as Accused Murderer Tells Court His name Is "Death to Traitors, Freedom for Britain"', *The Telegraph*, 18 June 2016. Available online http://www.telegraph.co.uk/news/2016/06/18/ jo-cox-mp-shot-thomas-mair-arrives-at-court-following-murder-cha/
4. For examples, see Harriet Sherwood, Vikram Dodd, Nadia Khomami, and Steven Morris, 'Cameron Condemns Post-Brexit Xenophobic and Racist Abuse', *The Guardian*, 27 June 2016. Available online: https://www.theguardian.com/uk-news/ 2016/jun/27/sadiq-khan-muslim-council-britain-warning-of-post-brexit-racism; and Jamie Bullen, 'Brexit: Facebook Page Highlights Racism after EU Referendum Vote Triggers Spike in Hate Crimes', *Evening Standard*, 27 June 2016. Available online: http://www.standard.co.uk/news/politics/brexit-facebook-page-highlights-racism-after-eu-referendum-vote-triggers-spike-in-hate-crimes-a3281951.html
5. Peter Yeung, 'EU Referendum: Reports of Hate Crime Increase 57% Following Brexit Vote', *The Independent*, 28 June 2016. Available online: http://www. independent.co.uk/news/uk/home-news/brexit-hate-crime-racism-reports-eu-referendum-latest-a7106116.html
6. Rajeev Syal, 'MP Jo Cox Wrote Passionate Defence of Immigration Days before Her Death', *The Guardian*, 19 June 2016. Available online: https://www.theguardian.com/uk-news/2016/jun/19/ jo-cox-passionate-defence-immigration-death-article-eu
7. For a list of attacks that have taken place since 9/11, see Nadia Khomami, 'Terrorist Attacks by Violent Jihadis in the US since 9/11', *The Guardian*, 5 December 2015. Available online: https://www.theguardian.com/us-news/2015/dec/05/ terrorist-attacks-by-islamists-in-the-us-since-911

8. See Oliver Laughland and Ryan Felton, "'It's All Just Poison Now": Flint Reels as Families Struggle through Water Crisis', *The Guardian*, 24 January 2016. Available online: https://www.theguardian.com/us-news/2016/jan/24/flint-michigan-water-crisis-lead-poisoning-families-children

9. See 'Gun Violence Archive'. Available online: http://www.gunviolencearchive.org/ ; 'Guns in the US: The Statistics Behind the Violence', *BBC News*, 5 January 2016. Available online: http://www.bbc.co.uk/news/world-us-canada-34996604

10. 'Donald J. Trump Addresses Terrorism, Immigration, and National Security', 13 June 2016. Available online: https://www.donaldjtrump.com/press-releases/donald-j.-trump-addresses-terrorism-immigration-and-national-security; 'Donald Trump on the Issues', *The Politics and Elections Portal*. Available online: http://2016.presidential-candidates.org/Trump/?on=terrorism

11. Rachel Pistol, 'Why Shinzo Abe's Pearl Harbor Visit Comes as Threat of Internment Returns', *Newsweek*, 26 December 2016. Available online: http://europe.newsweek.com/why-shinzo-abes-pearl-harbor-visit-comes-threat-internment-returns-536364; Rachel Pistol, '75 Years after Pearl Harbor, the Threat of Internment Returns', *The Huffington Post*, 1 January 2016. Available online: http://www.huffingtonpost.co.uk/rachel-pistol/75-years-after-pearl-harb_b_13896910.html

12. 'Immigration Reform That Will Make America Great Again', Available online: https://www.donaldjtrump.com/positions/immigration-reform

13. Julia Preston, Alan Rappeport, and Matt Richtel, 'What Would It Take for Donald Trump to Deport 11 Million and Build a Wall?', *The New York Times*, 19 May 2016. Available online: http://www.nytimes.com/2016/05/20/us/politics/donald-trump-immigration.html?_r=0

14. Greg Robinson, *A Tragedy of Democracy: Japanese Confinement in North America* (New York: Columbia University Press, 2009); Roger Daniels, *Concentration Camps, North America: Japanese in the United States and Canada during World War II* (Malabar, FL: Krieger, 1981).

15. William H. Sewell Jr., 'Marc Bloch and the Logic of Comparative History', *History and Theory* 6 (1967), 208.

16. Raymond Grew, 'On Reading Six Books in Search of Another', *Comparative Studies in Society and History* 11 (1969), 355.

17. George M. Frederickson, 'From Exceptionalism to Variability: Recent Developments in Cross-National Comparative History', *Journal of American History* 82 (1995), 587.

18. See A. W. B. Simpson, *In the Highest Degree Odious: Detention without Trial in Wartime Britain* (Oxford: Clarendon Press, 1992); Aaron L. Goldman, 'Defence Regulation 18B: Emergency Internment of Aliens and Political Dissenters in Great Britain during World War II', *The Journal of British Studies* 12, no. 2 (1973), 120–36.

19. Paul Thompson, 'Family Myth, Models, and Denials in the Shaping of Individual Life Paths', in *International Yearbook of Oral History and Life Studies, Volume II*, ed. Daniel Bertaux and Paul Thompson (Oxford: Oxford University Press, 1993), 13.

Chapter 1

1. E. S. Roscoe, 'Aliens in Great Britain', *Transactions of the Grotius Society 16* (1930), 66.
2. 'Regulators of Aliens Act 1793'.
3. 'Act for Establishing Regulations Respecting Aliens 1816'; 'Act for the Registration of Aliens 1836'; Roscoe, 'Aliens', 66.
4. Roscoe, 'Aliens', 278.
5. Some were transmigrants, often stopping en route to North America, but many eastern European Jews ended their journey in London and chose to settle in the East End [Catherine Jones, *Immigration and Social Policy in Britain* (London: Tavistock, 1977), 70, 74].
6. Lloyd Gartner, *The Jewish Immigrant in England, 1870–1914* (London: Vallentine Mitchell, 2001), 166. The Jews were also often destitute by the time they arrived in London, having spent their resources on travelling to the country. As time progressed, feelings of charity towards the refugees eroded. See David Cesarani, 'An Alien Concept? The Continuity of Anti-Alienism in British Society before 1940', in *The Internment of Aliens in Twentieth Century Britain*, ed. David Cesarani and Tony Kushner (London: Frank Cass, 1993), 28.
7. David Feldman, '"The Importance of Being English": Jewish Immigration and the Decay of Liberal England', in *Metropolis London: Histories and Representations since 1800*, ed. David Feldman and Gareth Stedman (London: Routledge, 1989), 61.
8. Jones, *Immigration*, 67.
9. Feldman, 'Importance', 78. David Feldman, *Englishmen and Jews, Social Relations and Political Culture 1840–1914* (New Haven: Yale University Press, 1994), 281.
10. 'Aliens Act 1905'.
11. Ibid.
12. Ibid.
13. Colin Holmes, *A Tolerant Country? Immigrants, Refugees and Minorities in Britain* (London: Faber, 1991), 106.
14. Ibid.
15. Ibid., 18–19; and Panikos Panayi, *Immigration, Ethnicity and Racism in Britain, 1815–1945* (Manchester: Manchester University Press, 1994), 106.

16. Helena Wray, 'The Aliens Act 1905 and the Immigration Dilemma', *Journal of Law and Society* 33 (2006), 319.

17. Gartner, *Immigrant*, 279.

18. Jill Pellew, 'The Home Office and the Aliens Act, 1905', *The Historical Journal* 32, no. 2 (1989), 384; Wray 'Dilemma', 303.

19. Pellew, 'Home Office', 384.

20. V. D. Lipman, *A History of the Jews in Britain since 1858* (Leicester: Leicester University Press, 1990), 73.

21. Cesarani, 'Alien Concept?', 31.

22. Holmes, *Tolerant?*, 24.

23. Tom Rees, 'Immigration Policies in the United Kingdom', in *'Race' in Britain: Continuity and Change*, ed. Charles Husband (London: Hutchinson, 1982), 79.

24. Roscoe, 'Aliens', 69.

25. Aaron L. Goldman, 'Defence Regulation 18B: Emergency Internment of Aliens and Political Dissenters in Great Britain during World War II', *The Journal of British Studies* 12, no. 2 (1973), 120.

26. There were multiple riots against non-whites in 1919. Cesarani, 'Alien Concept?', 37.

27. David Cesarani, 'Anti-alienism in England after the First World War', *Immigrants and Minorities* 6 (1987), 6.

28. It increased the restrictions on aliens in multiple ways which included making name changes illegal and making it illegal for an alien to hold a position of authority on a British merchant ship or fishing boat registered in the United Kingdom, and for former enemy aliens to own or have an interest in land in Great Britain, or any share or interest in any company owning a British ship, for three years after the passing of the Act. 'Aliens Restriction (Amendment) Act 1919'.

29. Ibid.

30. Cesarani, 'Anti-alienism', 5.

31. A further restriction added to the 1919 (Amendment) Act was passed in 1925, namely, the Special Restriction (Coloured Alien Seamen) Order, which closed a loophole that had allowed alien seamen the right to settle in Britain (Holmes, *Tolerant?*, 25; Rees, 'Immigration', 78).

32. Louise London, 'Britain and Refugees from Nazism: Policies, Constraints and Choices', in *European Immigrants in Britain, 1933–1950*, ed. Johannes-Dieter Steinert and Inge Weber-Newth (Munich: Saur, 2003), 75–76.

33. Ibid., 75.

34. Charmian Brinson and Richard Dove, *A Matter of Intelligence: MI5 and the Surveillance of Anti-Nazi Refugees 1933–50* (Manchester: Manchester University Press, 2014), 22.

35. However, there was still little understanding as to the scale of the problems for Jews in Germany and when refugees tried to describe the situation the reaction in Britain was often 'to assume that [refugees were] prejudiced than that they were blind ... [we] shut up' (Marion Berghahn, 'Jewish Refugees in Britain', in *European Immigrants in Britain*, 99). Even when refugees were granted entry, their 'freedom and security were far from complete' [Tony Kushner and Katharine Knox, *Refugees in an Age of Genocide* (London: Cass, 1999), 154].

36. Brinson and Dove, *Intelligence*, 22.

37. HO 213/103 Austrian refugees: memorandum (1938). HO 213/317 Concerns raised by the German Jewish Aid Committee about the immigration of 'mental cases' (1939).

38. Quote from a meeting with the Board of Deputies of British Jews as noted in HO 213/42 Meeting with Board of Deputies of British Jews (1938); see also Geoffrey Alderman, *Modern British Jewry* (Oxford: Oxford University Press, 1992), 295–96.

39. Note of meeting with President of General Medical Council in HO 213/264 Dentists: sharp increase in applicants for admission to Dental Register; note of meeting with President of General Medical Council (1935).

40. HO 213/265 Dentist: memorandum on current situation (1936). As A. J. Sherman has noted, much attention has been paid to 'the outspoken hostility of the British medical profession to refugee doctors, dentists and especially psychoanalysts' while few have remembered 'the inescapable reality that in a time of widespread unemployment no country in the world was prepared to accept large numbers of destitute immigrants'. See Sherman, *Island Refuge: Britain and Refugees from the Third Reich 1933–1939* (Ilford, Essex: Frank Cass., 1994), 6.

41. HO 213/257 Doctors: attitude of British medical bodies (1938).

42. Such an unyielding attitude led to at least one documented case of a doctor taking his own life in desperation at the fact he was informed he would not be able to practice in England. Ibid.

43. HO 213/266 Architects (1939).

44. Paul Jacobsthal, 'Memoirs of Professor Paul Jacobsthal, Onetime Internee of Hutchinson Camp', MS 11626; Marion Berghahn, *Continental Britons: German-Jewish Refugees from Nazi Germany* (Oxford: Berghahn Books, 2007), 78.

45. Students were able to secure time in Britain, provided that they promised to leave the country upon completion of their studies. Hebrew Christians were offered training in Britain provided they secured employment outside of the British Isles. See HO 213/256 Doctors: correspondence with International Hebrew Christian Alliance (1938).

46. See HO 213/267 Farm workers (1936) for a YMCA scheme that faltered at the first bureaucratic hurdle and HO 213/282 Channel Islands: agricultural training camp

for refugees (1939) for a GEC plan to train forty refugees in Alderney for future work in Northern Rhodesia.

47. Dr Moritz Meyer, a German Jewish doctor who trained in Britain, won a case against the Medical Board of Victoria, Australia, which had tried to keep him from practicing. Australians feared the court's decision would open up the floodgates of unwanted refugees who had qualified in Britain. Australian fear of mass influx of doctors. HO 213/255 Doctors: Australian fear of mass influx (1937). Each of the dominions had their own independent policy on aliens. See Sherman, *Refuge*, 14.

48. HO 213/95 Correspondence with German embassy (1938).

49. HO 213/105 Jewish refugees in France (1939). Between 1933 and 1939 it is estimated that 23,000 refugees were admitted to the Netherlands, 25,000 were admitted to Belgium, and 40,000 were absorbed by France. Sherman, *Refuge*, 264–65. See also Brinson and Dove, *Intelligence*, 22.

50. HO 213/3 Austrian refugees: revision of landing conditions (1938).

51. HO 213/94 British legal reaction to German race laws relating to Jewish emigration (1938).

52. Louise London, *Whitehall and the Jews, 1933–1948: British Immigration Policy, Jewish Refugees, and the Holocaust* (Cambridge: Cambridge University Press, 2003), 2.

53. HO 213/115 Temporary asylum for German immigrants to US: opinions of American Consul General in Berlin (1939).

54. Clare Ungerson, 'The Forgotten Four Thousand: Jewish Refugees in Sandwich in 1939', *Wiener Library Seminar*, 25 January 2011. See also 'Papers of Adolf Gruenwald, One Time Internee of Sefton Camp, Douglas', MS 11891; IWM, 'Evelyn Ruth Kaye Interview', 2007; Sherman, *Refuge*, 215; Peter Leighton-Langer, *The King's Own Loyal Enemy Aliens: German and Austrian Refugees in Britain's Armed Forces, 1939–45* (London: Vallentine Mitchell, 2006), 8.

55. London, *Whitehall*, 11; Brinson and Dove, *Intelligence*, 1; Sherman, *Refuge*, 7; Johannes-Dieter Steinert and Inge Weber-Newth, 'European Immigrants in Britain, 1933–50', in *European Immigrants in Britain*, 8.

56. Financial difficulties: note of meeting with Treasury, Unemployment Assistance Board and Ministry of Health in HO 213/294 Financial difficulties: note of meeting with Treasury, Unemployment Assistance Board and Ministry of Health (1939).

57. HO 213/295 Financial assistance from government: proposed methods (1940).

58. Panikos Panayi, 'An Intolerant Act by an Intolerant Society: The Internment of Germans in Britain during the First World War', in *Internment of Aliens*, 55.

59. Internees were permitted to appeal the decision that had put them behind barbed wire if they could obtain 'sureties from two British persons of standing'. Ibid., 56.

60. Ibid., 58.

61. Ibid.

62. Ibid., 59.

63. 4 September 1939 as quoted in Margaret Harkins, 'Alien Internment at Huyton during World War II', in *A Prominent Place: Studies in Merseyside History*, ed. John A. Davies and Janet E. Hollinshead (Liverpool: Liverpool Hope Press, 1999), 113.

64. Sir John Anderson explained the structure to Parliament, 20 September 1939, HO 213/453 Setting up (1939).

65. Scottish Tribunals for German and Austrian Refugees HO 213/454 Scotland (1939).

66. Ibid.; emphasis in the original.

67. Brinson and Dove, *Intelligence*, 44.

68. Wendy Ugolini, *Experiencing War as the 'Enemy Other': Italian Scottish Experience in World War II* (Manchester: Manchester University Press, 2014), 38.

69. HO 213/454.

70. For example, IWM, 'Ludwig Spiro Interview' (1979).

71. IWM, 'Margot Pottlitzer Interview' (1978).

72. Hilda Ogbe, *The Crumbs off the Wife's Table* (Ibadan: Spectrum, 2001), 14. Edith Horowitz, a Swiss national by birth, was classified 'B' without even attending a tribunal while her Austrian husband was placed in the 'C' category (WRI correspondence July 18, 1940 in 'Papers of Harry Johnson (Methodist Minister, Port St Mary) Relating to His Involvement with Rushen Internment Cam' 1940–1945, MS 09378).

73. Mark Lynton, *Accidental Journey: A Cambridge Internee's Memoir of World War II* (Woodstock: Overlook, 1995), 14. See also Margot Pottlitzer Interview; John A. Bather, 'Steven Vajda Interview', MS 11860.

74. Lou Baruch, 'Reminiscences of Lou Baruch Who Was Onboard the Arandora Star and Transported to the Tatura Camps', 2007, MS 11709.

75. A. Berriedale Keith, 'The War and the Constitution Part II', *The Modern Law Review* 4 (1940), 100; Ludwig Spiro Interview; 'Papers Relating to the Internment of Members of the Beermann Family', MS 11801.

76. Protected Areas included, but were not limited to, Liverpool (Harkins, 'Huyton', 117); Ramsgate (Letter from Johnson to Wellington October 19, 1940, Papers of Harry Johnson); Fife (SA2002.053. 'Taped interview with Orazio Caira by Dr Wendy Ugolini, 2 October 1999'. Held at the Department of Celtic and Scottish Studies Archive, University of Edinburgh); Hull (Rosemarie Dalheim, 'Papers of Rosemarie Dalheim, a Former Teenage Internee', 1940s, MS 11806).

77. Reports from 18 May to 10 July 1940 in Paul Addison and Jeremy A. Crang, eds, *Listening to Britain: Home Intelligence Reports on Britain's Finest Hour – May to September 1940* (London: Bodley Head, 2010). See also Berriedale, 'Constitution', 100; 'Mona Quillin Interview about Her Memories of Her Parents' Port St Mary Guest House Which Housed Internees during World War II', 2004, MS 11032; Beermann Family Papers. Fears of a Fifth Column were not only limited to Great

Britain. See Alfred-Maurice De Zayas, *The German Expellees: Victims in War and Peace* (London: Palgrave Macmillan, 1993), 21.

78. Wendy Ugolini, "'The Internal Enemy Other': Recovering the World War Two Narratives of Italian Scottish Women', *Journal of Scottish Historical Studies* 24 (2004), 150.

79. 'Women were left alone to make their own arrangements and had to find temporary owners to take over their businesses and organise new accommodation and schooling for their children in a very short period of time.' Ibid., 151.

80. Edith Abbott, 'Federal Immigration Policies, 1864–1924', *The University Journal of Business* 2, no. 2 (1924), 133.

81. The great Taiping rebellion, which began in 1848, 'paralyzed trade and industry in south-eastern China and brought famine and ruin to millions'. Maldwyn Allen Jones, *American Immigration* (Chicago: Chicago University Press, 1960), 204.

82. The 1790 Nationality Act, which had limited citizenship through naturalization to 'free white persons', was modified in 1870 to grant those of African American descent the right to naturalize. Bill Ong Hing, *Making and Remaking Asian America through Immigration Policy, 1850–1990* (Stanford, CA: Stanford University Press, 1993), 23.

83. Cited in Andrew Gyory, *Closing the Gate: Race, Politics, and the Chinese Exclusion Act* (Chapel Hill: University of North Carolina, 1998), 5.

84. 'An Act to execute certain treaty stipulations relating to Chinese (Chinese Exclusion Act) 1882'.

85. By 1870 the Chinese in California numbered 49,310, a total of 8.5 per cent of the population (Gyory, *Closing*, 7).

86. Ibid., 4–5.

87. Ibid., 138.

88. A score of 167 to 66 votes with 59 abstentions. Ibid., 238.

89. Ibid., 1.

90. Ibid., 257. The Chinese Exclusion Act was not the only action of Congress against immigrants in that year. The United States 'without intending to restrict immigration … took a hesitant but decisive step to control it', even from Europe. See John Higham, *Strangers in the Land: Patterns of American Nativism 1860–1925* (New York: Atheneum, 1974), 144. With the economic depression of the 1880s, workers felt that their jobs were being threatened by the influx of foreigners.

91. The Exclusion Act was renewed indefinitely in 1902 (Jones, *American Immigration*, 263). Any Chinese person believed to be in the country illegally was also liable to deportation unless they had registered themselves with the American authorities within one year of the initial Act passing. This was eventually extended by a further six months to allow more of the Californian Chinese population to register as the American government feared reprisals if it instigated a mass deportation of Chinese (Hing, *Making*, 25).

92. Jones, *American Immigration*, 204. Initially the Senate had wished to curtail both European and Japanese immigration by the introduction of a literacy test.

Eventually the literacy test was scrapped and the majority of the focus of the act of 1907 was centred on excluding all Japanese. See Higham, *Strangers*, 129–30.

93. Such measures, however, were not only to be found against the Japanese on the West Coast, but in December 1919 thousands of alien radicals on the East Coast were arrested and deported to Russia (Jones, *American Immigration*, 265).

94. Ibid., 262.

95. 'Act to regulate immigration 1917'.

96. King, *Making*, 71.

97. 'Act to regulate immigration 1917'. The literacy test had been a goal from the 1890s and indeed the premise of an immigrant needing to be able to read and write in English or another language was in play from 1896. See Henry Pratt Fairchild, 'The Literary Test and Its Making', *The Quarterly Journal of Economics* 31 (1917), 452–53.

98. Gerald L. Neuman, 'Habeas Corpus, Executive Detention, and the Removal of Aliens'. *Columbia Law Review* 98, no. 4 (1998), 1015. It would appear that America was determined to make all types of Indians unwelcome within the country.

99. Jones, *American Immigration*, 288.

100. Higham, *Strangers*, 264.

101. Ibid., 265.

102. Ibid., 267.

103. Ibid., 272.

104. Jones, *American Immigration*, 177–78.

105. King, *Making*, 204, 213.

106. Jones, *American Immigration*, 279.

107. 'Outstanding Features of the Immigration Act of 1924', *Columbia Law Review* 25, no. 1 (1925), 91. However, there was still a chance of refusal if on arrival in the United States the alien was to be found inadmissible under the immigration laws. 'Immigration Act of 1924 (Johnson-Reed Act)'.

108. Ibid., Sec. 15 (c) and (n). 'Picture brides' were an exclusively Japanese custom and so the idea of discriminating specifically against this type of marriage cannot be seen as anything other than evidence of anti-Japanese sentiment.

109. Jones, *American Immigration*, 277.

110. Yoshiko Uchida, *Desert Exile: The Uprooting of a Japanese American Family* (Seattle: University of Washington, 1982), 41–42. Monica Sone remembered how one summer when her family looked for a cottage to rent they were told, 'I'm sorry, but we don't want Japs around here' [Monica Sone, *Nisei Daughter* (Seattle: University of Washington, 1953), 114].

111. *Personal Justice Denied: Report of the Commission on Wartime Relocation and Internment of Civilians* (Seattle: Civil Liberties Public Education Fund/University of Washington, 1997), 44–45.

112. *Patria* was circulated by the Hearst International Film Service Corporation and *Shadows of the West* by the American Legion (ibid., 37).

113. Ibid., 41–43.
114. Cited in Michael Tunnell and George Chilcoat, *The Children of Topaz: The Story of a Japanese-American Internment Camp* (New York: Holiday House, 1996), 3.
115. *Justice Denied*, 44.
116. Uchida, *Exile*, 45.
117. Greg Robinson, *By Order of the President: FDR and the Internment of Japanese Americans* (Cambridge, MA: Harvard University Press, 2001), 11.
118. Ibid., 40.
119. Ibid., 43.
120. Munson concluded that the greatest threat was to the Japanese community were war to be declared as their white neighbours might take out their anger on them. Robinson, *Order*, 65–67; Michi Nishiura Weglyn, *Years of Infamy: The Untold Story of America's Concentration Camps* (Seattle: University of Washington, 1996), 34; *Justice Denied*, 52–53.
121. Peter Irons, *Justice at War: The Story of the Japanese American Internment Cases* (Oxford: Oxford University Press, 1983), 59; Paul R. Spickard, *Japanese Americans: The Formation and Transformations of an Ethnic Group*. New York: Twayne, 1996), 96–97; Regional Oral History Office, *Japanese-American Relocation Reviewed: Volume I, Decision and Exodus* (Berkeley: Bancroft Library, 1976), 5b.
122. *Justice Denied*, 47.
123. Ibid., 48.
124. Weglyn, *Infamy*, 27; Robinson, *Order*, 73.
125. Robinson, *Order*, 240.
126. Those arrested were subject to a hearing to determine whether they should remain in custody for the duration of the war. See Edward Ennis Interview, *Relocation Reviewed: Volume I*, 3c. The arrests were publicized by the FBI to reassure the American public. Bill Hosokawa, *Nisei: The Quiet American* (Boulder: Colorado University Press, 2002), 239.
127. According to the Ringle Report (Irons, *Justice*, 204).
128. Irons, *Justice*, 78; Honda Interview in *REgenerations Oral History Project: Rebuilding Japanese American Families, Communities, and Civil Rights in the Resettlement Era; Los Angeles Region: Volume II*, ed. Japanese American National Museum (Los Angeles, 2000), 36.
129. Jerry Kang, 'Denying Prejudice: Internment, Redress, and Denial', *UCLA Law Review* 51 (2004), 992.
130. For example, see 'FBI Tightens Curb on 256,000 Aliens', *The New York Times*, 1 April 1942.
131. Emily Roxworthy, *The Spectacle of Japanese American Trauma: Racial Performativity and World War II* (Honolulu: University of Hawaii Press, 2008), 80.
132. Letter written to John J. McCloy, Edward J. Ennis, US IMS, Dillon S. Myer, W. Wade Head, and John Provinse (Chief Community Services, WRA) from

Dr. T. G. Ishimaru, Poston General Hospital, 20 January 1943. 'Poston', 1943. See also Chikaraishi Interview in *REgenerations Oral History Project: Rebuilding Japanese American Families, Communities, and Civil Rights in the Resettlement Era; Chicago Region: Volume I*, ed. by Japanese American National Museum (Los Angeles, 2000), 77. Many philanthropists were caught in this trap as they had willingly contributed to the maintenance of the poor in their communities, which was construed to mean they were influential and therefore potentially subversive.

133. Funai, *REgenerations: Chicago*, 226–27.

134. The arrests of Germans, Italians, and Japanese were authorized by Presidential Proclamations 2525, 2526, and 2527, 7 and 8 December 1941.

135. Robert A. Wilson and Bill Hosokawa, *East to America: A History of the Japanese in the United States* (New York: William Morrow, 1980), 204; Robinson, *Order*, 257. Even the Supreme Court only chose to accept without close scrutiny that exclusion was a military necessity (*Justice Denied*, 50). See also WRA, *Collection 131 – 2.19* (1946).

136. The first such order was issued on 29 January 1942, with subsequent orders issued 2, 4, 5, 7 February 1942. See WRA, *Collection 131 – 1.1* (1942). Spickard, *Transformation*, 98. FDR's decision to sign EO 9066 was made 'with no consideration or weighing of the racial or constitutional implications of that action' (Robinson, *Order*, 257). Indeed, 'public response to [Executive Order 9066] was enthusiastic' (James L. Dickerson, *Inside America's Concentration Camps: Two Centuries of Internment and Torture* (Chicago: Lawrence Hill Books, 2010), 66).

137. The effective date of curfew order covering German and Italian aliens and all persons of Japanese ancestry in Military Area No. 1, requiring them to be in their places of residence between the hours of 8 pm and 6 am was 27 March 1941; forbidding possession of firearms, explosives, cameras, radio transmitting sets or shortwave receiving sets, and barring travel more than five miles from home without permit. See ibid.

138. Elena Tajima Creef, *Imaging Japanese America: The Visual Construction of Citizenship, the Nation, and the Body* (New York: New York University, 2004), 16.

139. *Justice Denied*, 114; Irons, *Justice*, 81–86.

140. *Justice Denied*, 116.

141. The National Lawyers' Guild saw internment as 'a minor item in the heaping quota of human misery which has been produced by the current war.' Irons, *Justice*, 132, 181.

142. Chikaraishi, *REgenerations: Chicago*, 81.

143. HO 213/117 USA regulations and procedures: State Department letter to British Embassy, New York (1939).

Chapter 2

1. HO 215/124 Classification of camps and segregation of internees: general matters (1940).

2. It is estimated that one in four Italians resident in Britain during the Second World War were arrested and interned. See Ugolini, 'Internal Enemy', 141.

3. Keiko Itoh, *The Japanese Community in Pre-war Britain: From Integration to Disintegration* (London: Routledge, 2013), 185.

4. Arrests varied from 3 am (Gaetano Rossi, 'Memories of 1940 Impressions of Life in an Internment Camp', 1991, M 28111) to a more reasonable 7 am ('Extract from Pinschof Journal Recalling Time Interned on Isle of Man', 2007, MS 11705). One internee was lucky enough to be spared arrest until after church (Chris Widdows, 'William Fritz Sommerfeld Interview', 2008, MS 11926). No special concessions were made even in the case of sick or heavily pregnant relatives; see P. Lachs, 'Memoirs of Unnamed Internee and Letter Requesting Help in Securing the Release of a Brother Interned on the Isle of Man', 1940–41, MS 11689; and Charmian Brinson, Anna Mueller-Haerlin, and Julia Winckler, *His Majesty's Loyal Internee: Fred Uhlman in Captivity* (Portland, OR: Vallentine Mitchell, 2009), 49. Arrests were often accompanied by searches of the internee and their property such as in the cases of 'Correspondence regarding the Internment of Elisabeth Bickel on the Isle of Man', 1940–2008, MS 11366; and Rosemarie Dalheim, 'Papers of Rosemarie Dalheim, a Former Teenage Internee', 1940s, MS 11806.

5. Lynton, *Accidental Journey*, 17.

6. 'Documentation Relating to Internment of Eugen Stern', 1939–40, MS 12411. Thoughts echoed by many, including Henry Mendel, as recorded by his daughter, Rachel Mendel, 'Behind Barbed Wire', 2009, MS 12140.

7. Dalheim, 'Papers'.

8. Renate Olins, 'Island Prison', in *What Did You Do during the War, Mummy?*, ed. Mavis Nicholson (Bridgend, Wales: Seren, 2010), 47–48.

9. Brinson et al., *Loyal Internee*, 50. Anna Bill-Jentszch experienced similar kindnesses from her local policemen in Anna Bill-Jentzsch, 'Account of Internment', 1998, MS 09990. Some particularly negative experiences of remaining in a cell for several days are included in Baruch, 'Reminiscences'; as well as examples of memories of being held at gunpoint. See also Rossi, 'Memories'. Other examples similar to Uhlman's include Lachs, 'Memoirs'; and 'Papers of the Klaffl Family Relating to the Internment of Rosemary "Bella" Klaffl, Her Sister Elizabeth (Betty) and Mother Maria Theresia in Rushen Camp during World War II', 1940–53, MS 11270.

10. Charmian Brinson, '"In the Exile of Internment" or "Von Versuchen, aus einer Not eine Tugend zu machen": German-Speaking Women Interned by the British during

the Second World War', in *Politics and Culture in Twentieth-Century Germany*, ed. William Niven and James Jordan (Rochester, NY: Camden House, 2003), 64.

11. 'Papers of Erna Nelki', 1941–2001, MS 12388. See also Julia Ruth Winckler, 'Two Sisters: A Photographic Project in Four Parts', 2002, MS 10688; and the use of Edinburgh Prison as mentioned in Joan Johnson, 'My Memories of Life in Rushen Internment Camp, May 29th 1940 to August 31st 1941: A Personal Experience', 1990, MS 08866. Scottish men were temporarily interned in Saughton Prison, 'but you were well treated. Very, very respectfully treated. Cannot say one word against them. I was there for six months'. SA1998.32/33. 'Taped Interview with Joseph Pia by Dr Wendy Ugolini, 1 August 1998', Held at the Department of Celtic and Scottish Studies Archive, University of Edinburgh.

12. Dalheim, 'Papers'. See also Bill-Jentszch, 'Internment'.

13. 'Pinschof Journal'. See also IWM, 'Eva Wittenberg Interview' (1991).

14. Baruch, 'Reminscences'.

15. Ibid. See also 'Papers Documenting the Internment and Lives of Ludwig and Inge Hess and Inge's Friend Mrs Helli Wimbush', 1989–2005, MS 11248; HO 215/124.

16. For examples see 'Beermann Family Papers', 1939–40, MS 11801; 'Letters from Herbert Forner to Family Members', 1940–44, MS 11952; 'Memoirs of Willy Leopold Hess, One Time Internee of Onchan Camp, Isle of Man, 1940–1', MS 11038; 'Correspondence Documenting the Internment of Walter and Leopold Fiala', 1940–41, MS 12125; Fritz Israel Heinemann, 'Fritz Heinemann at Onchan', 1940, MS 12196. Lingfield Racecourse was also used, as noted in Bather, 'Steven Vajda'; not forgetting York Racecourse, as in Fritz Lustig, 'Memoirs of Fritz Lustig Entitled "Internment in Peel, July to October 1940"', 2008, MS 11788. Those interned in Scotland were either held in prisons or in tents in fields. See SA1998.35. 'Taped Interview with Renzo Serafini by Dr Wendy Ugolini, 7 August 1998'. Held at the Department of Celtic and Scottish Studies Archive, University of Edinburgh; Orazio Caira Interview; Joseph Pia Interview.

17. Mendel, 'Barbed'; Tony Kushner, *Remembering Refugees Then and Now* (Manchester: Manchester University Press, 2006), 76–77; Lynton, *Accidental Journey*, 17. Not forgetting the prisons that were used, see Werner Kittel, 'Papers Relating to the Internment of the Gerlachs and Wolfgang Kittel', 2009, MS 12211; and 'Memoirs of Ludwig Hess'.

18. Brinson et al., *Loyal Internee*, 52.

19. Jacobsthal, 'Memoirs'.

20. Kushner, *Remembering*, 76.

21. Jacobsthal, 'Memoirs'. Further descriptions of the lack of decent accommodation at Warth Mills and the insensitive handling of the internees by the major in charge, including pilfering, can be found in Kushner, *Remembering*, 76–77; Camillo

D'Allesandro, 'Camp Life on the Isle of Man in World War II: Memoirs of an Italian Internee', 1981, MS 11185; IWM, 'Hellmuth Weissenborn Interview', 1978; and Rossi, 'Memories'.

22. Lachs, 'Memoirs'.

23. Ibid. Registered medical practitioners at Huyton drew up a similar list in June 1940, noting that there were thirty-nine patients aged between fifty and seventy with severe heart diseases, twenty diabetics, twenty with tuberculosis, twenty-one with gastrointestinal disorders, and nine with mental disorders (including suicidal tendencies and schizophrenia). See Harkins, 'Huyton', 120. Hellmuth Weissenborn noted that in his house in Hutchinson camp there was a man suffering from schizophrenia (Hellmuth Weissenborn Interview). See also Renzo Serafini Interview.

24. Jessica Feather, *Art behind Barbed Wire* (Liverpool: National Museums Liverpool, 2004), 8; Harkins, 'Huyton', 118.

25. Herbert Forner remarked on his hate of inactivity in 'Letters from Herbert Forner to Family Members', 1940–44, MS 11952; and in 'Letters Relating to Mr Aberbach Relating to Internment in Mooragh Camp', 1945, MS 11348, Huyton was summed up with the phrase 'Life at that camp was a bore and I felt rather depressed.'

26. For example, F. S. Loebl, who served as a street father at Huyton and was commended for his 'never-tiring energy, [his] foresight, and above all through the kindness with which [he] tackled the rather intricate material and personal problems which [he] had to encounter' ('Information Relating to Internees F S Loebl, Robert Loebl, and Herbert Loebl', 1940, 2008, MS 12197).

27. See Harry Cannell, 'Hardships Caused by the Internment Camps on the Isle of Man during the 1939 to 1945 War', 1996, MS 09555, for an example of a requisitioning letter. The standard letter was sent to all those whose houses fell within areas designated for barbed wire.

28. Ibid. The agreement signed by the boarding-house owners also stated that the furniture could be bought from the owners at any point during the war and that the owners were expected to return to running a boarding house once their property was returned. See also 'Papers of N. C. Callister re Requisition of 13 Hutchinson Square', 1940–45, MS 10661; and Isle of Man Government, 'Papers Relating to the Requisitioning of 13 Royal Avenue West, Onchan', 1940–47, MS 11720. In 1943, the Manx government took advantage of the agreement to purchase the furniture at 1940s rates, which represented a loss to many owners as furniture prices had risen during the intervening years.

29. Life continued much as usual for such boarding-house owners. For example, see Elizabeth Corrin, 'Recollections of Elizabeth Corrin or Her Childhood Experiences of Internees', 2003, MS 10778.

30. See Rossi, 'Memories'. The standard of accommodation could vary greatly; Erna Nelki, for example, shared the house bathroom with nineteen other women, but there were water jugs and wash basins in each room ('Papers of Erna Nelki').

31. Helmuth Weissenborn Interview.

32. Such cases were exaggerated in newspapers sympathetic to the plight of the refugee internee, for example, the *News Chronicle*, 15 October, 1941. A reply to the article was made in the *Daily Telegraph* by internee Renate De Garimberti, who asked the reader to remember that 'the beds are very big double beds' and therefore it was not as much of a hardship as the *Chronicle* made out. Dame Joanna Cruickshank, Commandant of the Rushen camp, explained that as soon as it became known a woman was a Nazi she was separated from Jewesses so that the camp could continue in harmony (*Manchester Guardian* interview reported in the *Isle of Man Times*, 25 December 1940). See also Cyril Cuthbert, 'Papers of Cyril R Cuthbert, One-Time Commandant of Married Internees Camp', 1941–45, MS 11196, Eva Wittenberg Interview; and 'Papers of Erna Nelki'.

33. Brinson et al., *Loyal Internee*, 86. Due to the dirtiness of the blankets, Willy Leopold Hess 'anxiously avoided any wool blanket contact directly with [his] skin', instead asking for a sleeping bag to help protect him at night ('Willy Leopold Hess Memoirs').

34. Baruch, 'Reminiscences'.

35. Mendel, 'Barbed'. Professor Jacobsthal in his memoirs remembers joking with his fellow internees that 'we often thought that it would have been much worse to have a voluntary holiday in this place'.

36. Even if their religious commitment was limited to wearing a yarmulke at religious meetings when external visitors were present (Rossi, 'Memories'). Each camp established its own Orthodox houses, with their own cooks. See Hellmuth Weissenborn Interview; Frank Jochanan, 'Inside Out: Isle of Man Revisited, 1940–2000', 2000, MS 10323; Jacobsthal, 'Memoirs'; 'Aberbach Letters'; Brinson et al., *Loyal Internee*, 90; and Max Sussman, 'A Young Internee on the Isle of Man 1940–1', 2007, MS 11751. The separate houses for those requiring kosher food were also mentioned in newspaper reports at the time, such as in the *Isle of Man Times*, 25 December 1940, quoting a piece from the *Manchester Guardian* (Cuthbert, 'Papers').

37. 'Account of Internment at P Camp, Hutchinson Square, Douglas', 1940s, MS 10739, which also mentions the creation of a camp cookbook containing one hundred recipes and 'influenced food favourably'. See also 'Aberbach Letters'; Lustig, 'Memoirs'; Ille Pinkus, 'Letters Written by Ille Pinkus', 1940; and Michael Corvin, 'Camp Tribune No 1 16 August 1941; published in Y Camp (Married Camp)', 1941, M 31545. Some cooks were feared rather than appreciated for having fine culinary skills. Willy Leopold Hess remembers the two cooks in House

18, Onchan Camp, of being 'fond of cigarette ends on the tongue which I suppose could easily land in the soup' ('Willy Leopold Hess Memoirs'). Poor food often came about as a result of poor management. Weissenborn recalled dining very well, particularly during the period one of the men in his house smuggled chickens from his labouring job into the kitchen (Hellmuth Weissenborn Interview). Some landlords and ladies in Port Erin and Port St Mary were generous with their charges, one even providing extra tinned fruit that they had hoarded in the cellar (Dalheim, 'Papers'). Perhaps the worst example of boarding-house owners taking advantage of the system however was with Inge Hess, who after giving birth to her daughter in camp had her milk ration so watered down by her landlady that upon inspection by the camp authorities it was declared that there were 'traces of milk in that water' ('Ludwig Hess Memoirs'). As Renate Olins remembers, 'Apparently [the landlord] got a pound a week for each of his residents, so the less food he gave us, the more profit he made' (Olins, 'Island Prison', 48–49).

38. Orazio Caira Interview. The fact that fruit was a highly prized commodity in camp is demonstrated by the fact that rewards for competitions were often a choice of either cigarettes or fruit; see '*The Camp*: Hutchinson Square Internment Camp Journal Issues 1–13/14', 1940, M 27059. Johanna Rieger complained that the food provided for the children was insufficient and it was essential that she supplemented their diet with fruit ('Johanna Luise Frida Rieger Correspondence', 1940, MS 12203). Inge Hess and her friend would sometimes pick plants from the roadside to clean and eat to supplement their diet ('Ludwig Hess Memoirs'). See also 'Klaffl Papers'; Pinkus, 'Letters'; Jacobsthal, 'Memoirs'; and D'Allesandro, 'Camp life' where Camillo noted that he developed a series of abscesses on his chin due the lack of vegetables and had cravings for anything green, even dandelion leaves.

39. See Pinkus, 'Letters' for regular requests for 'salamiwurst'; and D'Allesandro, 'Camp life' where Camillo asked his wife to send him special cakes. Walter Fiala enjoyed the cake sent to him by his fiancée ('Fiala Correspondence', 29 March 1941), as did Lou Baruch the piece of wedding cake he received through the post (Baruch, 'Reminiscences').

40. IWM, 'John Duffield Interview' (1979). See also *Isle of Man Times*, 21 October 1940.

41. Mendel, 'Barbed'; IWM, 'Claus Moser Interview' (1997). In general, relations were good between the guards and their charges [Orazio Caira Interview, HO 215/130 Camps: Huyton, Lancashire: standing orders; control of internees in hospital (1941)]. Shoemaking, tailoring, carpentry, and barbers' shops also sprang up in the camps [HO 215/149 Distinction between prisoner of war and civilian internment camps (1941)].

42. Notice dated 1 June 1940, as documented by Eugen Stern. This view was reflected by the majority of the Camp Commandants. The Commandant of P Camp was praised for displaying 'intelligent and sympathetic leadership' ('Account of P Camp'), for example. Huyton's Commandant was seen by one internee as 'sensible', with a 'very humane attitude' whereas the Commandant at Central Camp was considered to be 'very unfriendly, not to say hostile' by the same internee (Mendel, 'Barbed'). Another internee criticized the Commandant of Huyton for being 'ignorant' ('Loebl'). Major Daniel, of Hutchinson Camp, was seen by most as 'very helpful' (Hellmuth Weissenborn Interview). The Commandant of Warth Mills was 'a real rascal', perhaps reflecting the poor conditions at the camp (Rossi, 'Memories'). There were as many views of the Commandants, therefore, as there were internees. A representative of the International Red Cross reported that 'I should like to stress the fact that the task of these Commandants is by no means an easy one. They have not to deal with disciplined military units, which are used to receive and to carry out orders, but with a haphazard collection of civilian individuals, who, as each one has his special "case", have little tendency to form a community. Therefore a great deal of psychological understanding is needed to run such camps successfully' [HO 215/107 Isle of Man (1945)].

43. Brinson, 'Versuchen', 68.

44. For examples at Huyton, see 'Loebl'; and Lynton, *Accidental Journey*, 21–26. Isle of Man arrangements are detailed in Account of P Camp. See also 'Home Office Orders for Internment Camps' (1943).

45. *The Camp*, 20 October 1941. See also HO 215/149 Distinction between prisoner of war and civilian internment camps (1941); Renzo Serafini Interview.

46. If internees from their house were late for roll call, 'house fathers' could inflict punishments such as cleaning the floor; see Brinson et al., *Loyal Internee*, 69. The evening roll call was much preferred to the morning roll call where individuals might be fighting to use the limited bathrooms all at the same time ('Willy Leopold Hess Memoirs'). See also Rachel Pistol, 'Interview with David Brand about Dr. Angelo Lauria', 2014.

47. Brinson, 'Versuchen', 68.

48. Margot Hodge, 'Memories and Personal Experiences of My Internment on the Isle of Man in 1940', 1999, MS 10119. See also Pinkus, 'Letters'; Dalheim, 'Papers'; and Olins, 'Island Prison', 49. Sometimes some of the older internees with means would pay the younger internees to do some of the cleaning for them (Lustig, 'Memoirs'), but for the most part everyone did what was required of them, not always cheerfully, as recalled in Brinson et al., *Loyal Internee*, 95, where Uhlman described washing up as 'plain hell'.

49. Johnson, 'Memories'. Rev. Johnson did not limit himself just to providing religious services; he was also active in War Resisters' International, with whom

he corresponded regularly in the assistance of his temporary flock, as well as the Central Department for Interned Refugees. See 'Papers of Harry Johnson (Methodist Minister, Port St Mary) Relating to His Involvement with Rushen Internment Camp', 1940–45, MS 09378.

50. Dr Downey, Catholic archbishop of Liverpool, Rev. Henry Carter CBE, Methodist minister and honorary chairman of the Board and executive of the Christian Council for Refugees, were just two of the official visitors to Rushen Camp (ibid.; Orazio Caira Interview). The Methodist Church in Port Erin hosted many musical concerts for those at Rushen Camp (Brinson, 'Versuchen', 73).

51. See John Duffield Interview for examples in Onchan; Joseph Pia Interview; Itoh, *Japanese*, 186.

52. 'Home Office Orders'.

53. Mendel, 'Barbed'. In the married camp the town hall was used for Jewish services on Friday evenings and Saturday ('Mona Quillin Interview about Her Memories of Her Parents' Port St Mary Guest House Which Housed Internees during World War II', 2004, MS 11032).

54. 'Home Office Orders'. All letters were subject to processing by the censor's office in Liverpool, which could cause great delays, particularly for letters written in a foreign language. See also HO 215/130 Camps: Huyton, Lancashire: standing orders; control of internees in hospital (1941); Joseph Pia Interview.

55. Itoh, *Japanese*, 186.

56. 'Willy Leopold Hess Memoirs'. Comments were made by virtually all those interned about the delay of the post. Some examples include: Ille Pinkus chastising her mother for not writing to her more often, letters often arriving several weeks after dispatch (Pinkus, 'Letters'); William Fritz Sommerfeld receiving a parcel of letters 26 June 1940, the majority of which had been posted between 4 and 10 June (William Sommerfeld Interview); Paul Jacobsthal first hearing from his wife almost a month after his internment as none of his wires had gotten through (Jacobsthal, 'Memoirs'); and Henry Mendel finding it took some two to three months to receive messages from his wife and daughter in Switzerland (Mendel, 'Barbed').

57. See the feature articles 27 October, 3 and 17 November 1940 on the etchings in 'The Camp: Hutchinson Square Internment Camp Journal Issues 1–6, 8–16, 20', 1941, M 27060. Paul Jacobsthal mentions the poor light caused by ARP regulations in his 'Memoirs'.

58. Ink was more problematic but artists such as Weissenborn used margarine along with pigment as a substitute. A washing machine was press-ganged into use as an impromptu printing press using this ink mixture on lino cuttings in order to create printed items (Hellmuth Weissenborn Interview).

59. See newspaper report, 6 September 1940 entitled 'Governor among the Aliens' in 'Papers of Harry Johnson' regarding the creations of schoolchildren in the women's camp.

60. As mentioned in Mona Quillin Interview. Many a boarding-house owner returned to their homes after the war to discover much of what had been left in the house had been used for other purposes. See also Cannell, 'Hardships'.

61. Fred Uhlman created some sketches himself (Brinson et al., *Loyal Internee*, 62), but also recalls exhibitions of work by Ehrlich, Kramer, Fechenbach, Markiewicz, Kahn, Hirschenhauser, Blensdorf, and Haman (55). He was also familiar with the work of Kurt Schwitters who was interned in the same camp and was prone to recite poetry (53). Other artists included Hellmuth Weissenborn, responsible for starting the etching trend (Hellmuth Weissenborn Interview; and *The Camp*); Ernst Muller-Blensdorp, a wood carver (13 November 1940 issue of *The Camp*); Severino Tremator (Rossi, 'Memories'); and Paul Felix Franz Nietsche, who made the most of his internment to draw portraits (William Kaczynski, 'Papers of William Kaczynski, One Time Child Internee of Rushen Camp', 1940–2006, MS 11680).

62. Brinson et al., *Loyal Internee*, 87–88. Schwitters was also renowned for painting on cardboard during his internment (Hellmuth Weissenborn Interview).

63. *The Camp*, 1940.

64. Olins, 'Island Prison', 49; Margot Pottlitzer Interview; Dalheim, 'Papers'; 'Papers of the Klaffl family'; Mrs T. O'Rourke, 'Poems from Rushen Internment Camp', 1940–41, MS 09337; Pinkus 'Letters'; 'Elisabeth Bickel Correspondence'.

65. For examples of some of the academics interned, see the 'Oxford Group' listing in Jacobsthal, 'Memoirs'.

66. 'Willy Leopold Hess Memoirs'.

67. Reading rooms were only possible many months into internment when periodicals were finally allowed inside the camps. A subscription was required from each reader in order to purchase said periodicals, which gave it a slight air of exclusivity (24 November 1940 issue of *The Camp*). In another issue of the Hutchinson newspaper it was estimated that up to 60 per cent of the internees had at some point used the library facilities (14 January 1941 issue of *The Camp*). The National Central Library London, the Victoria and Albert Museum, and the Douglas Public Library provided 'books of a scientific nature' for the internees, and it was estimated that there were 7,600 volumes available to browse ('Account of P Camp'). Even when internees were transported abroad, as will be touched on later, the desire for libraries travelled with them (Baruch, 'Reminiscences'). Ille Pinkus complained that the books available in Rushen Camp were 'only bad books, just to learn English and occupy oneself' (Ille Pinkus, 'Letters'). See also Dalheim, 'Papers'.

68. 'Papers of Erna Nelki'. See also Hodge 'Memories'; Mendel, 'Barbed'; 'Willy Leopold Hess Memoirs'; and William Sommerfeld Interview.

69. *The Camp*, 27 October 1940. There was much relief that news was for the first time available instantly, instead of via out-of-date copies of newspapers (*The Camp*, 14 January 1941). See also Helmuth Weissenborn Interview. Even the Gestapo welcomed the introduction of newspapers into the camps, as noted in Gestapo,

'Copy of Gestapo Document Relating to British Internment Camps including Those on the Isle of Man', 1940, MS 09510.

70. Issue 1, 'The Camp'. The Technical School offered training in Technical and Electrical Skills, Maths, Physics, Technical Translation and English to equip its students to help in the war effort upon release – 'self preservation by learning' (Brinson et al., *Loyal Internee*, 18, 24–25). The Canadian government was keen to create a trade school at Sherbrooke [HO 215/161 Canada: B and C category internees (1941–43)].

71. 24 November 1940, *The Camp*; Ogbe, *Crumbs*, 17–19; Orazio Caira Interview.

72. Comments such as 'the children need school so badly' were commonplace at the beginning of internment, see letter dated 29 December 1940 in 'Rieger Correspondence'.

73. 'Papers of Erna Nelki'. Nelki notes that a special class was created for the children still traumatized after Kristallnacht with the help of a social worker. Renate Olins remembers Specht as being very strict but also that by the time Renate returned to school in London she had advanced further than her non-interned fellow pupils. See Olins, 'Island Prison', 49.

74. 'Papers of Erna Nelki'.

75. Dalheim, 'Papers' and 'Herbert Forner Letters'. For all the limitations, however, a mixed curriculum was offered, including English, Arithmetic, Geography, History, German, Handicraft, Gymnastics; see Jochanan, 'Inside Out'.

76. See Pinkus, 'Letters'; Johnson, 'Memories'; Dalheim, 'Papers'; and Ogbe, *Crumbs*, 19.

77. Brinson, 'Versuchen', 69–70.

78. The Skills Service Exchange was liquidated in November 1941 as the high number of releases made the scheme no longer viable (ibid.).

79. Regularly mentioned in *The Camp*; Rossi, 'Memories'; Mendel, 'Barbed'; and 'Sefton Review Nos 1 and 8'; Joseph Pia Interview.

80. Itoh, *Japanese*, 186.

81. 'Willy Leopold Hess Memoirs'. *The Camp* wrote that the actors 'have actually shown that they are able to give us proofs of their art in spite of these circumstances'. German and English recitals of famous works such as Faust were also commonplace (*The Camp*, 1940).

82. As the 'Bradda Glen' song went 'Nowadays on Bradda Glen, Holiday Camp without men, You see women left and right, Same by day and same by night' ('Beermann Papers').

83. Brinson et al., *Loyal Internee*, 22. That was not the only time Captain Daniels intervened for the benefit of one of his internees. Heinrich Fraenkel was greatly assisted in his work *Help Us Germans to Beat the Nazis!*, published by Victor Gollancz in 1941, by the provision of an attic room and a lifting of postal restrictions on his reading material (ibid., 21).

84. *The Camp*, Issue 1, 1940, which then went on to say incredulously, 'And all this on a boarding-house piano'! Fritz Lustig after receiving his cello spent the majority of his internment practicing and performing with fellow musicians in Peveril Camp in order to boost morale. See Robin Lustig, 'The Wandering Scribe'. Available online: http://www.wanderingscribes.com/#!Back-in-the-Isle-of-Man-after-74-years/c1ybh/837721C8-1C95-493B-88AB-AA3B1B9D748F

85. Henry Mendel commended a performance of 'The Silver Box', 5 August 1941 (Mendel, 'Barbed'). For references concerning the liberating feeling a visit to the pictures could have, see Kittel, 'Papers'; Dalheim, 'Papers'; Brinson et al., *Loyal Internee*, 70; John Duffield Interview; 'Papers of the Klaffl family'; and Pinkus, 'Letters'.

86. Lomnitz, '*Never Mind!*', 18.

87. Although there was a trial of a weekly postal collection between Rushen camp and the other Isle of Man camps for mail between wives and husbands, but not fiancés or other relatives in 1940 [HO 215/290 Communication between camps (1941)].

88. See, for example, the *Manchester Guardian*'s interview in *The Isle of Man Weekly Times*, 25 December 1940.

89. See 'Willy Leopold Hess Memoirs' for mention of discussion about travelling to Australia. Erna Nelki remembers the Australia meeting and also discussing emigration to British Honduras, San Domingo, or Ecuador on the second visit ('Papers of Erna Nelki'). The visits alternated between Port Erin and Douglas. See also Dalheim, 'Papers'.

90. 'Willy Leopold Hess Memoirs'.

91. *The Camp*, 27 October 1940. Industrious husbands and fathers would spend the intervening time working on gifts for their spouses or children. Frederick Beermann, for example, made his daughter, Edna, a rocking horse for one such visit ('Beermann Papers'). See also Olins, 'Island Prison', 50.

92. 'Camp Tribune', 16 August 1941. Consideration had been given to creating a married camp as early as 1940 [HO 215/124 Classification of camps and segregation of internees: general matters (1940)].

93. 'Rieger Correspondence'.

94. Dalheim, 'Papers'.

95. See Sussman, 'Young'; Cuthbert, 'Papers'; Dalheim 'Papers'; and 'Herbert Forner Letters'.

96. John Duffield Interview.

97. Brinson et al., *Loyal Internee*, 73.

98. Pistol, 'Brand Interview'.

99. See *The Isle of Man Times*, 5 December 1941 and 5 January 1942.

100. Susannah Helman, 'The Dunera Boys', *The National Library Magazine* (2010), 7.

101. Ronald Stent, *A Bespattered Page? The Internment of His Majesty's 'Most Loyal Enemy Aliens'* (London: Deutsch, 1980), 96; Connery Chappell, *Island of Barbed*

Wire: Internment on the Isle of Man in World War Two (London: Robert Hale, 2005), 28.

102. Numbers vary between sources. See, for example, Memorandum on Internment and Transfer Overseas of Aliens, July 27, 1940 [PREM 3/49 Arandora Star (1940)]. See also Terri Colpi, 'The Impact of the Second World War on the British Italian Community', in *The Internment of Aliens in Twentieth Century Britain*, ed. David Cesarani and Tony Kushner (London: Routledge, 1993), 178.

103. Colpi 'Impact', 178. HO 215/429 Deaths, funeral arrangements etc. for the *Arandora Star* (1942); HO 352/43 List of names of Italians who perished on the *Arandora Star* (1950); WO 361/4 Losses on SS *Arandora Star* (1940).

104. PREM 3/49; HO 213/438 Arandora Star embarkation lists (1940); HO 215/262 Voyage of HMT Dunera: promises allegedly made to volunteers; parliamentary question (1942); HO 215/265 Voyage of SS Ettrick: conditions in Canadian camps on arrival (1941); HO 215/266 Voyage of SS Sobieski: embarkation list (1940).

105. Louise Burleston, 'The State, Internment and Public Criticism in the Second World War', in *The Internment of Aliens in Twentieth Century Britain*, ed. David Cesarani and Tony Kushner (London: Frank Cass, 1993), 99.

106. Lynton, *Accidental Journey*, 33.

107. The *Dunera*, for example, was designed for 1,600 passengers including crew, yet 2,732 internees were sent aboard, excluding guards and crew; see Cyril Pearl, *The Dunera Scandal: Deported by Mistake* (London: Angus & Robertson, 1983), 19; Helman, 'Dunera', 3. Sleeping on the floor was the norm on all transport ships.

108. Lynton, *Accidental Journey*, 34.

109. Benzion Patkin, *The Dunera Internees* (Stanmore, NSW, Australia: Cassell, 1979), 37. One internee noted that 'on the boat luggage was strewn about and open cases everywhere looted by the soldiers' (Baruch, 'Reminiscences'). Another remembered 'the suitcases were opened forcefully by soldiers. Many things, sometimes everything were taken out, put into the pocket or thrown overboard' (Helman, 'Dunera', 3). The aggressive nature of the guards was toned down for the television mini-series 'The Dunera Boys', broadcast in the 1980s, and yet still made for uncomfortable viewing; Birgit Lang, 'The Dunera Boys: Dramatizing History from a Jewish Perspective', in *'Totally Un-English'? Britain's Internment of 'Enemy Aliens' in Two World Wars*, ed. Richard Dove (Amsterdam: The Yearbook of the Research Centre for German and Austrian Exile Studies Vol. 7, 2005), 183.

110. Baruch, 'Reminiscences'.

111. B. Fehle, 'Memorandum Relating to the Disaster of the SS Arandora Star', 1940, MS 09647. See also Maria Serena Balestracci, *Arandora Star: From Oblivion to Memory* (Parma: MUP, 2008); and Baruch 'Reminiscences'.

112. Fehle, 'Memorandum'.

113. According to the Snell Inquiry, lifeboats were provided for 750 of the persons aboard, rafts for a further 1,088, and there were also 2,000 lifejackets onboard; see Stent, *Bespattered*, 109.

114. Fehle, 'Memorandum'.

115. Joseph Pia Interview.

116. See ibid.; and Baruch 'Reminiscences'.

117. See 'Pinschof Journal'; 'Willy Leopold Hess Memoirs'; HO 215/161.

118. Jochanan, 'Inside Out'. See also Cuthbert, 'Papers'; Patkin, *Dunera*, 27; and Eric Koch, *Deemed Suspect: A Wartime Blunder* (London: Methuen, 1980), 38–39.

119. Nicole M. T. Brunnhuber, 'After the Prison Ships: Internment Narratives in Canada', in *'Totally Un-English'?*, 169.

120. Lynton, *Accidental Journey*, 38; HO 215/155 Canada: segregation of Nazi and non-Nazi internees (1941); HO 215/161.

121. Stent, *Bespattered*, 230.

122. June Nathan, 'Biographical Note about Ernst Geiduschek (Late Ernest Garson)', 2009, MS 12120.

123. Concerns were also expressed over bias towards Fascists by Camp Commandants. See HO 215/155; HO 215/161. The actor Robert Rietti, for example, was injured by members of the British Union of Fascists while in a prison in Liverpool ('Robert Rietti Obituary', *The Daily Telegraph*, 22 April 2015).

124. HO 215/161; HO 215/155.

125. 'Ludwig Hess Memoirs'. Hess also noted that 'you could easily have fried an egg on the walls at midday heat'. Conditions at Hay were such that members of the garrison were supplied with close-fitting tinted goggles for protection against dust storms. No such provision was made for the internees, however (Pearl, *Scandal*, 97).

126. For example, there was no paper or ink for writing letters to relatives initially in Australian camps, see Baruch, 'Reminiscences'. Replacing items like spectacles could also be a problem as it was not seen as 'high priority' by some Canadian Camp Commandants. See HO 215/161; Stent, *Bespattered*, 218.

127. Baruch, 'Reminiscences'.

128. Stent, *Bespattered*, 232–35; HO 215/161.

129. Stent, Bespattered, 232–35. See also F. A. Barker, 'Letter of Thanks for Medical Care Given by Dr Patrick Peel to Internees', 1945, MS 12380; Helman, 'Dunera', 4–5.

130. For example, friends of Yushiko Uchida 'had moved from Zone One to Dinuba, where they thought they would be safe ... found themselves subject to removal after all, and were eventually sent to a camp in Arizona. Had they not attempted the first move at all, they could have been with their Bay Area friends in Tanforan, and later Topaz, and saved themselves considerable expense as well'

(Uchida, *Exile*, 95). Hatsu (Matsumoto) Kanemoto's family also voluntarily relocated. As she describes: 'Then all of the sudden, one morning, in the newspaper it says we were going to be evacuated. So we had to run around, run around because we didn't want to go to camp at that time. We were going to go to Colorado. But it might have been easier if we went to camp. We really had to struggle when we went to Colorado.' See *REgenerations Oral History Project: Rebuilding Japanese American Families, Communities, and Civil Rights in the Resettlement Era: San Jose Region: Volume IV*, ed. Japanese American National Museum (Los Angeles, 2000), 34.

131. Dickerson, *Concentration*, 78.

132. Daniels, *Prisoners*, 48.

133. Curtis Munson had already reported to the president, prior to Pearl Harbor, along with the Honolulu FBI, that the majority of the Japanese population was trustworthy, and the FBI already had records regarding all those deemed suspect. Robinson, *Order*, 75–76, 94–95.

134. Weglyn, *Infamy*, 87.

135. Doris Berg Nye, 'My Memories of the War Years'. Available online: http://gaic. info/berg-story/. See also Carl Tiemann's story in Stephen Fox, *America's Invisible Gulag: A Biography of German American Internment & Exclusion in World War II* (New York: Peter Lang, 2000), 170–71.

136. *Justice Denied*, 278–79.

137. Ibid.

138. Weglyn, *Infamy*, 177. See also Dickerson, *Concentration*, 48; Berg Nye, 'Memories'.

139. Jeffery F. Burton, Mary M. Farrell, Florence. B. Lord, and Richard W. Lord, *Confinement and Ethnicity: An Overview of World War II Japanese American Relocation Sites* (Western Archeological and Conservation Center National Park Service US Department of the Interior, 2000).

140. 'Issei, Nisei, Kibei – Fortune Magazine Reviews the Program of the WRA and the Problems Created by the Evacuation from the West Coast of 110,000 People of Japanese Descent' (1944) in *Gerda Isenberg Papers 3.1*, (1944); Chikaraishi, *REgenerations: Chicago*, 78; Burton et al, *Confinement*.

141. Stephen Fox, *Uncivil Liberties: Italian Americans under Siege during World War II* (Parkland, FL: Universal Publishers, 2000), xi.

142. Takako Day, *Show Me the Way to Go Home: The Moral Dilemma of Kibei No No Boys in World War Two Incarceration Camps* (East Middlebury, VT: Wren Song Press, 2014), 4.

143. Uchida, *Exile*, 81.

144. Kando Ikeda, *Ikeda Family Papers 1.1*, 1942.

145. Fox, *Invisible Gulag*, 132.

146. Karen L. Riley, *Schools behind Barbed Wire: The Untold Story of Wartime Internment and the Children of Arrested Enemy Aliens* (Lanham, MD: Rowman & Littlefield, 2002), 155.

147. Fox, *Invisible Gulag*, 132.

148. The other countries who deported some or all of their enemy alien internees to the United States were Bolivia, Colombia, Costa Rica, the Dominican Republic, Ecuador, El Salvador, Guatemala, Haiti, Honduras, Nicaragua, Panama, and Peru. *Justice Denied*, 305, 307. See also Heidi Donald, *We Were Not the Enemy: Remembering the United States' Latin-American Civilian Internment Program of World War II* (Bloomington, IN: iUniverse, 2007).

149. See Mari Okazaki, *Journal April 24 to June 14, 1942* (California, 1942).

150. Terminal Islanders, for example, were given the minimum time to evacuate, leading to the creation of a highly antagonistic group in the relocation centres; see R. B. Cozzens (field assistant director Manzanar), 'Letter to Dillon Myer', 1943; 'Poston', 1943. According to official records, however, the decision for the evacuation of the Terminal Islanders was made 6 days prior (WRA, *131–1.1*).

151. Uchida, *Exile*, 59.

152. Sakamoto, *REgenerations: San Jose*, 293. See also Okazaki, *Journal*; Minoru Kiyota, *Beyond Loyalty: The Story of a Kibei* (Honolulu: University of Hawaii, 1997), 62. It was not only physical items that had to be left behind. Sumiko Kobayashi remembered leaving her dog, who she had been given on her eleventh birthday, with Spanish neighbours. When camp policy changed allowing pets she sent for Tippy, only to find she had run away 'probably because she didn't like Spanish food as much as Japanese food' (Rachel Pistol, 'Interview with Sumiko Kobayashi', 2015).

153. One family, who leased a hotel but owned the furniture and fixings inside, agreed to let a friend take care of their goods and rent the rooms out on their behalf, on the understanding that the profits would be sent to the family. This agreement worked for the first four months but thereafter not a penny was received. As the son explained after the war: 'This is typical of what happened. And we had no course of action to be able to collect the money outside of legal action. But nobody had money for legal action and being so far away, too.' See Chikaraishi, *REgenerations: Chicago*, 79. See also Koike, *REgenerations: San Jose*, 169. In direct contrast were the actions of Miss Hudson, a Caucasian friend of the Sugi family, who 'rented [the house] out, paid the property tax and insurance, and whatever costs out of the rent proceeds … So when the war ended and my parents were coming back, they notified her, and she had the renter move out, and had all the furniture that belonged to us which she had stored, moved back in place. She even had all of the utilities re-connected in my father's name – the water, gas, electricity, and some basic foods in the refrigerator'. See Hurt, *REgenerations: Los Angeles*, 134. See also Honda, *REgenerations: Los Angeles*, 61–62, 75.

154. 'The Wartime Handling of Evacuee Property', WRA, *131 – 2.19*.

155. The WRA concluded after the war that 'the wartime handling of evacuee property is a sorry part of the war record'. Ibid.

156. *Justice Denied*, 115; Irons, *Justice*, 87–93.

157. *Justice Denied*, 236–37; Weglyn, *Infamy*, 228; Irons, *Justice*, 93–99.

158. Mitchell T. Maki, Harry H. L. Kitano, and Megan S. Berthold, *Achieving the Impossible Dream: How the Japanese Americans Obtained Redress* (Chicago: University of Illinois Press, 1999), 37; Jeanne Wakatsuki Houston and James D. Houston, *Farewell to Manzanar* (New York: Bantam Books, 1973), 125.

159. *Justice Denied*, 100, 239; Houston, *Farewell*, 126; Irons, *Justice*, 99–103.

160. Communication regarding the details of time and location for departure was often contradictory and caused additional anguish for those being evacuated. See Okazaki, *Journal*.

161. Hatsuye Egami, *The Evacuation Diary of Hatsuye Egami* (Pasadena, CA: Intentional Productions, 1996), 20.

162. Mine Okubo, *Citizen 13660* (New York: Columbia University Press, 1946), 35. For more examples of the accommodation at Tanforan, see 'Letters Written by Two Japanese-American Schoolgirls from Internment Centers', 1942; and Uchida, *Exile*, 70. Fresno County Fair Ground was used as an Assembly Center and 'the most offensive aspect of our detention was the nauseating stench of urine emanating from the stable area and constantly in our nostrils' (Violet Kazue De Cristoforo, *Violet Kazue De Cristoforo Papers 1.1*, 1988). Tulare is described in Okazaki, *Journal*. At Merced 'Some doors [were] at least 2 inches too small for the doorway and in some places the rain water and mud seep in through the concrete'. The same internee said that when her family saw their living quarters they 'were so sick [they] couldn't, eat, walk, or talk. [They] couldn't even cry till later' (Unknown, 'Letter from Merced Assembly Center', 1942). The conditions at Salinas were no better, as described in Kitaji, *REgenerations San Jose*, 251. Despite these realities, Justice Tom Clark still claimed almost thirty years later that the stalls had been turned into 'nice apartments' (*Relocation Reviewed: Volume I*, 9b).

163. See Uchida, *Exile*, 75–76; Okazaki, *Journal*; and Amino, *REgenerations: Chicago*, 12. Not all the Assembly Centers were fortunate enough to have proper bathroom furniture and therefore were expected to use hastily constructed wooden latrines on 'hard, fresh-sawed, un-sandpapered wood'. See 'Letter from Merced'.

164. Egami, *Evacuation*, 27.

165. Kiyota, *Beyond*, 68.

166. Okazaki, *Journal*.

167. FBI raids and the resulting confiscation of hot plates and other such items led to much unrest in the camps, particularly in Santa Anita. See FBI, *Files Concerning the War Relocation Authority, 1942–1946 1.15*, 1943.

168. 'Letter from Merced'. A constant complaint was that 'the army food we were given was totally lacking in the fresh fruits and vegetables to which we were accustomed, uniformly unappetizing, and at times tainted because of the lack of refrigerators and the inexperience of the cooks' (*Cristoforo 1.1*; Sone, *Daughter*, 178; Okazaki, *Journal*). One mother from Santa Anita wrote: 'I don't know how I'm going to keep my children's health because, as I wrote before, Teddy doesn't eat a darn thing at the mess hall besides milk. At first I thought it was Tedd's fault for being so particular, but everyone with children between the ages of about six and seven complains. I don't blame them: even I wouldn't eat it if I weren't so hungry' (Okazaki, *Journal*). See also Ueno and Zaima, *REgenerations: San Jose*, 481, 633;

169. Uchida, *Exile*, 77. See also 'Letters from two schoolchildren'.

170. Uchida, *Exile*, 77. See also Okazaki, *Journal*; Okubo, *Citizen*, 38–39, 41.

171. Tunnell and Chilcoat, *Children*, 11.

172. Uchida, *Exile*, 86.

173. Ibid., 84; Okazaki, *Journal*.

174. Uchida, *Exile*, 93.

175. Tamie Tsuchiyama, 'Letters from Santa Anita Assembly Center', 1942.

176. FBI, *1.15*. The fact that rioting occurred was used by the press to bolster arguments for the exclusion of those of Japanese ancestry from the West Coast (Tsuchiyama, 'Letters').

177. It should be noted that Manzanar was classed as an Assembly Center until June 1, 1942 (WRA, *131–1.1*).

178. Some of the journeys lasted several days but sleeping berths were only available for infants or those suffering a severe disability. The military insisted that the blinds be drawn, supposedly for the safety of the internees. The trains were also shunted onto sidings whenever a higher priority train was on the tracks, leading to delays of sometimes up to ten hours (*Justice Denied*, 149–51).

179. Government officials labelled the centres as being in 'wilderness-type areas' (ibid.).

180. At Manzanar, 1,000 volunteers from Los Angeles arrived in March 1942 to prepare the camp for the arrival of a further 9,000 over the coming months. The internees were also responsible for constructing the administrative buildings for the Caucasian staff as these were not included in the original construction contracts (*Justice Denied*, 149–51, 158).

181. At several of the Centers there were exceptions, such as at Heart Mountain where the blocks were twice the size and had two mess halls, recreation halls, and washing and laundry facilities (ibid.). It should also be noted that there were, once again, no adapted toilet facilities for the use of children ('Manzanar (Miscellaneous)').

182. Ibid. Poston and Gila River were the hottest of the ten locations ('Poston', 1943), though in all locations temperatures often soared during the day and plummeted at night.

183. One woman in Topaz sustained extensive burns when roofing tar dripped into her apartment while she was resting ('Topaz Daily Log', 1942).

184. *Justice Denied*, 158. Larger apartments of up to twenty by twenty or twenty by twenty-five feet were available for larger families.

185. In Topaz in October 1942, 225 stoves were still needed yet only 53 were available ('Block Managers' Meeting Minutes, Topaz', 1942). In the week preceding Christmas at Poston regular fuel shortages were reported, leading to a rationing of oil (WRA, *Gila River 1.7*, 1943). Poston was still experiencing stove shortages in February 1943 ('Poston', 1943).

186. Ueno, *REgenerations: San Jose*, 476. See also Honda, *REgenerations: Los Angeles*, 63.

187. Honda, *REgenerations: Los Angeles*, 63 'They tried everything to control the wind and the dust. They plowed the empty areas, made irrigation ditches, and spread gravel between the barracks. But nothing was successful; the elements won out' (Okubo, *Citizen*, 184). See also Uchida, *Exile*, 109; 'Lila Wilson Interview' (1968); 'Manzanar (Miscellaneous)'.

188. Altitude caused problems not least with the cooking initially where the lower boiling point of water led to many meals of half-cooked rice (ibid.); and Ueno, *REgenerations: San Jose*, 477.

189. Lila Wilson Interview.

190. Amino, *REgenerations: Chicago*, 12; 'Poston', 1942.

191. 'Poston', 1942. Minoru Kiyota recalled finding three scorpions nesting in one of the toilets when he arrived at Topaz (Kiyota, *Beyond*, 75).

192. *Cristoforo 1.1*.

193. *San Francisco Chronicle*, 1 June 1943 in Charles F. Ernst, *Topaz Scrap Book* (1943). At Topaz, for example, the food was reported by the internees to be 'plain but edible' (*The Desert News*, 3 July 1943, in ibid.), though the standard varied drastically within the camp from 'Enough food, best taste' in Block 14 to 'As far as quantity goes, it's very scarce' in Block 22 ('Block Managers' Meeting Minutes, Topaz', 1942). See also 'Poston', 1942 and 1943, where 'the proof of insufficient diet is shown by the fact that many people are necessitated in taking vitamin pills in order to keep their health.'

194. Dillon S. Myer, *Collection 131 – 2.2*, 1944. See also *The Desert News*, 28 December 1942, in *Topaz Scrap Book*.

195. *San Francisco Chronicle*, 8 May 1943, in *Topaz Scrap Book* The *Christian Science Monitor* provided some balance to the debate when it published 24 June 1943: 'The fact that the average cost of food a day an inmate in the Relocation Centers compares almost exactly with the same cost in Alcatraz Federal Prison in San Francisco Bay ... supplies a fair answer to the question of how luxuriously these racially Japanese "guests" of the United States are faring' (ibid.).

196. Community Council, 'Topaz Council Meeting Minutes', 1943.

197. 'Manzanar (Miscellaneous)'. One young internee reported mostly surviving on apple butter and bread as she usually sat with a family of boys who grabbed food away from the women (Amino, *REgenerations: Chicago*, 15). See also Honda, *REgenerations: Los Angeles*, 64.

198. 'We never ate together as a family ... Food was there, so you just go there to eat' (Arii, *REgenerations: San Jose*, 23).

199. *Desert News*, 3 July 1943. At Heart Mountain there were a number of former agricultural workers from the Santa Clara valley in California who grew vegetables and grain on approximately 1,500 acres. See Cecilia M. Tsu, *Garden of the World: Asian Immigrants and the Making of Agriculture in California's Santa Clara Valley* (Oxford: Oxford University Press, 2013), 209.

200. Tunnell and Chilcoat, *Children*, 58. See also 'Official Report of the First General Assembly of Topaz, Sept. 11', 1942.

201. *Isenberg 3.1*.

202. 'Poston', 1942; Nobi Takahashi, 'Letters from Tanforan Assembly Center', 1942.

203. *Tulean Dispatch*, 18 June 1943, as cited in Burton et al., *Confinement*.

204. Ibid. See also 'Gila Anniversary Booklet "A Year at Gila" July 20th, 1943', in *Gila River 1.7*. Also *WRA, Collection 131 – 1.4*, 1943; 'Poston', 1943.

205. Kazuo Inouye, for example, went to top sugar beets in Montana where he was refused service on more than one occasion (Inouye, *REgenerations: Los Angeles*, 174). See also Ueno, *REgenerations: San Jose*, 490. An estimated 1,600 internees helped relieve labour shortages in the harvesting of sugar beet crops in eastern Oregon, Utah, Idaho, and Montana (WRA, *131 – 1.1*). See also 'Press Release, Topaz', 1942. Besides earning extra money some of the internees found the farmers very appreciative. For example, see Teraji, *REgenerations: Chicago*, 529.

206. Valerie J. Matsumoto, 'Japanese American Women during World War II', *Frontiers: A Journal of Women Studies* 8 (1984), 9.

207. Initially the payments to internees were in line with the payment of US Army Privates, but the Privates' payments increased to $30 per month, unlike the wages for the internees, leading to great discontent [Orin Starn, 'Engineering Internment: Anthropologists and the War Relocation Authority', *American Ethnologist* 13, no. 4 (1986), 708]. There was also controversy over a 'slave labour racket' at Tule Lake where Japanese Americans looked after children of the Caucasian staff for a much reduced rate [Richard Drinnon, *Keeper of Concentration Camps: Dillon S. Myer and American Racism* (Berkeley: University of California, 1987), 47]. See also Sone, *Daughter*, 179; Kiyota, *Beyond*, 68.

208. 'Poston', 1942.

209. 'Poston', 1943. As the internees at Topaz noted, 'Without an efficient organization, both the Administration and the residents as a whole would suffer a great deal' ('Topaz Council Meeting Minutes', 1943).

210. Subcommittees of the councils included those with a focus on food, education, health, and employment. See 'Topaz Council Meeting Minutes', 1943; 'Poston', 1942; and *Gila River 1.7*.

211. Thomas James, *Exile Within: The Schooling of Japanese Americans, 1942–1945* (Cambridge, MA: Harvard University Press, 1987), 47. See also Mayeda, *REgenerations: Chicago*, 445; FBI, *Files Concerning the War Relocation Authority, 1942–1946 1.9*, 1943. Despite the realities of the limitations of schooling within camp, distinguished educators wrote in professional journals about the high quality of the schooling (see Kehoe 1944 as quoted in Starn, 'Engineering', 770).

212. Schoolchild, 'Relocation, Its Challenge to Me', 1942. See also Sakamoto, *REgenerations: San Jose*, 297.

213. In Manzanar as many as forty to forty-three children would be herded into rooms designed for twenty-five to twenty-seven individuals and light levels were well below the minimum standard ('Manzanar (Miscellaneous)').

214. 'Topaz Daily Log' 1942; 1943.

215. Teacher retention was an issue across mainland America. The average tenure at Poston in 1942–43 was 4.8 months. Caucasian teachers could choose whereabouts they lived in Cam. Those teachers who had moved to the centres for ideological reasons tended to reside within internee barracks whereas those attracted by money lived in comparative luxury in the administrators' quarters (James, *Exile*, 50, 3). See also Tunnell and Chilcoat, *Children*, 42; Honda, *REgenerations: Los Angeles*, 64.

216. *Topaz Scrap Book.*

217. Honda, *REgenerations: Los Angeles*, 67. See also Koike, *REgenerations Oral History Project: Rebuilding Japanese American Families, Communities, and Civil Rights in the Resettlement Era; San Diego Region: Volume III*, ed. Japanese American National Museum (Los Angeles, 2000), 182; and *Gila River 1.7*. In winter some centres constructed ice rinks (Okubo, *Citizen*, 158). During the summer months it was possible for groups to picnic in areas outside the camp (WRA, *Manzanar Weekly Reports*, 1943). In Manzanar a group of men started a camp fishing club whose tale has been turned into a film that has toured the United States (Manzanar Fishing Club website, http://www.fearnotrout.com).

218. Honda, *REgenerations: Los Angeles*, 57.

219. Nat R. Griswold, 'Rohwer: From Final Report: Historical Statistical-Functional Report of Community Activities Section' (Berkeley, 1945), 38.

220. Egami, *Evacuation*, 39.

221. Griswold, 'Rohwer'. See also WRA, 'Manzanar Weekly Reports', 1943; 'Manzanar (Miscellaneous)'; 'Poston', 1942; 'Poston', 1943.

222. Emily Colborn-Roxworthy, "'Manzanar, the Eyes of the World Are upon You': Performance and Archival Ambivalence at a Japanese American Internment Camp', *Theatre Journal* 59, no. 2 (2007), 204.

223. Roxworthy, *Spectacle*, 158.

224. Colborn-Roxworthy, 'Manzanar', 213.

225. Ibid., 200.

226. Ibid., 214.

227. Roxworthy, *Spectacle*, 175.

228. See Okazaki, *Journal*; 'Notes on Community Government', 31 December 1943 in 'Poston', 1943. Vegetable plots, or 'Victory Gardens' were encouraged but one internee asked, 'What can you do with only 7 packages of seeds (beans, peas, carrots, radishes, squashes, chickory, lettuce)? ... each Recreational Center will only receive enough seeds to occupy a space of 5' x 6'. Now what in the name of Heaven can you do with that!' (Nobi Takahashi, 'Letters from Tanforan Assembly Center', 1942). See also 'Manzanar (Miscellaneous)'.

229. WRA, *Collection 131 – 1.2*, 1942. *Victory Bulletin*, 30 June 1943, in *Topaz Scrap Book*.

230. Okazaki, 'Letters'; 'Manzanar (Miscellaneous)'; 'Topaz Daily Log', 1942; Honda, *REgenerations: Los Angeles*, 65.

231. Some of the more racist of those in command of the operation of the camps called for segregation of the camps to ensure that no more 'Japs' could be born in America (Drinnon, *Keeper*, 65). See also *Cristoforo 1.1*; and Community Council, 'Topaz Community Government', 1942.

232. Manzanar and Amache (Granada) cemeteries are still the focal point for remembrance services to this day. Topaz residents were particularly against using the cemetery in camp and the dead were sent to Salt Lake City for cremation where they were held for burial (Okubo, *Citizen*, 162).

233. At least one child was run over in camp (Community Council, 'Topaz Council Meeting Minutes' 20 September 1943). There were also several deaths related to trucks in camp, for example, the man crushed behind a dump truck at Tule Lake (*San Francisco Chronicle*, 29 October 1943, in *Topaz Scrap Book*) and a man who was thrown off a farm truck and suffered serious injury ('Topaz Council', 1943). In Arkansas, the main source of winter heat came from wood burning stoves. Inadequate training on wood felling led to the death of a man in January 1943 [Russell Bearden, 'The False Rumor of Tuesday: Arkansas's Internment of Japanese-Americans'. *The Arkansas Historical Quarterly* 41 (1982), 333]. Construction projects were also dangerous. Kingo Mitsuayasu was admitted to hospital in a critical condition after one end of the high school wall he was helping construct collapsed ('Topaz Daily Log', 1943).

234. As a result of the Wakasa shooting, day sentries were abolished at Topaz and the use of firearms restricted. This, however, did not stop further 'near misses' occurring. See 'Topaz Daily Log', 1943; Community Council, 'Central Utah Project Council', 1944. Elsewhere there was a case of an internee being shot at by a civilian while working in the woods outside Jerome, as well as several incidents of

assault at other camps when internees were working beyond the perimeter fence, and two internees en route to Lordsburg were shot 'trying to escape'. See Bearden, 'False', 338; Burton et al., *Confinement*; 'Topaz Council', 1943.

235. Tunnell and Chilcoat, *Children*, 28.

236. The two internees who died in the shooting were eighteen and twenty-one years old. Common Ground, 'What Happened at Manzanar', 1943. See also Ueno, *REgenerations: San Jose*, 481–88; FBI, *1.15*.

237. Poston was the scene of multiple beatings that involved hospitalization. All the victims had pro-American ties. See FBI, *1.15* and WRA, 'Tule Lake'.

238. Kataji, *REgenerations: San Jose*, 250; WRA, 'Tule Lake'.

239. FBI, *1.15*.

240. FBI, *Files concerning the War Relocation Authority, 1942–1946 1.1* (1942).

241. The WRA believed that segregation could be carried out in such a way that there was no bias against those who openly admitted to supporting Japan in the war effort (*Gila River 1.1*). It should be noted that no one of German or Italian ancestry was required to complete the loyalty questionnaire (Dickerson, *Concentration*, 226).

242. Cozzens, 'Letter to Dillon Myer'. See also *Justice Denied*, 192; Drinnon, *Keeper*, 78; and *San Francisco Chronicle*, 14 April 1943 (*Topaz Scrap Book*).

243. *Justice Denied*, 195; Kiyota, *Beyond*, 96.

244. *Justice Denied*, 192. Registration was never completed at Tule Lake, for example, where approximately 3,000 internees refused to register.

245. 'Utah Project Council', 1944. Significantly in 1942 provision had been made to exempt from internment any Italian or German aliens who had a relative who was serving or had died in the armed forces. This was never extended to the Japanese Americans (Morton Grodzins, *Americans Betrayed: Politics and the Japanese Evacuation* (Chicago: Chicago University Press, 1949), 282).

246. *Justice Denied*, 193. Some Nisei were assigned to 1800 Engineer Service Battalion along with Germans and Italians over whom the army wanted to keep close watch [David J. O'Brien and Stephen S. Fugita, *The Japanese American Experience* (Bloomington: Indiana University Press, 1991), 68]. See also 'Block Managers' Meeting Minutes, Topaz', 1944.

247. Roxworthy, *Spectacle*, 14

248. O'Brien and Fugita, *Experience*, 69.

249. Prior to the Loyalty Questionnaire only 2,255 applications for repatriation and expatriation were made, in contrast to the 6,673 applications made in 1943 (*Justice Denied*, 251).

250. *Gila River 1.1*. See also 'Poston', 1943 and 1944; *San Francisco Chronicle*, 23 June 1943 (*Topaz Scrap Book*). Those deemed loyal from Tule Lake were transferred to other camps.

251. Kiyota, *Beyond*, 81–82.

252. Ibid., 96.

253. *Isenberg 3.1.*

254. Day, *Show Me*, 25.

255. See Kiyota, *Beyond*, 48, 59–60.

256. Day, *Show Me*, 24.

257. Ibid., 35.

258. See WRA, 'Tule Lake', 1943; Cozzens, 'Letter to Dillon *Myer*'; FBI, *1.15*; Kaneko, *REgenerations: Chicago*, 316.

259. Day, *Show Me*, 118.

260. Ibid., 121; Kiyota, *Beyond*, 109–10.

261. In some ways the 18,000 internees at Tule Lake were considered to be 'insurance' for the 10,000 American civilians in the hands of the Japanese [*Gerda Isenberg papers 3.8* (1944)].

262. *Tulean Dispatch*, 16 October 1943; 'Tule Lake (Correspondence)' 1944; Weglyn, *Infamy*, 205.

263. Day, *Show Me*, 118; Kiyota, *Beyond*, 104.

264. Kiyota, *Beyond*, 105.

265. Ibid., 109.

266. The jailhouse was built by the internees and was a cause of much controversy. See Drinnon, *Keeper*, 110–15; *Cristoforo 1.1*; 'Tule Lake (Correspondence)'; Ueno, *REgenerations: San Jose*, 499, 522; and Weglyn, *Infamy*, 206.

267. Weglyn, *Infamy*, 166.

268. Ibid., 167–69; Day, *Show Me*, xix.

269. Toyo Suyemoto, *I Call to Remembrance: Toyo Suyemoto's Years of Internment* (Piscataway, NJ: Rutgers University Press, 2007), 79.

270. For examples, see Claus Moser Interview; and Lynton, *Accidental Journey*.

271. 'Papers of Harry Johnson'.

272. Hellmuth Weissenborn Interview.

Chapter 3

1. House of Commons Debate, *Hansard*, 10 July 1940, vol. 362, 1209. Cazalet continued, 'Vital keymen have been interned, and we have locked up engineers and scientists who were making a real contribution to winning the war; boys at school have been taken away, their education uncompleted, and, if it is true – I hope it may be contradicted – worst of all, in some cases we have actually mixed in the same camps, Nazis and Jews.'

2. See, for example, debates in the House of Commons, *Hansard*, 10 July 1940, vol. 362, 1208–306; 7 November 1940, vol. 365, 1504–31; 20 November 1940, vol. 365, 1988–93W.

3. 'Victor Gollancz: Eleanor Rathbone', *AJR*, February (1946), 13.

4. As George Strauss noted, under the first White Paper 'Einstein, Thomas Mann, and Toscanini would have to remain interned' (Stent, *Bespattered*, 208).

5. Hellmuth Weissenborn Interview; 'Fiala Correspondence'; Ludwig Spiro Interview; Goldman, '18B', 126; 'Adolf Gruenwald Papers'; Joseph Pia Interview.

6. Stent, *Bespattered*, 209.

7. Ibid., 210.

8. *The Camp*, 16 June 1941.

9. Ille Pinkus, a sixteen-year-old, wrote of her joy at being reclassified to a 'C' on 18 January 1941 (Pinkus, 'Letters'). See also Ludwig Spiro Interview; Celeste Sidoli, 'Letter from Internee in Palace Camp, Douglas', 1941, MS 10042; 'Harry Johnson Papers'; Bill-Jentzsch, 'Internment'; Orazio Caira Interview.

10. See Hodge, 'Memories'; and Georg Kohlberg and Karola Kohlberg, 'Correspondence between Internees Georg Kohlberg and His Fiancee Karola Krey', 1939–41, MS 10131.

11. 22 February 1941 'Sefton Review Nos 1 and 8'.

12. Stent, *Bespattered*, 226–27.

13. Ibid.; Maximilian Koessler, 'Enemy Alien Internment: With Special Reference to Great Britain and France', *Political Science Quarterly* 57 (1942), 111; '*The Camp* Issues 1–6, 8–16, 20'; Nathan, 'Ernst Geiduschek'.

14. Stent, *Bespattered*, 229.

15. Koch's published works include his account of internment: Koch, *Suspect*.

16. Mendel, 'Barbed'; Baruch, 'Reminiscences'. Major Julian Layton, the Home Office liaison officer, was despatched to Australia to try and make release run as smoothly as possible (Helman, 'Dunera', 3–4).

17. Stent, *Bespattered*, 238–39; Patkin, *Dunera*, 137.

18. Stent, *Bespattered*, 238–39. See also Brunnhuber, 'After', 176; Pearl, *Scandal*, 217; Helman, 'Dunera', 4.

19. Lynton, *Accidental Journey*, 53. Another example of poor record keeping can be seen in Evelyn Ruth Kaye Interview.

20. As Lynton notes in *Accidental Journey*, 'I left [SS] *Thysville* in Liverpool in mid-February 1941, with about one hundred and twenty pounds in winnings and wages, having been interned with ten shillings nine months earlier. Financially speaking, the internment had been a success.' Ibid., 58.

21. Stent, *Bespattered*, 213–14.

22. For more information on the 18B detainees, who were British fascists as opposed to enemy aliens, see Goldman, '18B', 120–36; 'Papers relating to Franz Joseph Buch, an 18B detainee in Peveril Camp, Peel', 1940–43, MS 12384; Simpson, *Odious*; Cuthbert, 'Papers'; Margot Pottlitzer Interview; HO 213/7 The internment of citizens of friendly nations (1942).

23. Chappell, *Island*, 122–23; Joseph Pia Interview.

24. Chappell, *Island*, 130–32.

25. Steven Vajda Interview; Ronald Stent Interview. Other examples include Max-Otto Ludwig Loewenstein who changed his name to Mark Lynton (Lynton, *Accidental Journey*, 3), and Jacob Schartenburg who became Walter Sharman ['Papers of Jacob Schartenburg (later Walter Sharman)', 1940s, MS 12413]. also Nathan, 'Ernst Geiduschek'; 'Adolf Gruenwald Papers'; See Helen Fry, *Denazification: Britain's Enemy Aliens, Nazi War Criminals and the Reconstruction of Post-war Europe* (Stroud, Gloucestershire: The History Press, 2010), 15–16. Indeed, my own grandfather changed his name from Fritz to Frederick in order to disguise his Austrian roots.

26. Dalheim, 'Papers'.

27. Bill-Jentzsch, 'Internment'.

28. Orazio Caira Interview.

29. Camillo D'Allesandro married an Englishwoman and lived in Oxford both before his internment and after his release (D'Allesandro, 'Camp life'). Margot Hodge, a trainee nurse, returned to St. James' Hospital in Leeds post-internment to resume her training (Hodge, 'Memories'). See also Jacobsthal, 'Memoirs'; and 'Papers Documenting the Life and Internment of Domenico Traversari, an Italian Interned on the Isle of Man, 1940–1945: include copies of correspondence relating to Traversari's attempts to gain release, a handwritten transcription of an account of his life by his eleven-year-old grandson (1978) and colour copies of portraits of Domenico and Cesira his wife, painted on the Isle of Man during his internment', 1943–44, 1978, MS 11273.

30. Ugolini, *Experiencing*, 199.

31. Wendy Ugolini, '"Spaghetti Lengths in a Bowl?" Recovering Narratives of Not "Belonging" amongst the Italian Scots', *Immigrants and Minorities* 31 (2013), 226.

32. Ibid., 227.

33. Renzo Serafini Interview; Joseph Pia Interview; Orazio Caira Interview.

34. Sussman, 'Young'. See also Claus Moser Interview.

35. Hans Sturm, 'Through Stormy Seas to Calm Waters: Memories of a German Jehovah's Witness Interned on the Isle of Man during World War II', 2000, MS 11641. Herbert Loebl qualified as an electrical engineer after the war and started his own business manufacturing scientific instruments, ultimately earning an OBE for Services to Exports, the Citizens' Medal of Bamberg, the German Cross of the Order of Merit, and the Bavarian Cross of the Order of Merit ('Loebl'). Moses Aberbach continued his interrupted studies at the University of Leeds and moved on to postgraduate study ('Aberbach Letters').

36. Eva Wittenberg Interview.

37. 'Papers of Erna Nelki'.

38. Margot Pottlitzer Interview.

39. Lustig, 'Memoirs'.

40. Brinson et al., *Loyal Internee*, 159.

41. Fry, *Denazification*, 172.

42. Joseph Pia Interview.

43. 'Elisabeth Bickel Correspondence'.

44. Hellmuth Weissenborn Interview; Ludwig Spiro Interview.

45. Lachs, 'Memoirs'. Much pressure was put on younger men to sign up. See letter dated 31 March 1941 in 'Harry Johnson Papers'; Renzo Serafini Interview.

46. Joseph Pia Interview.

47. Ugolini, *Experiencing*, 149–50.

48. Ibid., 156.

49. Leighton-Langer, *King's*, 8.

50. Ibid., 9. As there was no Pioneer Corps in Canada, internees were unable to sign up to any of the Canadian Armed Forces and had to return to Britain to enlist [HO 215/218 Listing of luggage before embarkation to prevent bogus compensation claims (1943–45)].

51. Ugolini, *Experiencing*, 160.

52. Ultimately 'not everyone was a hero. Not everyone even had the opportunity to do anything heroic. But in choosing to be a soldier or a member of the women's services each one did the only sensible thing open to him or her in order to oppose the Nazis effectively'. Ibid., 23, 238. See also Bather, 'Steven Vajda'; Lustig, 'Memoirs'.

53. Ugolini, *Experiencing*, 159, 172.

54. Leighton-Langer, *King's*, 24. Fritz Lustig made a similar observation: 'One step from being guarded to being entitled to wear the same uniform as the chap who had been guarding us!'

55. Winckler, 'Sisters'.

56. Fry, *Denazification*, 18.

57. Ugolini, *Experiencing*, 159–60.

58. See Lustig, 'Memoirs'.

59. Fry, *Denazification*, 16–17.

60. Ibid., 35.

61. HO 215/221 Losses sustained during transfers to Isle of Man in May 1941; HO 215/209 Departmental opinions on compensation liability for internees' losses: voyage of SS Ettrick (1941–42); HO 215/213 Voyage of HMT Dunera: compensation for loss or damage (1941); HO 215/199 Australia: property claims of HMT Dunera passengers on release (1941). The government was worried in case further compensation claims would be made when internees returned to Britain from Canada and Australia, which led to lists being compiled of luggage before an internee left any of the camps in the Dominions (HO 215/218).

62. Approximately £12 was given to each internee. Stent, *Bespattered*, 133. War Office policy was to settle claims of £10 or under and to give two-thirds of any amount over £10 (HO 215/213). See also Helman, 'Dunera', 4.

63. Johnson, 'Memories'; Cannell, 'Hardships'; HO 215/222.

64. Anti-alien feeling was monitored via organizations such as the AJR. See 'The First Five Years', *AJR*, May (1946), 33.

65. Ogbe, *Crumbs*, 59; 'Loebl'; Sussman, 'Young'; Brinson et al., *Loyal Internee*, 159; Olins, 'Island Prison', 53; Winckler, 'Sisters'.

66. Eva Wittenburg Interview; Lustig, 'Memoirs'; 'Ludwig Hess Memoirs'; 'Is Naturalisation Good for This Country? A Discussion in the Home Service of the BBC', *AJR*, October (1946), 75; 'Naturalisation', *AJR*, December (1946), 89.

67. Joseph Pia Interview; Orazio Caira Interview.

68. WRA, 'Tule Lake'.

69. Greg Robinson, *After Camp: Portraits in Midcentury Japanese American Life and Politics* (Berkeley, CA: University of California, 2012), 75. See also Okubo, *Citizen*, 205.

70. Okubo, *Citizen*, 206–7; Chikaraishi, *REgenerations: Chicago*, 81.

71. Matsumoto, 'Women', 10. See also 'Topaz Daily Log', 1942; Griswold, 'Rohwer'.

72. Robinson, *After*, 52. According to a Nisei student at the University of Texas, their quota was eight students in the whole university – a not uncommon limitation ('Letter to Topaz from relocated student', 1942).

73. Matsumoto, 'Women', 11.

74. 'Letter to Topaz from relocated student'.

75. Robinson, *After*, 46; *Gerda Isenberg papers 2.1* (1944).

76. Uyehata, *REgenerations: San Jose*, 570.

77. See Adam Schrager, *The Principled Politician: The Ralph Carr Story* (Golden, CO: Fulcrum, 2008); *Gerda Isenberg papers 3.4* (1942). Also worthy of note were the Attorney General of Utah and Mayor Harry Cain for their pro-internee attitude (Wilson and Hosokawa, *East*, 211).

78. Kanemoto, *REgenerations: San Jose*, 149; Teraji, *REgenerations: Chicago*, 532.

79. Other pro-Nisei hirers included the Briggs Manufacturing Company, the Essex Wire Company, Gar Wood Industries, and the Ex-cell-o Company (Robinson, *After*, 49). McClurg's publishing house approached the WRA expressing interest in hiring former internees because of the strong Japanese work ethic (Amino, *REgenerations: Chicago*, 41).

80. *Justice Denied*, 195.

81. Ibid., 196.

82. James C. McNaughton, *Nisei Linguists: Japanese Americans in the Military Intelligence Service during World War II* (Washington DC: Department of the Army, 2006), 106.

83. *Justice Denied*, 197. Maki et al., *Achieving*, 42.

84. 'Topaz Council', 1944.

85. Eric L. Muller, *Free to Die for Their Country: The Story of the Japanese American Draft Resisters in World War II* (Chicago: University of Chicago, 2001), 4.

86. The only exception was Judge Louis E. Goodman who declared that to prosecute the twenty-six men from Tule Lake who appeared before him was 'shocking to his conscience' and 'a violation of due process'. Ibid., 5.

87. President Truman pardoned the draft resisters in 1947. Ibid., 6. See also 'Central Utah Project Council'; Community Council, 'Topaz Council Meeting Minutes', 1944; Teraji, *REgenerations: Chicago*, 549; Maki et al., *Achieving*, 40. Despite the pardon some felt that the stigma still affected their employment opportunities (Mayeda, *REgenerations: Chicago*, 503).

88. Hurt, *REgenerations: Los Angeles*, 120; Community Council, 'Topaz Council', 1944.

89. McNaughton, *Linguists*, 5, 8.

90. Ito, *REgenerations: San Diego*, 108–12. 'The only reason you join is, because you figure that, you owe something to your country, yeah? That's the only reason I can think of. I had no other reason why I joined. The only reason is, because I'm an American, and that's why I joined' (Yoshioka, *REgenerations: San Diego*, 323). The fact the unit was the most decorated in American history has been noted in several television shows, including an episode of the Hawaii Five-0 remake (*Hawaii Five-O 'Ho'onani Makuakane' 'Honor Thy Father'* (2013). [TV programme] CBS. 13 December).

91. Dickerson, *Concentration*, 192; McNaughton, *Linguists*, 139.

92. Some of the Nisei were so disillusioned with America that they 'went for broke' because they felt that there was little to which to return. See Ito, *REgenerations: San Diego*, 112.

93. McNaughton, *Linguists*, 24, 26–27.

94. Ibid., 144.

95. Ibid., 143.

96. Ibid., 207.

97. Ibid., 456; Kiyota, *Beyond*, 195.

98. McNaughton, *Linguists*, 141.

99. Ibid., 113.

100. Reported remarks of General Charles Willoughby, MacArthur's chief of staff for intelligence in ibid., 460.

101. Matsumoto, 'Women', 11; Harry K. Honda, *REgenerations: Los Angeles*, 29.

102. Rose Honda, *Regenerations: Los Angeles*, 61–62.

103. *Gerda Isenberg papers 2.6* (1945).

104. Rose Honda's father, for example, was offered a job as a gardener through boarding house contacts (Rose Honda, *REgenerations: Los Angeles*, 68). Masayo (Yasui) Arii received an offer of domestic work from a Jewish lady who wanted to help (Arii, *REgenerations: San Jose*, 25). See also Community Council, *Heart Mountain 1.1* (1944); Yonemitsu, *REgenerations: San Diego*, 283.

105. Generously called 'Relocation Assistance Grants'. Community Council, 'Topaz Council Meeting Minutes', 1945.

106. Aimee Chin, 'Long-Run Labor Market Effects of Japanese American Internment during World War II on Working-Age Male Internees', *Journal of Labor Economics* 23, no. 3 (2005), 521.

107. Several internees had placed their money in Japanese banks before the war and these assets had been frozen. The number of yen to the dollar naturally increased exponentially, wiping the value of the savings. After the war the JACL assisted in negotiating a better exchange rate for these depositors. The only financial assistance available was from the Veterans Administration who gave $20 a week to veterans for up to a year if they were out of work (Harry Honda, *REgenerations: Chicago*, 31, 34).

108. Yoshioka, *REgenerations: San Diego*, 320. Similarly, the six members of the Suzuki family lived in two rooms of a house and shared a bathroom with another couple on their arrival to the Windy City (Amino, *REgenerations: Chicago*, 20). See also Chikaraishi, *REgenerations: Chicago*, 83.

109. Amino, *REgenerations: Chicago*, 20.

110. Harry Honda, *REgenerations: Los Angeles*, 19.

111. Amino, *REgenerations: Chicago*, 46; Robinson, *After*, 50.

112. Harry Honda, *REgenerations: Los Angeles*, 12

113. Ibid.

114. Robinson, *After*, 50; Harry Honda, *REgenerations: Los Angeles*, 29; Hurt, *REgenerations: Los Angeles*, 121.

115. Robinson, *After*, 50.

116. Hariko Sugi's father, for example, was dependent on his wife picking up whatever work she could find in order to support him as he was too old to work (Hurt, *REgenerations: Los Angeles*, 122).

117. 'Topaz Council Meeting Minutes', 1945.

118. Dillon Myer gave several talks in Pasadena to encourage tolerance towards those of Japanese ancestry returning to the West Coast. See Dillon S. Myer, *Collection 131 – 2.4*, 1944; Dillon S. Myer, *Collection 131 – 2.5*, 1944.

119. Chikaraishi, *REgenerations: Chicago*, 83. Katie Koga found that the Japanese were an unknown quantity in Chicago. Her landlady said 'Ooh, gosh, she talks just like me!' on meeting her (Hironaka, *REgenerations: San Diego*, 97).

120. 'Manzanar (Miscellaneous)'; Uchida, *REgenerations: San Jose*, 439. Government federal housing projects were established on the West Coast in order to provide temporary housing to the returning internees. Voorhies, *REgenerations: San Diego*, 205.

121. Hurt, *REgenerations: Los Angeles*, 134. The Honda family had their property returned by the family that had employed the father. They also supplied the Honda family with a car for a minimal price on their return from internment (ibid., 61–62). See also William Yardley, 'Bob Fletcher Dies at 101; Helped Japanese Americans', *The New York Times*, 6 June 2013, for an account of how

Yardley maintained the farms of three Japanese households during internment. Available online: http://www.nytimes.com/2013/06/07/us/bob-fletcher-dies-at-101-saved-farms-of-interned-japanese-americans.html?smid=fb-share&_r=2

122. Koike, *REgenerations: San Diego*, 169.

123. Ibid., 173.

124. Hurt, *REgenerations: Los Angeles*, 134; Voorhies, *REgenerations: San Diego*, 202–8; Berg Nye, 'Memories'. There were occasional warehouse fires in several of the camps in which internees lost their property that had been transported there for safekeeping. See FBI, *Files concerning the War Relocation Authority, 1942–1946 1.7* (1943); 'Topaz Daily Log', 1943; WRA, *Manzanar Weekly Reports* (1944).

125. Chikaraishi, *REgenerations: Chicago*, 79.

126. WRA, *Collection 131 – 1.7*, 1945.

127. WRA, *131 – 2.19*.

128. Robinson, *After*, 6.

129. Sakamoto, *REgenerations: San Jose*, 307. See also Harry Honda, *REgenerations: Los Angeles*, 35; Regional Oral History Office, *Volume I*, 20.

130. Irons, *Justice*, 348. Harry Honda's parents received approximately $2,000 on their evacuation claim, for example (Harry Honda, *REgenerations: Chicago*, 16).

131. Dickerson, *Concentration*, 237–38.

132. Izumi, Masumi. 'Prohibiting "American Concentration Camps": Repeal of the Emergency Detention Act and the Public Historical Memory of the Japanese American Internment'. *The Pacific Historical Review* 74 (2005), 168, 172.

133. As cited in Creef, *Imaging*, 14.

134. Maki et al., *Achieving*, 117.

135. Ibid., 120.

136. Ibid., 123.

137. Ibid., 128.

138. Kang, *Denying*, 935–36, 944.

139. Ibid., 947–48.

140. Maki et al., *Achieving*, 136.

141. *Justice Denied*, xvii.

142. Ibid.

143. Ibid., xviii.

144. Maki et al., *Achieving*, 194.

145. Ibid., 195.

146. Daniels, *Coming*, 303.

147. Amino, *REgenerations: Chicago*, 64.

148. Yonemitsu, *REgenerations: San Diego*, 300; David Yoo, 'Captivating Memories: Museology, Concentration Camps, and Japanese American History', *American Quarterly* 48 (1996), 697.

149. Pistol, 'Kobayashi Interview'.

150. Elazar Barkan, *The Guilt of Nations: Restitution and Negotiating Historical Injustices* (Baltimore: Johns Hopkins, 2001), 30; Daniels, *Coming*, 303. As Attorney General Richard Thornburgh said on presenting a reparations cheque to a survivor, 'By finally admitting a wrong, a nation does not destroy its integrity but, rather, reinforces the sincerity of its commitment to the Constitution and hence to its people' (Maki et al., *Achieving*, 213).

151. It was not until President Clinton's time in office that the Japanese Latin Americans were offered restitution. Dickerson, *Concentration*, 229; Maki et al., *Achieving*, 222. Interestingly, the Italian community brought about the Wartime Violation of Italian Americans Civil Liberties Act in 2001 but no reparation was made (Dickerson, *Concentration*, 231).

152. 'A Bill for the relief of Bertha Berg'. S. 790, 103rd Congress, First Session, 19 April 1993.

153. Rhoda E. Howard-Hassmann, 'Getting to Reparations: Japanese Americans and African Americans', *Social Forces* 83, no. 2 (2004), 833.

154. See the 'Go for Broke' National Education Center's website for how the apology was positively received: http://www.goforbroke.org/about_us/about_us_educational_history.php

Chapter 4

1. Hodge, 'Memories'.

2. Helman, 'Dunera', 7.

3. Koch, *Suspect*, xiv.

4. Olins, 'Island Prison', 50.

5. Ibid., 52–53.

6. Rachel Pistol, 'Interview with Gaby Koppel', 2012.

7. Hellmuth Weissenborn Interview. Another internee was glad to 'see the back of this place' (Josef Levy, 'English Exercise Book of Josef Levy', 1940s, MS 09401). Another internee 'never spoke about the month spent in Holloway Prison, but her Isle of Man stories generally were quite positive' (Winckler, 'Sisters'.).

8. D'Allesandro, 'Camp Life'.

9. 'Loebl'.

10. Ibid.

11. 'Elisabeth Bickel Correspondence'.

12. Pistol, 'Brand Interview'.

13. For example, see Jochanan, 'Inside Out'.

14. Fritz Lustig, 'Memories, Memories …', *AJR*, November 2014.

15. Rossi, 'Memories'.

16. It was not uncommon for survivors of the tragedy to view British politicians with contempt thereafter (Frank Whitford, 'Sir Eduardo Paolozzi obituary', *The Guardian*, 22 April 2005).

17. Balestracci, *Arandora Star*, 328. See also the information on the Colonsay website focusing on the tragedy. Available online: http://www.colonsay.org.uk/About/Arandora-Star

18. 'Wales Breaks Its Silence … from Memories to Memorials' exhibition toured Wales in 2010. Available online: http://www.arandorastarwales.us/Arandora_Star_Memorial_Fund_in_Wales/HOME.html

19. 'The Arandora Star Tragedy'. Available online: http://www.mazzinigaribaldiclub.org/arandora_star.html

20. 'Italian Cloister Garden'. Available online: http://www.italiancloister.org.uk/why1.htm Not forgetting the memorial chapel in Bardi, Italy. See 'Mazzini Garibaldi Charitable Foundation'. Available online: http://www.mgfoundation.com/mazzini-garibaldi-projects-arandora.html

21. See 'Mazzini Garibaldi Charitable Foundation'; 'Wales Breaks Its Silence … from Memories to Memorials'.

22. 'The Arandora Star Campaign for an Apology Facebook Group'. Available online: https://www.facebook.com/groups/788468851172264/?ref=ts&fref=ts; 'Arandora Star Facebook Group'. Available online: https://www.facebook.com/groups/67868197405/?ref=ts&fref=ts

23. Ugolini, *Experiencing*, 199.

24. Alexander Ramati, *Barbed Wire on the Isle of Man: The Wartime British Internment of Jews* (London: Harcourt, 1980), 218.

25. Ibid., 230–31.

26. David Baddiel, *The Secret Purposes* (London: Little, Brown & Company, 2004); Francine Stock, *A Foreign Country* (London: Chatto & Windus, 1999).

27. Natasha Solomons, *Mr Rosenblum's List: Or Friendly Guidance for the Aspiring Englishman* (London: Sceptre, 2010).

28. Natasha Solomons, 'Inspirations – Mr Rosenblum's List'. Available online: http://natashasolomons.com/inspirations-rosenblum/

29. 'David Baddiel'. Available online: http://www.bbc.co.uk/whodoyouthinkyouare/past-stories/david-baddiel.shtml

30. 'Francine Stock: Break in transmission', *The Guardian*, 8 March 1999.

31. *Who Do You Think You Are? – Tamzin Outhwaite* (2014), [TV programme] BBC, 21 August; *Great British Railway Journeys – Heysham to Snaefell* (2012), [TV programme] BBC, 27 January.

32. *Behind the Wire* (2000), [Radio programme] BBC Radio 4, 19 October. See also *Desert Island Discs* (1988), [Radio programme] BBC Radio 4, 6 November.

33. Lang, 'Dunera Boys', 183.

34. Ibid., 187.

35. *Foyle's War – The German Woman* (2002), [TV programme] ITV, 27 October.

36. Not to neglect the work of renowned sculptor Sir Eduardo Paolozzi, the only male survivor of his family's internment (Whitford, 'Paolozzi').

37. 'Kurt Schwitters Exhibition Curated by Professor Fran Lloyd'. Available online: http://fada.kingston.ac.uk/news/kurt-schwitters-exhibition-curated-by-professor-fran-lloyd/; 'Kurt Schwitters Internment Camp Art Exhibition Opens', *BBC News*, 27 September 2013. Available online: http://www.bbc.co.uk/news/world-europe-isle-of-man-23974500; Tate Britain, 'Schwitters in Britain'. Available online: http://www.tate.org.uk/whats-on/tate-britain/exhibition/schwitters-britain. The AJR and Jewish Museum held an exhibition entitled 'Continental Britons' in 2002 which included a section on internment. AJR, 'Continental Britons'. Available online: http://www.ajr.org.uk/continental-britons? A resurgence of interest in Schwitters has also led to the republication of his 'fairy tales'. See Kurt Schwitters, *Lucky Hans and Other Merz Fairy Tales (Oddly Modern Fairy Tales)* (Princeton, NJ: Princeton University Press, 2014).

38. The exhibition also toured Birkenhead that same year. 'Forced Journeys: Artists in Exile in Britain c. 1933–45'. Available online: http://www.ashgate.com/isbn/9780900157134; Ben Uri Museum, 'Forced Journeys on Tour'. Available online: http://www.benuri.org.uk/public/?event-details=8

39. Such as Andrew Graham-Dixon, 'Schwitters in Britain, at Tate Britain, Review', *The Telegraph*, 6 February 2013. Available online: http://www.telegraph.co.uk/culture/art/art-reviews/9852499/Schwitters-in-Britain-at-Tate-Britain-review.html; Brian Sewell, 'Brian Sewell on: Schwitters in Britain, Tate Britain – Review', *Evening Standard*, 31 January 2013. Available online: http://www.standard.co.uk/goingout/exhibitions/brian-sewell-on-schwitters-in-britain-tate-britain-review-8474403.html

40. For documents relating to the Home Office, War Office, and MI5 the National Archives in Kew, London, hold the documents, though a significant number of copies can be found in the Manx National Archives. The Imperial War Museum holds an unrivalled collection of oral history of former internees captured from 1979 onwards.

41. Cresswell, Yvonne, ed., *Living with the Wire* (Douglas, Isle of Man: Manx National Heritage, 1994). In the summer of 2015, Rushen Heritage has opened an exhibition about the all-female cam. See Rushen Heritage, 'Friend or Foe?' Available online: http://www.rushenheritage.org/calendar-item/friend-or-foe/

42. 'Second World War Internee Records for the Isle of Man', *AJR*, February (2008).

43. Manx National Heritage, 'Living with the Wire: Civilian Internment on the Isle of Man', *Isle of Man News*, 10 November 2010. Available online: www.manx.net/isle-of-man-news/706/living-with-the-wire-civilian-internment-on-the-isle-of-man

44. Walker Art Gallery, 'Art behind Barbed Wire'. Available online: http://www.liverpoolmuseums.org.uk/walker/exhibitions/barbedwire/index.aspx; Feather, *Art*. See also Corinne Field, 'The Walker Reveals a Wartime Life behind Barbed Wire', *Culture 24*, 24 March 2004. Available online: http://www.culture24.org.uk/places-to-go/north-west/liverpool/art20510

45. Ed Vulliamy, 'The Dispossessed Speak to Us Still', *The Guardian*, 29 February 2004. Available online: http://www.theguardian.com/artanddesign/2004/feb/29/art1

46. Dunera Museum, 'Hay Prisoner of War and Internment Camp Interpretive Centre'. Available online: http://www.hay.nsw.gov.au/Museums/DuneraMuseum/tabid/99/Default.aspx; Visit New South Wales, 'Dunera Museum – Prisoner of War and Internment Camp Interpretive Centre – Hay'. Available online: http://www.visitnsw.com/destinations/country-nsw/griffith-area/hay/attractions/dunera-museum-at-hay-railway-station

47. Lucy Nash, 'Exhibition Remembers Dunera Boys 70 Years on', *ABC News*, 14 February 2010. Available online: http://www.abc.net.au/news/2010-02-12/exhibition-remembers-dunera-boys-70yrs-on/330272; National Library of Australia, 'The Dunera Boys 70 Years on'. Available online: https://www.nla.gov.au/exhibitions/dunera-boys; Migration Heritage Centre, '1941 Dunera Boys Hay Internment Camp Collection'. Available online: http://www.migrationheritage.nsw.gov.au/exhibition/objectsthroughtime/dunera/

48. 'Friends of the Dunera Boys'. Available online: https://www.facebook.com/groups/281170982833/?fref=ts

49. Some of those interned in Canada still kept in touch in the years after internment. For example, see Joe Pieri, *Isle of the Displaced: An Italian-Scot's Memoirs of Internment in the Second World War* (Glasgow: Neil Wilson Publishing, 1997), 145.

50. Martha Nakagawa, 'Mabel Imai Tomita: How One Family Was Ripped Apart at Tule Lake', *Rafu Shimpo*, 31 August 2014.

51. Ansel Adams, John Armor, and Peter Wright, *Manzanar* (New York: Times Books, 1988), 115; Mary Jo Patterson, 'Released', *Drew Magazine*, September 2012. Available online: http://www.drewmagazine.com/2012/09/released/

52. Starn, 'Engineering', 708.

53. Adams et al., *Manzanar*, xvii.

54. Ibid., xviii.

55. Creef, *Imaging*, 22.

56. Adams et al., *Manzanar*, xviii.

57. *Impounded*, eds Okihiro and Gordon, 5–6.

58. The government had hoped that a photographic record 'could protect against false allegations of mistreatment and violations of international law, but it carried the risk … of documenting actual mistreatment'. Ibid., 19–21.

59. Adams et al., *Manzanar*, xx; *Impounded*, eds Okihiro and Gordon, 21.

60. The other being Zanruder's film of President Kennedy's assassination. See Karen Ishizuka and Patricia Zimmerman, eds, *Mining the Home Movie: Excavations in Histories and Memories* (Berkeley: University of California, 2007), 15.

61. Okubo, *Citizen*.

62. Creef, *Imaging*, 87.

63. Smithsonian American Art Museum, 'Exhibitions: The Art of Gaman: Arts and Crafts from the Japanese American Internment Camps, 1942–1946'. Available online: http://americanart.si.edu/exhibitions/archive/2010/gaman/

64. Ibid.

65. Bellevue Arts Museum, 'The Art of Gaman: Arts and Crafts from the Japanese American Internment Camps, 1942–1946'. Available online: http://www.bellevuearts.org/exhibitions/current/art_of_gaman/index.html; Maliika Rao, 'These Crafts Made by Japanese-American Prisoners Will Renew Your Faith in Human Ingenuity', *The Huffington Post*, 15 August 2014. Available online: http://www.huffingtonpost.com/2014/08/15/art-of-gaman-arts-crafts-japanese-interment-camps_n_5655381.html

66. Oishi, *Hiroshi*, 10.

67. Dave Tatsuno, creator of the only home movie from a relocation center, *Topaz*, was involved in the making of the movie. David Guterson, *Snow Falling on Cedars* (San Diego: Harcourt, 1994).

68. Guterson won the PEN/Faulkner Award for Fiction. The books are both 'a courtroom drama with racial conflict … as well as being a regional novel that portrays a particular time in U.S. history' [Richard Wasowski, *Snow Falling on Cedars Notes* (New York: Wiley, 2000), 5].

69. Danielle Steel, *Silent Honor* (London: Bantam Books, 1996).

70. Julie Otsuka's *When the Emperor Was Divine* (New York: Penguin, 2013) was a *New York Times* Notable Book, a *San Francisco Chronicle* Best Book of the Year, a Barnes & Noble Discover Great New Writers finalist, and has recently been added to the National Endowment for the Arts. 'The Big Read' Library (Julie Otsuka, 'About Julie Otsuka'. Available online: http://www.julieotsuka.com/about/)

71. Otsuka, *When the Emperor Was Divine*.

72. Otsuka, 'About'.

73. Jamie Ford, *Hotel on the Corner of Bitter and Sweet* (New York: Ballantine Books, 2009). Ford was the winner of the 2010 Asian/Pacific American Award for Literature.

74. Suzanne Lieurance, *The Lucky Baseball: My Story in a Japanese-American Internment Camp* (Berkeley Heights, NJ: Enslow, 2009). See also Ken Mochizuki, *Baseball Saved Us* (New York: Lee & Low Books, 1995).

75. For example, see *Unfinished Business* (1986), [Documentary film] Dir. Steven Okazaki, which focuses on the legal challenges to internment; *The Untold Story: Internment of Japanese Americans in Hawaii* (2012), [Documentary film] Dir. Ryan Kawamoto, which documents martial law in Hawaii; *Valor with Honor* (2010), [Documentary film] Dir. Burt Takeuchi, which documents the 442nd Regiment; and *Old Man River* (1998), [Documentary film] Dir. Allan Holzman, in which the actress Cynthia Gates Fujikawa traces the history of her father. These examples are merely the tip of the documentary iceberg.

76. 'The Manzanar Fishing Club'. Available online: http://www.fearnotrout.com/pages/the-film; part of the publicity for the film has been garnered through its Facebook page, making the subject accessible and relevant to the next generation. 'The Manzanar Fishing Club Facebook Page'.

77. For example, see Bosley Crowther, 'Movie Review: Bad Day at Black Rock', *The New York Times*, 2 February 1955.

78. Bosley Crowther, 'Movie Review: Go for Broke!', *The New York Times*, 25 May 1951.

79. *Magnum P.I. – Forty Years from Sand Island* (1983) [TV programme] CBS, 24 February.

80. *Cold Case – Family 8108* (2007), [TV programme] CBS, 9 December.

81. 'Hawaii Five-O'.

82. 'Allegiance: The Musical'. Available online: http://www.allegiancemusical.coMm/ ; Curtis M. Wong, 'George Takei to Make Broadway Debut in "Allegiance": Musical about Japanese-American Internment Experience', *The Huffington Post*, 5 February 2015. Available online: http://www.huffingtonpost.com/2015/02/05/george-takei-allegiance-broadway-_n_6624528.html

83. Anne Marie Welsh, 'Theater Review: "Allegiance" Gives Japanese Internment a Soft Focus', *Los Angeles Times*, 20 September 2012. Available online: http://articles.latimes.com/2012/sep/20/entertainment/la-et-cm-old-globe-review-20120921

84. Gerald Yamada, 'Open Letter about "Allegiance"', *Japanese American Veterans Association*, 10 September 2012. Available online: http://resisters.com/wordpress/wp-content/uploads/2012/09/JAVA_letter.pdf

85. Charles Isherwood, 'Review: "Allegiance", a Musical History Lesson about Interned Japanese-Americans', *The New York Times*, 8 November 2015. Available online: http://www.nytimes.com/2015/11/09/theater/review-allegiance-a-musical-history-lesson-about-interned-japanese-americans.html

86. Yamada, 'Open Letter'.
87. Alexis Soloski, 'Allegiance Review: George Takei Can't Save Broadway's Mediocre Pledge', *The Guardian*, 9 November 2015. Available online: http://www.theguardian.com/stage/2015/nov/08/allegiance-review-broadway-unexceptional-pledge-george-takei
88. Colborn-Roxworthy, 'Manzanar', 194.
89. Ibid., 196.
90. Burton et al., *Confinement*.
91. The auditorium was built in 1944 and used for many years as a heavy equipment garage by the county, before being restored to its present condition (National Park Service, 'Manzanar National Historic Site'. Available online: http://www.nps.gov/manz/historyculture/index.htm)
92. Colborn-Roxworthy, 'Manzanar', 191.
93. Ibid.
94. Ibid.
95. 'The Manzanar Committee'. Available online: http://www.manzanarcommittee.org/The_Manzanar_Committee/Home.html
96. Burton et al., *Confinement*, chapter 13.
97. National Park Service, 'Tule Lake Segregation Center Becomes National Monument', 5 December 2008. Available online: http://www.nps.gov/tule/parknews/new-park-announced.htm
98. 'Tule Lake Committee'. Available online: http://www.tulelake.org/; 'Tule Lake Pilgrimage Facebook Group'. Available online: https://www.facebook.com/groups/5857573804/?fref=ts Tule Lake is not the only camp represented on Facebook; see also 'Heart Mountain Interpretive Center Facebook Page'. Available online: https://www.facebook.com/heartmountainwy?fref=ts; and 'Minidoka National Historic Site Facebook Page'. Available online: https://www.facebook.com/pages/Minidoka-National-Historic-Site/151975884819492?fref=ts
99. For example, see 'Tule Lake Committee Files Lawsuit to Stop the Fence at Airport', *Pacific Citizen*, 24 October 2014. Available online: http://www.patrickcho.com/pacificcitizen/tule-lake-committee-files-lawsuit-to-stop-the-fence-at-airport/ 'Tulelake Municipal Airport Stakeholder Engagement Process'. Available online: https://docs.google.com/a/co.modoc.ca.us/viewer?a=v&pid=sites&srcid=Y28ubW9kb2MuY2 EudXN8Y291bnR5LW9 mLW1vZG9jfGd4OjY3M2ZhZTVmZDZ iMGZkZGU
100. 'Amache Preservation Group'. Available online: http://www.amache.org/pilgrimage; 'Amache Preservation Society Facebook Page'. Available online: https://www.facebook.com/AmachePreservationSociety?fref=ts
101. The farmer, Mervin Williams, continues to own parts of the former camp site. Burton et al., *Confinement*.

102. Restoration is planned to start as early as late 2015. See 'Tule Lake Committee'; National Park Service, 'Tule Lake Unit, World War II Valor in the Pacific National Monument'. Available online: http://parkplanning.nps.gov/parkHome.cfm?parkID =535&CFID=8551309&CFTOKEN=8943984823429af6-B8C5A5A9-D7A6-E7E0-DD00D94DA6828199&jsessionid=1127B8D1EA09D9FA7D0C32DE70C49984. ParkPlanning

103. 'National Park Service Press Release', 12 June 2014. Available online: http://www. nps.gov/news/release.htm?id=1600

104. Ibid. and National Park Service, 'Japanese American Confinement Sites'. Available online: http://www.nps.gov/jacs/

105. See National Park Service, 'Honouluili National Monument'. Available online: http://www.nps.gov/hono/learn/historyculture/index.htm; and Frances Kai-Hwa Wang, 'Oahu's Honouliuli Internment Camp Designated National Monument', *NBC News*, 21 February 2015. Available online: http://www.nbcnews.com/news/asian-america/ oahus-honouliuli-internment-camp-designated-national-monument-n311086

106. 'Minoru Yasui Awarded Presidential Medal of Freedom', *Northwest Asian Weekly* 34, no. 48 (2015), 23 November.

107. 'Possible Presidential Medal of Freedom to Honor Endo', *Northwest Asian Weekly* 34, no. 30 (2015), 20 July.

108. Frances Kai-Hwa Wang, 'Campaign Urges USPS to Create Stamp in Honor of Japanese-American WWII Soldiers', *NBC News*, 11 November 2015. See also 'They Deserve a Stamp'. Available online: http://theydeserveastamorg/

109. 'Stamp Honoring Tuskegee Airman to Be Dedicated in Special Ceremony at North Carolina Civil Rights Museum'. Available online: http://uspsstamps.com/ blog/2014/7/25

110. National Park Service, 'Minidoka National Historic Site'. Available online: http:// www.nps.gov/miin/index.htm; Burton et al., *Confinement*.

111. Burton et al., *Confinement*.

112. Ibid.

113. John Sammon, 'Memorial Planned to Commemorate Tanforan Site', *Nikkei West*, 12 November 2015. Available online: http://nikkeiwest.com/1/?p=2397

114. 'Go for Broke National Education Center'. Available online: http://www. goforbroke.org/about_us/about_us_educational_history.php

115. Annual Cherry Blossom Freedom Walks are arranged to 'raise awareness about the Japanese American experience during World War II and to highlight the vigilant role that American citizens must continue to play in preserving the constitutional rights of all Americans' and start from the memorial. See the National Japanese American Memorial Foundation website at http://www.njamf.com/

116. National Japanese American Memorial Foundation.

117. See Yamato, *Moving*, for the story of how this feat was accomplished.

118. 'California Museum'. Available online: http://www.californiamuseum.org/
     uprooted-japanese-americans-during-wwii An exhibition of the same name
     was in Ontario, Oregon, for the last three months of 2014 and included lesson
     plans for the exhibition to be incorporated into mainstream teaching. See
     'Uprooted: Japanese American Farm Labor Camps during World War II'. Available
     online: http://www.uprootedexhibit.com/
119. The preparations for this exhibition ultimately led to the publication of Hatsuye
     Egami's *Evacuation Diary*, itself unusual because fewer diaries and memoirs have
     been published by Issei internees. See Egami, *Evacuation*, 10.
120. 'Densho'. Available online: http://www.densho.org/
121. 'Japanese American Relocation Digital Archives'. Available online: http://www.
     calisphere.universityofcalifornia.edu/jarda/
122. Yoo, 'Captivating', 681.
123. Ibid., 694, 697.
124. For example, see Gail Sakurai, *Japanese American Internment Camps*
     (Toronto: Children's Press, 2002); Susan Dudley Gold, *Korematsu v. United
     States: Japanese-American Internment* (New York: Marshall Cavendish
     Benchmark, 2006); Bryan J. Grapes, ed., *Japanese American Internment Camps*
     (San Diego: Greenhaven, 2001).
125. Uchida, *Exile*, 154.
126. Yonemitsu, *REgenerations: San Diego*, 300–01.
127. Patterson, *Released*.
128. Bather, 'Vajda Interview'.
129. 'Britain's Promise to Remember: The Prime Minister's Holocaust Commission
     Report', January 2015. Available online: https://www.gov.uk/government/uploads/
     system/uploads/attachment_data/file/398645/Holocaust_Commission_Report_
     Britains_promise_to_remember.pdf

Conclusion

1. See Chapter 3 of Erika Lee and Judy Yung, *Angel Island: Immigrant Gateway to
   America* (Oxford: Oxford University Press, 2010). Japanese and Japanese Americans
   landing at Angel Island were likely to be detained only for a day or two, unlike other
   Asian nationalities such as the Chinese.
2. See WO 361/4 Losses on SS *Arandora Star* (1940).
3. Sophie Brown, 'Daily Mail Headline from 1938 Draws Comparisons with Current
   Reporting of Calais Migrant Crisis', *The Huffington Post UK*, 31 July 2015. Available
   online: http://www.huffingtonpost.co.uk/2015/07/31/daily-mail-1938-jews_n_
   7909954.html

4. Brendan Carlin, 'Free Hotels for the Calais Stowaways in Soft Touch Britain: Outrage as Immigrants Illegally Entering UK Get Cooked Meals and £35 Cash a Week within Days of Arrival', *The Mail on Sunday*, 1 August 2015. Available online: http://www.dailymail.co.uk/news/article-3182519/Welcome-soft-touch-UK-Outrage-immigrants-illegally-entering-UK-free-hotel-rooms-cooked-meals-35-cash-week-days-arrival.html

5. As quoted in Anne Karpf, 'We've Been Here Before', *The Guardian*, 8 June 2002. Available online: http://www.theguardian.com/uk/2002/jun/08/immigration.immigrationandpublicservices

6. For example, see Tal Kopan, 'Donald Trump: Syrian Refugees a "Trojan Horse"', *CNN*, 16 November 2015. Available online: http://edition.cnn.com/2015/11/16/politics/donald-trump-syrian-refugees/

7. Jennifer Steinhauer, 'Senate Blocks Bill on Tougher Refugee Screening', 20 January 2016. Available online: http://www.nytimes.com/2016/01/21/us/politics/senate-refugee-screening-bill-syria-iraq.html?_r=0

Bibliography

Primary Sources

Manx National Archives, Douglas, Isle of Man

'17 Camp Location Plans and Restricted Access Areas from Isle of Man Government Circulars Relating to Aliens, Internees or Detainees'. 1939–45. M 29812.

'Account of Internment at P Camp, Hutchinson Square, Douglas'. 1940s. MS 10739.

'Alien Internment Camps in the United Kingdom'. M 23044.

Aliens Registration Office. 'Documentation regarding Otto Israel Putzel'. 1939–47. MS 11800.

Barker, F. A. 'Letter of Thanks for Medical Care Given by Dr Patrick Peel to Internees'. 1945. MS 12380.

Baruch, Lou. 'Reminiscences of Lou Baruch Who Was Onboard the Arandora Star and Transported to the Tatura Camps'. 2007. MS 11709.

Bather, John A. 'A Conversation with Steven Vajda'. 1994. MS 11860.

Bill-Jentzsch, Anna. 'Account of Internment'. 1998. MS 09990.

Breitbarth, Rudolf. 'Correspondence from Internee Rudolf Breitbarth to His Wife Erna and Daughter Marianne'. 1940. MS 11656.

Buresova, Jana. 'Photographs of Locations in Douglas and Port Erin with Connections to Internment in WWII'. 2009. MS 12174.

'*The Camp*: Hutchinson Square Internment Camp Journal Issues 1–13/14'. 1940. M 27059.

'*The Camp*: Hutchinson Square Internment Camp Journal Issues 1–6, 8–16, 20'. 1941. M 27060.

Cannell, Harry. 'Hardships Caused by the Internment Camps on the Isle of Man during the 1939 to 1945 War'. 1996. MS 09555.

Cohen, Gerda. 'Telegram from Gerda Cohen Advising Husband, Heinrich, of His Release'. 1941. MS 12382.

'Correspondence Documenting the Internment of Walter and Leopold Fiala'. 1940–41. MS 12125.

'Correspondence regarding the Internment of Elisabeth Bickel on the Isle of Man'. 1940–2008. MS 11366.

Corrin, Elizabeth. 'Recollections of Elizabeth Corrin or Her Childhood Experiences of Internees'. 2003. MS 10778.

Corvin, Michael. 'Camp Tribune No 1 16 August 1941; Published in Y Camp (Married Camp)'. 1941. M 31545.

Cove, Ernest G. 'Letter from Ernest G Cove to Hugo Dachinger'. 1940. MS 10593.

Cuthbert, Cyril. 'Papers of Cyril R Cuthbert, One Time Commandant of Married Internees Camp'. 1941–45. MS 11196.

Dalheim, Rosemarie. 'Papers of Rosemarie Dalheim, a Former Teenage Internee'. 1940s. MS 11806.

D'Allesandro, Camillo. 'Camp Life on the Isle of Man in World War II: Memoirs of an Italian Internee'. 1981. MS 11185.

Deeble, Ashley. 'Papers Relating to Philipp Heinrich Greb'. MS 12103.

'Documentation Relating to Internment of Eugen Stern'. 1939–40. MS 12411.

'Documents from Central Internment Camp, Douglas'. 1940. MS 09477.

'Extract from Pinschof Journal Recalling Time Interned on Isle of Man'. 2007. MS 11705.

'Extract of Account Book Showing Cash Sales to "Alien" Internees at H. J. Qualtrough's Shoe Shop, Port St Mary. Copy of fishing permit held by H. J. Qualtrough'. 1940; 1945. MS 09296.

Fehle, B. 'Memorandum Relating to the Disaster of the SS Arandora Star'. 1940. MS 09647.

Gestapo. 'Copy of Gestapo Document Relating to British Internment Camps including Those on the Isle of Man'. 1940. MS 09510.

Heinemann, Fritz Israel. 'Fritz Heinemann at Onchan'. 1940. MS 12196.

Hodge, Margot. 'Memories and Personal Experiences of my Internment on the Isle of Man in 1940'. 1999. MS 10119.

'Home Secretary goes to Internment Island and sees the Tynwald Ceremony'. 1942. M 32219.

'Information Relating to Internees F S Loebl, Robert Loebl, and Herbert Loebl'. 1940; 2008. MS 12197.

Isle of Man Government. 'Papers Relating to the Requisitioning of 13 Royal Avenue West, Onchan'. 1940–47. MS 11720.

Jacobsthal, Paul. 'Memoirs of Professor Paul Jacobsthal, Onetime Internee of Hutchinson Camp'. MS 11626.

Jochanan, Frank. 'Inside Out: Isle of Man Revisited, 1940–2000'. 2000. MS 10323.

'Johanna Luise Frida Rieger Correspondence'. 1940. MS 12203.

Johnson, Joan. 'My memories of life in Rushen Internment Camp, May 29th 1940 to August 31st 1941: a personal experience'. 1990. MS 08866.

Kaczynski, William. 'Papers of William Kaczynski, One Time Child Internee of Rushen Camp'. 1940–2006. MS 11680.

Kissack, Rex. 'Papers of Rex and Elizabeth Kissack Relating to Gladys M. Workman and the German Internee Hermann Scholz'. 1938–1940; 1999–2005. MS 10127.

Kittel, Werner. 'Papers Relating to the Internment of the Gerlachs and Wolfgang Kittel'. 2009. MS 12211.

Kohlberg, Georg, and Kohlberg, Karola. 'Correspondence between Internees Georg Kohlberg and His Fiancee Karola Krey'. 1939–41. MS 10131.

Lachs, P. 'Memoirs of Unnamed Internee and Letter Requesting Help in Securing the Release of a Brother Interned on the Isle of Man'. 1940–41. MS 11689.

Lanczy, Gynla A. 'Statement by a Hungarian Cavalry Officer Interned in Mooragh Camp Sent to the Society of Friends'. 1941. MS 10947.

'Letter to J E Schmitz, House 41 P Camp from his Wife Friedi'. 1941. MS 11191.

'Letters from German Academic Bruno Kress'. 1940–44. MS 12073.

'Letters from Herbert Forner to Family Members'. 1940–44. MS 11952.

'Letters relating to Mr Aberbach relating to Internment in Mooragh Camp'. 1945. MS 11348.

Levy, Josef. 'English Exercise Book of Josef Levy'. 1940s. MS 09401.

Lustig, Fritz. 'Memoirs of Fritz Lustig Entitled "Internment in Peel, July to October 1940"'. 2008. MS 11788.

Magee, Mac. 'Barbed Wire Isle'. 1941. M 32172.

'Memoirs of a Japanese Internee in the Isle of Man, 1941–2'. 1965. MS 08584.

'Memoirs of Willy Leopold Hess, One Time Internee of Onchan Camp, Isle of Man'. 1940–41. MS 11038.

Mendel, Rachel. 'Behind Barbed Wire'. 2009. MS 12140.

'Mona Quillin Interview about Her Memories of Her Parents' Port St Mary Guest House Which Housed Internees during World War II'. 2004. MS 11032.

Nathan, June. 'Biographical Note about Ernst Geiduschek (Late Ernest Garson)'. 2009. MS 12120.

'Newspaper Article Detailing Love Story between Margaret Crosby and Her Italian Husband Renato Constantini'. MS 11676.

'Onchan Internment Camp Currency'. 1940s. MS 08685.

O'Rourke, Mrs T. 'Poems from Rushen Internment Camp'. 1940–41. MS 09337.

'Papers Documenting the Internment and Lives of Ludwig and Inge Hess and Inge's friend Mrs Helli Wimbush'. 1989–2005. MS 11248. 'Papers Relating to Franz Joseph Buch, an 18B Detainee in Peveril Camp, Peel'. 1940–43. MS 12384.

'Papers Documenting the Life and Internment of Domenico Traversari, an Italian Interned on the Isle of Man, 1940–1945: include copies of correspondence relating to Traversari's attempts to gain release, a handwritten transcription of an account of his life by his eleven year old grandson (1978) and colour copies of portraits of Domenico and Cesira his wife, painted on the Isle of Man during his internment'. 1943–44; 1978. MS 11273.

'Papers of Adolf Gruenwald, One Time Internee of Sefton Camp, Douglas'. MS 11891.

'Papers of Erna Nelki'. 1941–2001. MS 12388.

'Papers of Harry Johnson (Methodist Minister, Port St Mary) Relating to His Involvement with Rushen Internment Camp'. 1940–45. MS 09378.

'Papers of Jacob Schartenburg (Later Walter Sharman)'. 1940s. MS 12413.

'Papers of N. C. Callister re Requisition of 13 Hutchinson Square'. 1940–45. MS 10661.

'Papers of the Klaffl Family Relating to the Internment of Rosemary "Bella" Klaffl, Her Sister Elizabeth (Betty) and Mother Maria Theresia in Rushen Camp during World War II'. 1940–53. MS 11270.

'Papers Relating to the Internment of Dr Arthur Wolff (Onchan Camp)'. 1940–41.
    MS 11607.
'Papers Relating to the Internment of the Beermann family'. 1939–40. MS 11801.
'Permits Issued during World War II to N. Maddrell for Internment Camp Access and
    A. Maddrell for Night Fishing'. 1942; 1944. MS 11208.
'Port Erin Internment Camp'. 1941–45. MS 08841.
'Printed Booklet Entitled "Home Office Orders for Internment Camps" (revised edition
    with amendments up to 30 June 1943)'. 1943. MS 11293.
'Red Cross Reports on Isle of Man Internment Camps'. 1941–45. MS 12105.
Rossi, Gaetano. 'Memories of 1940 Impressions of Life in an Internment Camp'. 1991.
    M 28111.
Schapira, Rudolph. 'Letter from Rudolph Schapira, Peveril Camp, Peel to Heinz
    Schapira, Mortimer, Berks'. 1940. MS 11020.
'Sefton Review 11 November 1940, No. 1 and 24 February 1941, No. 8'. 1940–41.
    M 31547.
Shimmin, Roy. 'Your Roots: A Story for My Children'. 1940. MS 11520.
Sidoli, Celeste. 'Letter from Internee in Palace Camp, Douglas'. 1941. MS 10042.
Sturm, Hans. 'Through Stormy Seas to Calm Waters: Memories of a German Jehovah's
    Witness Interned on the Isle of Man during World War II'. 2000. MS 11641.
Sussman, Max. 'A Young Internee on the Isle of Man 1940–1'. 2007. MS 11751.
Verdiers, Edwin. 'A Hutchinson Camp March'. 1940s. MS 12198.
'Walter Fischer at Onchan Camp'. 1938–41. MS 12317.
'Weekly Summaries of Weekly Returns of Internees Held in Douglas, Onchan, Peel and
    Ramsey Internment Camps'. 1940–45. MS 06472.
'What War Has Brought to the Isle of Man'. 1941. M 29464.
Widdows, Chris, 'William Fritz Sommerfeld interview'. 2008. MS 11926.
Winkler, Julia, 'Johanna Lichtenstern interview'. 2002. MS 10602.
Winckler, Julia Ruth, 'Two Sisters: A Photographic Project in Four Parts'. 2002.
    MS 10688.
Women's Internment Camp, 'Permit Issued for Woman to Leave the Camp Once a
    Month for Hairdressing visit'. 1943. MS 11863.

National Archives, Kew

CAB 65/10/4 Conclusions of a Meeting of the War Cabinet Held in the Prime Minister's
    Room, House of Commons (Annexe), on Thursday, November 7, 1940, at 12 Noon
    (1940).
CAB 66/13/12 'Arandora Star' Inquiry (1940).
HO 213/3 Austrian refugees: revision of landing conditions (1938).
HO 213/5 Proposed moves to register foreign domestic servants (1938).
HO 213/7 The internment of citizens of friendly nations (1942).
HO 213/19 'London Gazette' lists: wartime economy measures (1939).

HO 213/40 Members of foreign political organisations (1937).

HO 213/41 Members of foreign political organisations (1937).

HO 213/42 Meeting with Board of Deputies of British Jews (1938).

HO 213/43 A memo that relates to the meeting between the Board of Deputies and Sir Samuel Hoare (1938).

HO 213/45 Minors and orphans (1940).

HO 213/88 Treatment of Italian consuls: memorandum (1940).

HO 213/91 Treatment of stateless aliens: correspondence with Berlin Passport Control (1936).

HO 213/93 Persecuted Jews: correspondence with Danzig Consulate-General (1937).

HO 213/94 British legal reaction to German race laws relating to Jewish emigration (1938).

HO 213/95 Correspondence with German Embassy (1938).

HO 213/97 Hungarian Jews: correspondence with Passport Control Officer, Budapest (1938).

HO 213/98 Written undertakings by potential refugees (1938).

HO 213/100 The issue of awarding visas to German Jewish refugees who were passing through Britain on their way to the United States (1938).

HO 213/101 Issue to German Jews under arrest (1938).

HO 213/102 Italian Jewish refugees (1939).

HO 213/103 Austrian refugees: memorandum (1938).

HO 213/105 Jewish refugees in France (1939).

HO 213/106 Political refugees in Slovakia (1939).

HO 213/108 British Committee for Refugees from Czecho-Slovakia: correspondence (1939).

HO 213/115 Temporary asylum for German immigrants to USA: opinions of American Consul General in Berlin (1939).

HO 213/117 USA regulations and procedures: State Department letter to British Embassy, New York (1939).

HO 213/155 Blood and Honour Law: memorandum; correspondence with Foreign Office (1936).

HO 213/157 Obligatory registration of German nationals living abroad: memorandum on effects of failure to comply (1938).

HO 213/159 Status of Germans nationalized abroad: departmental opinions (1940).

HO 213/223 Statistics: refusal to provide German Consuls with specific information on whereabouts of their nationals (1938).

HO 213/227 Refugees in Richborough camp, Kent (1939).

HO 213/228 LCC evacuation scheme (1940).

HO 213/231 Tribunals to review cases of enemy aliens: memorandum of guidance of appointees (1939).

HO 213/240 Internment of recalcitrants (1940).

HO 213/255 Doctors: Australian fear of mass influx (1937).

HO 213/256 Doctors: correspondence with International Hebrew Christian Alliance (1938).

HO 213/257 Doctors: attitude of British medical bodies (1938).

HO 213/262 Doctors: admission to HM forces in wartime (1939).

HO 213/264 Dentists: sharp increase in applicants for admission to Dental Register; note of meeting with President of General Medical Council (1935).

HO 213/265 Dentist: memorandum on current situation (1936).

HO 213/266 Architects (1939).

HO 213/267 Farm workers (1936).

HO 213/268 Co-ordinating Committee for Refugees (1939).

HO 213/275 The introduction of a stamped letter 'J' on German Jewish passports, restriction on Jews returning to Germany if they travelled abroad (1938).

HO 213/281 Channel Islands: potential Jewish refugees (1938).

HO 213/282 Channel Islands: agricultural training camp for refugees (1939).

HO 213/294 Financial difficulties: note of meeting with Treasury, Unemployment Assistance Board and Ministry of Health (1939).

HO 213/295 Financial assistance from government: proposed methods (1940).

HO 213/299 Financial assistance from government: summary (1940).

HO 213/317 Concerns raised by the German Jewish Aid Committee about the immigration of 'mental cases' (1939).

HO 213/354 Treatment of aliens in time of war: repatriation of Germans and Austrians (1938).

HO 213/438 *Arandora Star* Embarkation Lists (1940).

HO 213/447 Admission in wartime from German and other countries (1939).

HO 213/453 Setting up (1939).

HO 213/454 Scotland (1939).

HO 213/455 Completion of work (1940).

HO 213/456 Advisory Committee Internment of Aliens (1940).

HO 213/458 Czechoslovakia (1940).

HO 213/460 Facilities for the media (1940).

HO 213/464 War refugees: discussions (1939).

HO 213/476 Expenses: repatriation of internees (1940).

HO 213/478 Disposal of cash (1939).

HO 213/479 German youths of 17 and under (1939).

HO 215/21 Overseas internees: financial responsibility for repatriation expenses and removal to different internment locations (1943).

HO 215/105 Conditions in camps: Isle of Man; questions from International Red Cross (1943).

HO 215/107 Isle of Man (1945).

HO 215/124 Classification of camps and segregation of internees: general matters (1940).

HO 215/130 Camps: Huyton, Lancashire: standing orders; control of internees in hospital (1941).

HO 215/149 Distinction between prisoner of war and civilian internment camps (1941).

HO 215/155 Canada: segregation of Nazi and non-Nazi internees (1941).

HO 215/161 Canada: B and C category internees (1941–43).

HO 215/170 Movement of internees abroad: released internees landed at Bombay en route from Australia (1943).

HO 215/184 Draft rules and regulations: voucher money (1941).

HO 215/192 Removal of aliens from aliens protected areas in the event of invasion (1941).

HO 215/199 Australia: property claims of HMT Dunera passengers on release (1941).

HO 215/200 Isle of Man: government circulars relating to internment camps (1942–45).

HO 215/209 Departmental opinions on compensation liability for internees' losses: voyage of SS Ettrick (1941–42).

HO 215/213 Voyage of HMT Dunera: compensation for loss or damage (1941).

HO 215/215 Disposal of Remainder of Italian Property (1946).

HO 215/218 Listing of luggage before embarkation to prevent bogus compensation claims (1943–45).

HO 215/221 Losses sustained during transfers to Isle of Man in May 1941.

HO 215/222 Billeting of internees: Isle of Man: allowances to householders (1941–44).

HO 215/223 Internees detained in prisons (1941).

HO 215/225 Provision for the destitute (1941).

HO 215/229 Care after release (1941).

HO 215/262 Voyage of HMT *Dunera*: promises allegedly made to volunteers; parliamentary question (1942).

HO 215/265 Voyage of SS *Ettrick*: conditions in Canadian camps on arrival (1941).

HO 215/266 Voyage of SS *Sobieski*: embarkation list (1940).

HO 215/268 Shipping accommodation for alien refugees emigrating to the USA: minutes of meeting held at the Home Office in January 1941 (1941).

HO 215/272 Statistics: numbers interned in the UK and abroad (1944).

HO 215/278 Dissemination of information on classification of internees (1943).

HO 215/429 Deaths, funeral arrangements etc. for the *Arandora Star* (1942).

HO 352/43 List of names of Italians who perished on the *Arandora Star* (1950).

HO 396 Aliens Department: Internees Index.

PREM 3/49 *Arandora Star* (1940).

WO 361/4 Losses on SS *Arandora Star* (1940).

Special Collections, UCLA

Carter, Genevieve. *Collection 131 – 3.2.* 1944.

Kuroki, Ben. *Collection 131 – 2.1.* 1944.

Myer, Dillon S. *Collection 131 – 2.2.* 1944; *2.3.* 1945; *2.4.* 1944; *2.5.* 1944.

Department of the Interior Information Service. *Collection 131 – 2.14.* 1944.

WRA. *Collection 131 – 1.1.* 1942; *1.2.* 1942; *1.3.* 1942; *1.4.* 1943; *1.5.* 1943; *1.6.* 1944; *1.7.* 1945; *2.8.* 1946; *2.10.* 1945; *2.11.* 1945; *2.17.* 1942; *2.19.* 1946; *2.20.* 1943; *2.21.* 1944.

Bancroft Library, UC Berkeley

Bishop, Cleo D. 'Teachers Monthly Report to Dept. Heads, Topaz High School, January 27'. 1945.
'Block Managers Meeting Minutes, Topaz'. 1942; 1943; 1944; 1945.
Common Ground. 'What Happened at Manzanar'. 1943.
Community Council. 'Central Utah Project Council'. 1944.
Community Council. *Heart Mountain 1.1.* 1944; *1.2.* 1944; *1.4.* 1945.
Community Council. 'Topaz Community Government'. 1942.
Community Council. 'Topaz Council Meeting Minutes'. 1943; 1944; 1945.
Cozzens, R. B. (Field Assistant Director Manzanar). 'Letter to Dillon Myer'. 1943.
De Cristoforo, Violet Kazue. *Violet Kazue de Cristoforo papers 1.1.* 1988; *1.3.* 1988.
Ernst, Charles F. *Topaz Scrap Book.* 1943.
FBI. *Files concerning the War Relocation Authority, 1942–1946 1.1.* 1942; *1.3.* 1942; *1.5.* 1943; *1.7.* 1943; *1.9.* 1943; *1.11.* 1943; *1.12.* 1943; *1.13.* 1943; *1.15.* 1943.
Ferguson, Charles F. 'Letter to Ralph Merritt'. 1943.
Gerda Isenberg papers 2.1; 2.12. 1944; *2.21; 2.6.* 1945; *3.1.* 1944; *3.2.* 1943; *3.4.* 1942; *3.8.* 1944.
Ikeda, Kando. *Ikeda family papers 1.1.* 1942; *1.8.* 1942.
Ikeda family papers 1.7.
The Japanese on the Pacific Coast: A Factual Study of Events December 7, 1941 to September 1, 1942 with Suggestions for the Future. Los Angeles: Statement for the Los Angeles County Committee for Church and Community Cooperation, 1942.
'Letter to Topaz from relocated student'. 1942.
'Letters written by two Japanese-American schoolgirls from internment centers'. 1942.
'Lila Wilson Interview'. 1968.
'Manzanar (Miscellaneous)'.
'Manzanar Free Press'. 1943.
Masaoka, Joe, and Tanaka, Togo. *Manzanar Project Report No. 82.* 1942.
'Official Report of the First General Assembly of Topaz, Sept. 11'. 1942.
Okazaki, Mari. *Journal April 24 to June 14, 1942.* California, 1942.
Okazaki, Mari. 'Letters from Fresno Assembly Center (Tanforan)'. 1942.
Okazaki, Mari. 'Police Record of Complaints: Tulare Assembly Center'. 1942.
'Poston'. 1942; 1943; 1944; 1945.
'Press Release, Topaz'. 1942.
San Francisco Office WRA. 'Report of Meeting, April 7, at Salt Lake City, with Governors, Attorneys General, and Other State and Federal Officials of 10 Western States'. 1942.

Schoolchild. 'Relocation, Its Challenge to Me'. 1942.

Sugihara, George. *Education in Topaz*.

Takahashi, Nobi. 'Letters from Tanforan Assembly Center'. 1942.

Tanaka, Togo, and Masaoka, Joe. *Manzanar Project Report No. 76*. 1942.

Tanaka, Togo, and Masaoka, Joe. *Progress Report No. 68*. 1942.

Thomas, Norman. *Democracy and Japanese Americans*. New York: The Post War World Council, 1942.

'Topaz Correspondence'. 1944; 1945.

'Topaz Daily Log'. 1942; 1943.

'Topaz Photo Book'.

'Topaz Times'. 1944.

A Touchstone of Democracy: The Japanese in America. New York: Council for Social Action of the Congregational Christian Churches, 1942.

'Tule Lake (Correspondence)'. 1944.

Tsuchiyama, Tamie. 'Letters from Santa Anita Assembly Center'. 1942.

Unknown. 'Letter from Merced Assembly Center'. 1942.

WRA. *Gila River 1.1*. 1943; *1.7*. 1943; *1.8*. 1943; *1.9*. 1944.

WRA. *Heart Mountain 1.6*. 1943.

WRA. 'Manzanar Weekly Reports'. 1943; 1944; 1945.

WRA. 'Poston'. 1942.

WRA. 'Relocation Manual'.

WRA. 'Some Interesting Facts on Manzanar'. 1943.

WRA. 'Tule Lake'.

Private Collections

Pinkus, Ille. 'Letters written by Ille Pinkus'. 1940. Courtesy of Gaby Koppel.

Printed Primary Sources

Abbott, Edith. 'Federal Immigration Policies, 1864–1924'. *The University Journal of Business* 2 (1924): 133–56.

Abbott, Edith. 'Federal Immigration Policies, 1864–1924. II'. *The University Journal of Business* 2 (1924): 347–67.

Adams, Ansel, Armor, John and Wright, Peter. *Manzanar*. New York: Times Books, 1988.

Addison, Paul, and Crang, Jeremy A., eds. *Listening to Britain: Home Intelligence Reports on Britain's Finest Hour – May to September 1940*. London: Bodley Head, 2010.

Bentwich, Norman. *I Understand the Risks: The Story of the Refugees from Nazi Oppression Who Fought in the British Forces in the World War*. London: Victor Gollancz, 1950.

Berriedale Keith, A. 'The War and the Constitution Part II'. *The Modern Law Review* 4 (1940): 82–103.

'A Bill for the Relief of Bertha Berg'. S. 790, 103rd Congress, First Session, 19 April 1993.

Bryant, Margaret. 'Review'. *International Affairs Review Supplement* 19, no. 3/4 (1940): 195.

Columbia Law Review. 'Outstanding Features of the Immigration Act of 1924'. *Columbia Law Review* 25, no. 1 (1925): 90–95.

Cresswell, Yvonne, ed. *Living with the Wire*. Douglas, Isle of Man: Manx National Heritage, 1994.

Crowther, Bosley. 'Movie Review: Bad Day at Black Rock'. *The New York Times*, 2 February 1955.

Crowther, Bosley. 'Movie Review: Go for Broke!'. *The New York Times*, 25 May 1951.

Day, Takako. *Show Me the Way to Go Home: The Moral Dilemma of Kibei No No Boys in World War Two Incarceration Camps*. East Middlebury, VT: Wren Song Press, 2014.

'A Demobbed Officer Writes: Problems of Adjustment'. *AJR* July (1946): 49.

Donald, Heidi. *We Were Not the Enemy: Remembering the United States' Latin-American Civilian Internment Program of World War II*. Bloomington, IN: iUniverse, 2007.

Egami, Hatsuye. *The Evacuation Diary of Hatsuye Egami*. Pasadena, CA: Intentional Productions, 1996.

'Employment Problems'. *AJR* April (1946): 25.

'Ex-German Jews in the News'. *AJR* July (1956): 9.

Fair, Faith. 'Mr. Yamamoto – New Jersey Town Runs Him Out'. *Life* (1944): 13–14.

Farnham, K. H. 'Prince Frederick of Prussia: Reminiscences of a Fellow-Internee'. *AJR* June (1966): 12.

'FBI Tightens Curb on 256,000 Aliens'. *The New York Times*, 1 April 1942.

'The First Five Years'. *AJR* May (1946): 33.

Frankenschwerth, Kurt. 'Released'. *AJR* September (1960): 9.

Freyhan, Max. 'The Refugee's Arrival'. *AJR* August (1946): 60.

Garner, James W. 'Treatment of Enemy Aliens'. *The American Journal of International Law* 13 (1919): 22–59.

Gordon, Linda, and Okihiro, Gary Y., eds. *Impounded: Dorothea Lange and the Censored Images of Japanese American Internment*. New York: W. W. Norton, 2006.

Grenville, Anthony. 'Internment in Australia'. *AJR* July (2013): 1–2.

Griswold, Nat R. *Rohwer: From Final Report: Historical Statistical-Functional Report of Community Activities Section*. Berkeley, 1945.

Heathcote, Francis. 'In an Internment Camp'. *The Spectator* September 19 (1941): 16.

House of Commons Debates. *Hansard* 10 July 1940, vol. 362, 1208–306; 7 November 1940, vol. 365, 1504–31; 20 November 1940, vol. 365, 1988–93W.

House of Lords Debate. *Hansard* 24 October 1939, vol. 114, 1487.

Ichihashi, Yamato. *Japanese in the United States: A Critical Study of the Problems of the Japanese Immigrants and Their Children*. Stanford, CA: Stanford University Press, 1932.

'In War and Peace'. *AJR* May (1946): 37.

'Is Naturalisation Good for This Country? A Discussion in the Home Service of the BBC'. *AJR* October (1946): 75.

Isle of Man Times. 21 October 1940; 25 December 1940; 5 December 1941; 5 January 1942.

Judex. *Anderson's Prisoners.* London: Victor Gollancz, 1940.

Kahn, Leo. 'Isle of Man Twenty Years Ago'. *AJR* September (1960): 7.

Kahn, Leo. *Obliging Fellow.* London: Nicholson & Watson, 1946.

Kapp, Yvonne, and Mynatt, Margaret. *British Policy and the Refugees, 1933–1941.* London: Cass, 1997.

Kempner, Robert M. W. 'Review'. *The American Journal of International Law* 35, no. 4 (1941): 743–44.

Kiyota, Minoru. *Beyond Loyalty: The Story of a Kibei.* Honolulu: University of Hawaii, 1997.

Koch, Eric. *Deemed Suspect: A Wartime Blunder.* London: Methuen, 1980.

Koessler, Maximilian. 'Enemy Alien Internment: With Special Reference to Great Britain and France'. *Political Science Quarterly* 57 (1942): 98–127.

Lafitte, François. *The Internment of Aliens,* 2nd ed. London: Libris, 1988.

Lomnitz, Alfred. *'Never Mind, Mr. Lom!' or The Uses of Adversity.* London: Macmillan, 1941.

Lustig, Fritz. 'Memories, Memories . . .' *AJR* November (2014). Available online: http://www.ajr.org.uk/journal/issue.Nov14/article.16172 (accessed 24 August 2016).

Lynton, Mark. *Accidental Journey: A Cambridge Internee's Memoir of World War II.* Woodstock: Overlook, 1995.

Miller, Joaquin. 'The Chinese and the Exclusion Act'. *The North American Review* 173, no. 541 (1901): 782–89.

'Naturalisation'. *AJR* December (1946): 89.

'New Publications'. *International Affairs Review Supplement* 19, no. 6 (1941): 325–27.

Ogbe, Hilda. *The Crumbs off the Wife's Table.* Ibadan: Spectrum, 2001.

Okimoto, Paul M. *Oh! Poston, Why Don't You Cry For Me? And Other Stops Along the Way.* Xlibris Corporation, 2011.

Okubo, Mine. *Citizen 13660.* New York: Columbia University Press, 1946.

Olins, Renate. 'Island Prison'. In *What Did You Do during the War, Mummy?*, edited by Mavis Nicholson, 46–54. Bridgend, Wales: Seren, 2010.

Patterson, Mary Jo. 'Released'. *Drew Magazine* September (2012). Available online: http://www.drewmagazine.com/2012/09/released/ (accessed 16 April 2015).

Perry, Donald R. 'Aliens in the United States'. *Annals of the American Academy of Political and Social Science* 223, Minority Peoples in a Nation at War (1942): 1–9.

Pieri, Joe. *Isle of the Displaced: An Italian-Scot's Memoirs of Internment in the Second World War.* Glasgow: Neil Wilson Publishing, 1997.

Pratt Fairchild, Henry. 'The Literary Test and Its Making'. *The Quarterly Journal of Economics* 31, no. 3 (1917): 447–60.

Rathbone, Eleanor. *Falsehoods and Facts about the Jews*. London: Victor Gollancz, 1944.

Rathbone, Eleanor. *Rescue the Perishing; A Summary of the Position regarding the Nazi Massacres of Jewish and Other Victims and of Proposals for Their Rescue: An Appeal, a Programme and a Challenge*. London: The National Committee for Rescue from Nazi Terror, 1943.

Roscoe, E. S. 'Aliens in Great Britain'. *Transactions of the Grotius Society* 16 (1930): 65–72.

Satow, Ernest. 'The Treatment of Enemy Aliens'. *Problems of the War* 2 (1916): 1–10.

Schaefer, Ernst. 'Aspects of Community Life: Some Recollections'. *AJR* September (1960): 7–8.

'Second World War Internee Records for the Isle of Man'. *AJR* February (2008).

Sone, Monica. *Nisei Daughter*. Seattle: University of Washington, 1953.

'Ten Years Ago'. *AJR* June (1950): 1.

Uchida, Yoshiko. *Desert Exile: The Uprooting of a Japanese American Family*. Seattle: University of Washington, 1982.

'Victor Gollancz: Eleanor Rathbone'. *AJR* February (1946): 13.

The Virginia Law Register. 'Appeals. Alien, Returning from Temporary Visit Abroad, Can Bring with Him His Wife, notwithstanding Admission of Quota'. *The Virginia Law Register* 10 (1924): 71–72.

Wakatsuki Houston, Jeanne, and Houston, James D. *Farewell to Manzanar*. New York: Bantam Books, 1973.

Warner Parker, A. 'The Ineligible to Citizenship Provisions of the Immigration Act of 1924'. *The American Journal of International Law* 19, no. 1 (1925): 23–47.

WRA. 'Japanese Evacuation Proclamation'. 1941.

Legislation

'Act for Establishing Regulations Respecting Aliens 1816'.

'Act for the Registration of Aliens 1826'.

'Act for the Registration of Aliens 1836'.

'An Act to Execute Certain Treaty Stipulations Relating to Chinese (Chinese Exclusion Act) 1882'.

'An Act to Regulate the Immigration of Aliens to, and the Residence of Aliens in, the United States 1917'.

'Aliens Act 1905'.

'Immigration Act of 1924 (Johnson-Reed Act)'.

'Presidential Proclamation – Alien Enemies – Japanese, No. 2525, December 7, 1941'.

'Presidential Proclamation – Alien Enemies – German, No. 2526, December 8, 1941'.

'Presidential Proclamation – Alien Enemies – Italians, No. 2527, December 8, 1941'.

'Regulators of Aliens Act 1793'.

Films, Television Programmes and Radio Broadcasts

Bad Day at Black Rock (1955). [Film] Dir. John Sturges. USA: Metro-Goldwyn-Mayer.

Behind the Wire (2000). [Radio programme] BBC Radio 4. 19 October.

British Intelligence (1940). [Film] Dir. Terry O. Morse and William Nigh. USA: Warner Brothers.

Cold Case – Family 8108 (2007). [TV programme] CBS. 9 December.

Come See the Paradise (1990). [Film] Dir. Alan Parker. USA: Twentieth Century Fox.

Desert Island Discs (1988). [Radio programme] BBC Radio 4. 6 November.

The Dunera Boys (1985). [TV programme] Network 10. October 3.

Foyle's War – The German Woman (2002). [TV programme] ITV. 27 October.

Go For Broke! (1951). [Film] Dir. Robert Pirosh. USA: Metro-Goldwyn-Mayer.

Great British Railway Journeys – Heysham to Snaefell (2012). [TV programme] BBC. 27 January.

Hawaii Five-O 'Ho'onani Makuakane' 'Honor Thy Father' (2013). [TV programme] CBS. 13 December.

Magnum P.I. – Forty Years from Sand Island (1983). [TV programme] CBS. 24 February.

Manzanar Fishing Club (2012). [Film] Dir. Cory Shiozaki. USA: From Barbed Wire to Barbed Hooks/Talk Story Media.

Old Man River (1998). [Documentary film] Dir. Allan Holzman.

Snow Falling on Cedars (1999). [Film] Dir. Scott Hicks. USA: Universal Pictures.

Topaz (1945). [Film] Dir. Dave Tatsuno. USA.

Unfinished Business (1986). [Documentary film] Dir. Steven Okazaki.

The Untold Story: Internment of Japanese Americans in Hawaii (2012). [Documentary film] Dir. Ryan Kawamoto.

Valor with Honor (2010). [Documentary film] Dir. Burt Takeuchi.

Who Do You Think You Are? – David Baddiel (2004). [TV programme] BBC. 23 November.

Who Do You Think You Are? – Tamzin Outhwaite (2014). [TV programme] BBC. 21 August.

Interviews

IWM. 'Claus Moser Interview'. 1997.

IWM. 'Eva Wittenberg Interview'. 1991.

IWM. 'Evelyn Ruth Kaye Interview'. 2007.

IWM. 'Hellmuth Weissenborn Interview'. 1978.

IWM. 'John Duffield Interview'. 1979.

IWM. 'Ludwig Spiro Interview'. 1979.

IWM. 'Margot Pottlitzer Interview'. 1978.

Pistol, Rachel, 'Interview with David Brand about Dr. Angelo Lauria'. 2014.

Pistol, Rachel, 'Interview with Gaby Koppel'. 2012.

Pistol, Rachel, 'Interview with Sumiko Kobayashi'. 2015.

REgenerations Oral History Project: Rebuilding Japanese American Families, Communities, and Civil Rights in the Resettlement Era; Chicago Region: Volume I, ed. Japanese American National Museum (Los Angeles, 2000).

REgenerations Oral History Project: Rebuilding Japanese American Families, Communities, and Civil Rights in the Resettlement Era; Los Angeles Region: Volume II, ed. Japanese American National Museum (Los Angeles, 2000).

REgenerations Oral History Project: Rebuilding Japanese American Families, Communities, and Civil Rights in the Resettlement Era; San Diego Region: Volume III, ed. Japanese American National Museum (Los Angeles, 2000).

REgenerations Oral History Project: Rebuilding Japanese American Families, Communities, and Civil Rights in the Resettlement Era: San Jose Region: Volume IV, ed. Japanese American National Museum (Los Angeles, 2000).

Regional Oral History Office, *Japanese-American Relocation Reviewed: Volume I, Decision and Exodus* (Berkeley: Bancroft Library, 1976).

Regional Oral History Office, *Japanese-American Relocation Reviewed: Volume II, The Internment* (Berkeley: Bancroft Library, 1976).

SA1998.32/33. 'Taped interview with Joseph Pia by Dr Wendy Ugolini, 1 August 1998'. Held at the Department of Celtic and Scottish Studies Archive, University of Edinburgh.

SA 1998.35. 'Taped interview with Renzo Serafini by Dr Wendy Ugolini, 7 August 1998'. Held at the Department of Celtic and Scottish Studies Archive, University of Edinburgh.

SA2002.053. 'Taped interview with Orazio Caira by Dr Wendy Ugolini, 2 October 1999'. Held at the Department of Celtic and Scottish Studies Archive, University of Edinburgh.

Secondary Sources

AJR. 'Continental Britons'. Available online: http://www.ajr.org.uk/continental-britons? (accessed 22 August 2016).

Alberti, Johanna. *Eleanor Rathbone*. London: Sage, 1996.

Alderman, Geoffrey. *Modern British Jewry*. Oxford: Oxford University Press, 1992.

'Allegiance: The Musical'. Available online: http://www.allegiancemusical.com/ (accessed 16 April 2015).

'Amache Preservation Group'. Available online: http://www.amache.org/ (accessed 15 April 2015).

'Amache Preservation Society Facebook Page'. Available online: https://www.facebook.com/AmachePreservationSociety?fref=ts (accessed 10 February 2015).

'The Arandora Star Campaign for an Apology Facebook Group'. Available online: https://www.facebook.com/groups/788468851172264/?ref=ts&fref=ts (accessed 10 February 2015).

Arandora Star Facebook Group'. Available online: https://www.facebook.com/groups/ 67868197405/?ref=ts&fref=ts (accessed 10 February 2015).

'The Arandora Star Tragedy'. Available online: http://www.mazzinigaribaldiclub.org/ arandora_star.html (accessed 10 February 2015).

'The Arandora Star – Remembered at Last'. Available online: http://www. ancoatslittleitaly.com/Arandora-Star.html (accessed 10 February 2015).

Aulich, James. *War Posters: Weapons of Mass Communication*. London: Thames & Hudson, 2007.

Azuma, Eiichiro. *Between Two Empires: Race, History, and Transnationalism in Japanese America*. Oxford: Oxford University Press, 2005.

Balestracci, Maria Serena. *Arandora Star: From Oblivion to Memory*. Parma: MUP, 2008.

Barkan, Elazar. *The Guilt of Nations: Restitution and Negotiating Historical Injustices*. Baltimore: Johns Hopkins, 2001.

Bartrop, Paul R., ed. *The Dunera Affair: A Documentary Resource Book*. Melbourne, Australia: Jewish Museum of Australia, 1990.

Bearden, Russell. 'The False Rumor of Tuesday: Arkansas's Internment of Japanese-Americans'. *The Arkansas Historical Quarterly* 41 (1982): 327–39.

Bellevue Arts Museum. 'The Art of Gaman: Arts and Crafts from the Japanese American Internment Camps, 1942–1946'. Available online: http://www.bellevuearts. org/exhibitions/current/art_of_gaman/index.html (accessed 10 February 2015).

Ben Uri Museum. 'Forced Journeys on Tour'. Available online: http://www.benuri.org. uk/public/?event-details=8 (accessed 10 February 2015).

Berg Nye, Doris. 'My Memories of the War Years'. Available online: http://gaic.info/ berg-story/ (accessed 9 July 2016).

Berghahn, Marion. *Continental Britons: German-Jewish Refugees from Nazi Germany*. Oxford: Berghahn Books, 2007.

Berghahn, Marion. 'Jewish Refugees in Britain'. In *European Immigrants in Britain, 1933–1950*, edited by Johannes-Dieter Steinert and Inge Weber-Newth, 87–104. Munchen: Saur, 2003.

Black, Eugene C. *The Social Politics of Anglo-Jewry 1880–1920*. Oxford: Blackwell, 1988.

Brinson, Charmian. '"In the Exile of Internment" or "Von Versuchen, aus einer Not eine Tugend zu Machen": German-Speaking Women Interned by the British during the Second World War'. In *Politics and Culture in Twentieth-Century Germany*, edited by William Niven and James Jordan, 63–87. Rochester, NY: Camden House, 2003.

Brinson, Charmian. '"Loyal to the Reich": National Socialists and Others in the Rushen Women's Internment Camp'. In *'Totally Un-English'? Britain's Internment of 'Enemy Aliens' in Two World Wars*, edited by Richard Dove, 101–19. Amsterdam: The Yearbook of the Research Centre for German and Austrian Exile Studies Vol. 7, 2005.

Brinson, Charmian, and Dove, Richard. *A Matter of Intelligence: MI5 and the Surveillance of Anti-Nazi Refugees 1933–50*. Manchester: Manchester University Press, 2014.

Brinson, Charmian, Mueller-Haerlin, Anna, and Winckler, Julia. *His Majesty's Loyal Internee: Fred Uhlman in Captivity*. Portland, OR: Vallentine Mitchell, 2009.

'Britain's Promise to Remember: The Prime Minister's Holocaust Commission Report'. January 2015. Available online: https://www.gov.uk/government/uploads/system/uploads/attachment_data/file/398645/Holocaust_Commission_Report_Britains_promise_to_remember.pdf (accessed 20 August 2016).

Broom, Leonard, and Kitsuse, John I. *The Managed Casualty: The Japanese-American Family in World War II*. Berkeley: University of California, 1956.

Brown, Sophie. 'Daily Mail Headline from 1938 Draws Comparisons with Current Reporting of Calais Migrant Crisis'. *The Huffington Post UK*. 31 July 2015. Available online: http://www.huffingtonpost.co.uk/2015/07/31/daily-mail-1938-jews_n_7909954.html (accessed 2 March 2016).

Brunnhuber, Nicole M. T. 'After the Prison Ships: Internment Narratives in Canada'. In *'Totally Un-English'? Britain's Internment of 'Enemy Aliens' in Two World Wars*, edited by Richard Dove, 165–78. Amsterdam: The Yearbook of the Research Centre for German and Austrian Exile Studies Vol. 7, 2005.

Bullen, Jamie. 'Brexit: Facebook Page Highlights Racism after EU Referendum Vote Triggers Spike in Hate Crimes. *Evening Standard*, 27 June 2016. Available online: http://www.standard.co.uk/news/politics/brexit-facebook-page-highlights-racism-after-eu-referendum-vote-triggers-spike-in-hate-crimes-a3281951.html (accessed 27 June 2016).

Burleston, Louise. 'The State, Internment and Public Criticism in the Second World War'. In *The Internment of Aliens in Twentieth Century Britain*, edited by David Cesarani and Tony Kushner, 102–24. London: Frank Cass, 1993.

Burton, Jeffery F., et al. *Confinement and Ethnicity: An Overview of World War II Japanese American Relocation Sites*. Western Archeological and Conservation Center National Park Service US Department of the Interior, 2000.

Calavita, Kitty. 'The Paradoxes of Race, Class, Identity, and "Passing": Enforcing the Chinese Exclusion Acts, 1882–1910'. *Law & Social Inquiry* 25 (2000): 1–40.

'California Museum'. Available online: http://www.californiamuseum.org/uprooted-japanese-americans-during-wwii (accessed 10 February 2015).

Carlin, Brendan. 'Free Hotels for the Calais Stowaways in Soft Touch Britain: Outrage as Immigrants Illegally Entering UK Get Cooked Meals and £35 Cash a Week within Days of Arrival'. *The Mail on Sunday*, 1 August 2015. Available online: http://www.dailymail.co.uk/news/article-3182519/Welcome-soft-touch-UK-Outrage-immigrants-illegally-entering-UK-free-hotel-rooms-cooked-meals-35-cash-week-days-arrival.html (accessed 2 March 2016).

Carr, Robert K. 'Review'. *The American Political Science Review* 43 (1949): 1042–43.

Cesarani, David. 'An Alien Concept? The Continuity of Anti-alienism in British Society before 1940'. In *The Internment of Aliens in Twentieth Century Britain*, edited by David Cesarani and Tony Kushner, 25–52. London: Frank Cass, 1993.

Cesarani, David. 'Anti-alienism in England after the First World War'. *Immigrants and Minorities* 6 (1987): 5–29.

Cesarani, David. 'Dual Heritage or Duel of Heritages? Englishness and Jewishness in the Heritage Industry'. In *The Jewish Heritage in British History: Englishness and Jewishness*, edited by Tony Kushner, 29–41. London: Frank Cass., 1992.

Cesarani, David, and Kushner, Tony. 'Alien Internment in Britain during the Twentieth Century: An Introduction'. In *The Internment of Aliens in Twentieth Century Britain*, edited by David Cesarani and Tony Kushner, 1–24. London: Frank Cass, 1993.

Chappell, Connery. *Island of Barbed Wire: Internment on the Isle of Man in World War Two*. London: Robert Hale, 2005.

Colborn-Roxworthy, Emily. '"Manzanar, the Eyes of the World Are upon You": Performance and Archival Ambivalence at a Japanese American Internment Camp'. *Theatre Journal* 59, no. 2 (2007): 189–214.

Colpi, Terri. 'The Impact of the Second World War on the British Italian Community'. In *The Internment of Aliens in Twentieth Century Britain*, edited by David Cesarani and Tony Kushner, 167–87. London: Routledge, 1993.

Connelly, Mark. *We Can Take It! Britain and the Memory of the Second World War*. Harlow: Pearson Longman, 2004.

Cooper, Phillip J. *By Order of the President: The Use and Abuse of Executive Direct Action*. Lawrence: University of Kansas, 2002.

Creef, Elena Tajima. *Imaging Japanese America: The Visual Construction of Citizenship, the Nation, and the Body*. New York: New York University, 2004.

Daniels, Roger. *Coming to America: A History of Immigration and Ethnicity in American life*. New York: HarperCollins, 1990.

Daniels, Roger. *Concentration Camps, North America: Japanese in the United States and Canada during World War II*. Malabar, FL: Krieger, 1981.

Daniels, Roger. *Prisoners without Trial: Japanese Americans in World War II*. New York: Hill & Wang, 1993.

'Densho'. Available online: http://www.densho.org/ (accessed 10 February 2015).

De Zayas, Alfred-Maurice. *The German Expellees: Victims in War and Peace*. London: Palgrave Macmillan, 1993.

Dickerson, James L. *Inside America's Concentration Camps: Two Centuries of Internment and Torture*. Chicago: Lawrence Hill Books, 2010.

'Donald J. Trump Addresses Terrorism, Immigration, and National Security'. 13 June 2016. Available online: https://www.donaldjtrump.com/press-releases/donald-j.-trump-addresses-terrorism-immigration-and-national-security (accessed 28 June 2016).

'Donald Trump on the Issues'. Available online: http://2016.presidential-candidates.org/Trump/?on=terrorism (accessed 28 June 2016).

Donnelly, Mark. *Britain in the Second World War*. London: Routledge, 1999.

Dove, Richard. 'A Matter Which Touches the Good Name of This Country'. In '*Totally Un-English'? Britain's Internment of 'Enemy Aliens' in Two World Wars*, edited by

Richard Dove, 11–16. Amsterdam: The Yearbook of the Research Centre for German and Austrian Exile Studies Vol. 7, 2005.

Dowd Hall, Jacquelyn. 'Documenting Diversity: The Southern Experience'. *The Oral History Review* 4 (1976): 19–28.

Drinnon, Richard. *Keeper of Concentration Camps: Dillon S. Myer and American Racism*. Berkeley: University of California, 1987.

Dudley Gold, Susan. *Korematsu v. United States: Japanese-American Internment*. New York: Marshall Cavendish Benchmark, 2006.

Dunera Museum. 'Hay Prisoner of War and Internment Camp Interpretive Centre'. Available online: http://www.hay.nsw.gov.au/Museums/DuneraMuseum/tabid/99/Default.aspx (accessed 10 February 2015).

Eckerson, Helen F. 'Immigration and National Origins'. *Annals of the American Academy of Political and Social Science* 367 (1966): 4–14.

Eisenberg, Ellen. *The First to Cry Down Injustice: Western Jews and Japanese Removal during WWII*. Plymouth: Lexington Books, 2008.

Endelman, Todd M. 'Review: Jews, Aliens and Other Outsiders in British History'. *The Historical Journal* 37 (1994): 959–69.

Estlack, Russell W. *The Aleut Internments of World War II: Islanders Removed from Their Homes by Japan and the United States*. Jefferson, NC: McFarland, 2014.

'EU Referendum: Immigration Target "Impossible" in EU, Vote Leave Says'. *BBC News*, 20 June 2016. Available online: http://www.bbc.co.uk/news/uk-politics-eu-referendum-36573220 (accessed 25 June 2016).

Fahrmeir, Andreas. 'Immigration and Immigration Policy in Britain from the Nineteenth to the Twentieth Centuries'. In *European Immigrants in Britain, 1933–1950*, edited by Johannes-Dieter Steinert and Inge Weber-Newth, 43–57. Munich: Saur, 2003.

Feather, Jessica. *Art behind Barbed Wire*. Liverpool: National Museums Liverpool, 2004.

Feldman, David. *Englishmen and Jews, Social Relations and Political Culture 1840–1914*. New Haven: Yale University Press, 1994.

Feldman, David. '"The Importance of Being English": Jewish Immigration and the Decay of Liberal England'. In *Metropolis London: Histories and Representations since 1800*, edited by David Feldman and Gareth Stedman, 56–84. London: Routledge, 1989.

Field, Corinne. 'The Walker Reveals a Wartime Life behind Barbed Wire'. *Culture 24*, 24 March 2004. Available online: http://www.culture24.org.uk/places-to-go/north-west/liverpool/art20510 (accessed 10 February 2015).

'Forced Journeys: Artists in Exile in Britain c. 1933–45'. Available online: http://www.ashgate.com/isbn/9780900157134 (accessed 10 February 2016).

Fox, Stephen. *America's Invisible Gulag: A Biography of German American Internment & Exclusion in World War II*. New York: Peter Lang, 2000.

Fox, Stephen. *Uncivil Liberties: Italian Americans under Siege during World War II*. Parkland, FL: Universal Publishers, 2000.

'Francine Stock: Break in Transmission'. *The Guardian*, 8 March 1999. http://www. theguardian.com/books/1999/mar/08/costabookaward.features11 (accessed 10 February 2015).

Frederickson, George M. 'From Exceptionalism to Variability: Recent Developments in Cross-National Comparative History'. *Journal of American History* 82, no. 2 (1995): 587–604.

Friedlander, Albert H. 'Immigrants and Refugees. Keynote Address'. In *European Immigrants in Britain, 1933–1950*, edited by Johannes-Dieter Steinert and Inge Weber-Newth, 19–27. Munich: Saur, 2003.

'Friends of the Dunera Boys'. Available online: https://www.facebook.com/groups/ 281170982833/?fref=ts (accessed 7 December 2015).

Fry, Helen. *Denazification: Britain's Enemy Aliens, Nazi War Criminals and the Reconstruction of Post-War Europe*. Stroud, Gloucestershire: History Press, 2010.

Gainer, Bernard. *The Alien Invasion: The Origins of the Aliens Act of 1905*. London: Heinemann, 1972.

Gartner, Lloyd P. *The Jewish Immigrant in England, 1870–1914*. London: Vallentine Mitchell, 2001.

Gillman, Leni, and Gillman, Peter. *'Collar the Lot!' How Britain Interned and Expelled Its Wartime Refugees*. London: Quartet Books, 1980.

'Go for Broke National Education Center'. Available online: http://www.goforbroke.org/ about_us/about_us_educational_history.php (accessed 10 February 2015).

Goldman, Aaron L. 'Defence Regulation 18B: Emergency Internment of Aliens and Political Dissenters in Great Britain during World War II'. *The Journal of British Studies* 12 (1973): 120–36.

Graham-Dixon, Andrew. 'Schwitters in Britain, at Tate Britain, Review'. *The Telegraph*, 6 February 2013. Available online: http://www.telegraph.co.uk/culture/art/art-reviews/9852499/Schwitters-in-Britain-at-Tate-Britain-review.html (accessed 16 January 2016).

Grapes, Bryan J., ed. *Japanese American Internment Camps*. San Diego: Greenhaven, 2001.

Greenberg, Cheryl. 'Black and Jewish Responses to Japanese Internment'. *Journal of American Ethnic History* 14 (1995): 3–37.

Grew, Raymond. 'On Reading Six Books in Search of Another'. *Comparative Studies in Society and History* 11, no. 3 (1969): 355–64.

Grodzins, Morton. *Americans Betrayed: Politics and the Japanese Evacuation*. Chicago: Chicago University Press, 1949.

'Gun Violence Archive'. Available online: http://www.gunviolencearchive.org/ (accessed 28 June 2016).

'Guns in the US: The Statistics behind the Violence'. *BBC News*, 5 January 2016. Available online: http://www.bbc.co.uk/news/world-us-canada-34996604 (accessed 28 June 2016).

Gyory, Andrew. *Closing the Gate: Race, Politics, and the Chinese Exclusion Act*. Chapel Hill: University of North Carolina, 1998.

Harkins, Margaret. 'Alien Internment at Huyton buring World War II'. In *A Prominent Place: Studies in Merseyside History*, edited by John A. Davies and Janet E. Hollinshead, 113–24. Liverpool: Liverpool Hope Press, 1999.

Harris, Jose. 'War and Social History: Britain and the Home Front during the Second World War'. *Contemporary European History* 1 (1992): 17–35.

Harvey, Robert. *Amache: The Story of Japanese Internment in Colorado during World War II*. Dallas: Taylor Trade Publishing, 2004.

'Heart Mountain Interpretive Center Facebook Page'. Available online: https://www. facebook.com/heartmountainwy?fref=ts (accessed 10 February 2015).

Helman, Susannah. 'The Dunera Boys'. *The National Library Magazine* (2010): 3–7.

Higham, John. *Strangers in the Land: Patterns of American Nativism 1860–1925*. New York: Atheneum, 1974.

Hing, Bill Ong. *Making and Remaking Asian America through Immigration Policy, 1850–1990*. Stanford, CA: Stanford University Press, 1993.

Hoch, Paul K. 'No Utopia: Refugee Scholars in Britain'. *History Today* 35, no. 11 (1985): 53–56.

Holmes, Colin. *Anti-Semitism in British Society, 1876–1939*. London: Edward Arnold, 1979.

Holmes, Colin. 'British Government Policy towards Wartime Refugees'. In *Europe in Exile : European Exile Communities in Britain, 1940–1945*, edited by Jose Gotovitch and Martin Conway, 11–34. Oxford: Bergahn Books, 2001.

Holmes, Colin. *John Bull's Island: Immigration & British Society, 1871–1971*. Basingstoke: Macmillan, 1988.

Holmes, Colin. *A Tolerant Country? Immigrants, Refugees and Minorities in Britain*. London: Faber, 1991.

Hoobler, Dorothy, and Hoobler, Thomas. *The Japanese American Family Album*. Oxford: Oxford University Press, 1995.

Hosokawa, Bill. *Nisei: The Quiet Americans*. Boulder: Colorado University Press, 2002.

Howard, John. *Concentration Camps on the Home Front: Japanese Americans in the House of Jim Crow*. Chicago: Chicago University Press, 2008.

Howard-Hassmann, Rhoda E. 'Getting to Reparations: Japanese Americans and African Americans'. *Social Forces* 83, no. 2 (2004): 823–40.

Hughes, Trevor. 'Colo. Internment Camp Marks "Terrible Mistake" in WWII'. *USA Today*, 17 May 2014.

'Immigration Reform That Will Make America Great Again'. Available online: https:// www.donaldjtrump.com/positions/immigration-reform (accessed 25 June 2016).

Irons, Peter. *Justice at War: The Story of the Japanese American Internment Cases*. Oxford: Oxford University Press, 1983.

Isherwood, Charles. 'Review: "Allegiance", a Musical History Lesson about Interned Japanese-Americans'. *The New York Times*, 8 November 2015. Available online: http://www.nytimes.com/2015/11/09/theater/review-allegiance-a-musical-history-lesson-about-interned-japanese-americans.html (accessed 16 January 2016).

Ishizuka, Karen, and Zimmerman, Patricia, eds. *Mining the Home Movie: Excavations in Histories and Memories*. Berkeley: University of California, 2007.

'Isle of Colonsay'. Available online: http://www.colonsay.org.uk/About/Arandora-Star (accessed 10 February 2015).

'Italian Cloister Garden'. Available online: http://www.italiancloister.org.uk/why1.htm (accessed 24 June 2015).

Itoh, Keiko. *The Japanese Community in Pre-war Britain: From Integration to Disintegration*. London: Routledge, 2013.

Iyenaga, T., and Sato, Kenoske. *Japan and the California Problem*. New York: G.P. Putnam's, 1973.

Izumi, Masumi. 'Prohibiting "American Concentration Camps": Repeal of the Emergency Detention Act and the Public Historical Memory of the Japanese American Internment'. *The Pacific Historical Review* 74 (2005): 165–93.

James, Thomas. *Exile Within: The Schooling of Japanese Americans, 1942–1945*. Cambridge, MA: Harvard University Press, 1987.

'Japanese American National Museum'. Available online: http://www.janm.org/about/ (accessed 10 February 2015).

'Japanese American Relocation Digital Archives'. Available online: http://www. calisphere.universityofcalifornia.edu/jarda/ (accessed 10 February 2015).

Jones, Catherine. *Immigration and Social Policy in Britain*. London: Tavistock, 1977.

Jones, F. C. 'Review'. *International Affairs (Royal Institute of International Affairs 1944–)* 26 (1950): 553–54.

Jones, Maldwyn Allen. *American Immigration*. Chicago: Chicago University Press, 1960.

Kang, Jerry. 'Denying Prejudice: Internment, Redress, and Denial'. *UCLA Law Review* 51 (2004): 933–1013.

Karpf, Anne. 'We've Been Here Before'. *The Guardian*, 8 June 2002. Available online: http://www.theguardian.com/uk/2002/jun/08/immigration. immigrationandpublicservices (accessed 23 August 2016).

Kenyon, Georgina. 'Australian Army Infected Troops and Internees in Second World War'. *BMJ: British Medical Journal* 318 (1999): 1233.

Khomami, Nadia. 'Terrorist Attacks by Violent Jihadis in the US since 9/11'. *The Guardian*, 5 December 2015. Available online: https://www.theguardian.com/us-news/2015/dec/05/terrorist-attacks-by-islamists-in-the-us-since-911 (accessed 25 August 2016). Available online: https://www.theguardian.com/us-news/2015/dec/05/terrorist-attacks-by-islamists-in-the-us-since-911 (accessed 28 June 2016).

King, Desmond. *Making Americans: Immigration, Race, and the Origins of the Diverse Democracy*. Cambridge, MA: Harvard University Press, 2000.

Kitano, Harry H. L. *Japanese Americans: The Evolution of a Subculture*. Englewood Cliffs, NJ: Prentice, 1969.

Kocka, Jürgen. 'Comparison and Beyond'. *History and Theory* 42, no. 1 (2003): 39–44.

Kopan, Tal. 'Donald Trump: Syrian Refugees a "Trojan Horse"'. *CNN*, 16 November 2015. Available online: http://edition.cnn.com/2015/11/16/politics/donald-trump-syrian-refugees/ (accessed 3 February 2016).

'Kurt Schwitters Exhibition Curated by Professor Fran Lloyd'. Available online: http://fada.kingston.ac.uk/news/kurt-schwitters-exhibition-curated-by-professor-fran-lloyd/ (accessed 10 February 2015).

'Kurt Schwitters Internment Camp Art Exhibition Opens'. *BBC News*, 27 September 2013. Available online: http://www.bbc.co.uk/news/world-europe-isle-of-man-23974500 (accessed 10 February 2015).

Kushner, Tony. 'Clubland, Cricket Tests and Alien Internment, 1939–40'. In *The Internment of Aliens in Twentieth Century Britain*, edited by David Cesarani and Tony Kushner, 79–101. London: Frank Cass, 1993.

Kushner, Tony. 'Heritage and Ethnicity: An Introduction'. In *The Jewish Heritage in British History: Englishness and Jewishness*, edited by Tony Kushner, 1–28. London: Frank Cass, 1992.

Kushner, Tony. *The Persistence of Prejudice: Antisemitism in British Society during the Second World War*. Manchester: Manchester University Press, 1989.

Kushner, Tony. *Remembering Refugees Then and Now*. Manchester: Manchester University Press, 2006.

Kushner, Tony, and Knox, Katharine. *Refugees in an Age of Genocide*. London: Cass, 1999.

Lang, Birgit. 'The Dunera Boys: Dramatizing History from a Jewish Perspective'. In *'Totally Un-English'? Britain's Internment of 'Enemy Aliens' in Two World Wars*, edited by Richard Dove, 179–191. Amsterdam: The Yearbook of the Research Centre for German and Austrian Exile Studies Vol. 7, 2005.

Laughland, Oliver, and Felton, Ryan. '"It's All Just Poison Now": Flint Reels as Families Struggle through Water Crisis'. *The Guardian*, 24 January 2016. Available online: https://www.theguardian.com/us-news/2016/jan/24/flint-michigan-water-crisis-lead-poisoning-families-children (accessed 28 June 2016).

LaViolette, Forrest E. 'Review'. *Pacific Affairs* 22, no. 4 (1949): 442.

Lebzelter, Gisela C. *Political Anti-Semitism in England 1918–1939*. London: Macmillan, 1978.

Lee, Erika, and Yung, Judy. *Angel Island: Immigrant Gateway to America*. Oxford: Oxford University Press, 2010.

Leighton-Langer, Peter. *The King's Own Loyal Enemy Aliens: German and Austrian Refugees in Britain's Armed Forces, 1939–45*. London: Vallentine Mitchell, 2006.

Lipman, V. D. *A History of the Jews in Britain since 1858*. Leicester: Leicester University Press, 1990.

Lipman, V. D. *Social History of the Jews in England 1850–1950*. London: Watts, 1954.

London, Louise. 'Britain and Refugees from Nazism: Policies, Constraints and Choices'. In *European Immigrants in Britain, 1933–1950*, edited by Johannes-Dieter Steinert and Inge Weber-Newth, 73–86. Munich: Saur, 2003.

London, Louise. *Whitehall and the Jews, 1933–1948: British Immigration Policy, Jewish Refugees, and the Holocaust*. Cambridge: Cambridge University Press, 2003.

Lustig, Robin. 'The Wandering Scribe'. Available online: http://www.wanderingscribes.com/#!Back-in-the-Isle-of-Man-after-74-years/c1ybh/837721C8-1C95-493B-88AB-AA3B1B9D748F (accessed 2 April 2015).

Mackay, Robert. *The Test of War: Inside Britain 1939–45*. London: UCL Press, 1999.

Maki, Mitchell T., Kitano, Harry H. L., and Berthold, Megan S. *Achieving the Impossible Dream: How the Japanese Americans Obtained Redress*. Chicago: University of Illinois Press, 1999.

Manx National Heritage. 'Living with the Wire: Civilian Internment on the Isle of Man'. *Isle of Man News*, 10 November 2010. Available online: www.manx.net/isle-of-man-news/706/living-with-the-wire-civilian-internment-on-the-isle-of-man (accessed 24 June 2015).

'The Manzanar Committee'. Available online: http://www.manzanarcommittee.org/The_Manzanar_Committee/Home.html (accessed 21 April 2015).

'Manzanar Fishing Club'. Available online: http://www.fearnotrout.com (accessed 10 February 2015).

'The Manzanar Fishing Club Facebook Page'. Available online: https://www.facebook.com/TheManzanarFishingClub (accessed 10 February 2015).

Matsumoto, Valerie J. 'Japanese American Women during World War II'. *Frontiers: A Journal of Women Studies* 8 (1984): 6–14.

'Mazzini Garibaldi Charitable Foundation'. Available online: http://www.mgfoundation.com/mazzini-garibaldi-projects-arandora.html (accessed 24 June 2015).

McNaughton, James C. *Nisei Linguists: Japanese Americans in the Military Intelligence Service during World War II*. Washington, DC: Department of the Army, 2006.

Meehan, Patricia. *A Strange Enemy People: Germans under the British 1945–50*. London: Peter Owen, 2001.

Migration Heritage Centre, '1941 Dunera Boys Hay Internment Camp Collection'. Available online: http://www.migrationheritage.nsw.gov.au/exhibition/objectsthroughtime/dunera/ (accessed 10 February 2015).

'Minidoka National Historic Site Facebook Page'. Available online: https://www.facebook.com/pages/Minidoka-National-Historic-Site/151975884819492?fref=ts (accessed 10 February 2015).

'Minidoka Pilgrimage Facebook Page'. Available online: https://www.facebook.com/minidokapilgrimage?ref=br_rs (accessed 10 February 2015).

'Minoru Yasui Awarded Presidential Medal of Freedom', *Northwest Asian Weekly* 34, no. 48 (2015), 23 November. Available online: http://www.nwasianweekly.com/2015/11/minoru-yasui-awarded-presidential-medal-of-freedom/ (accessed 15 December 2015).

Modell, John. *The Economics and Politics of Racial Accommodation: The Japanese of Los Angeles, 1900–1942*. Chicago: University of Illinois Press, 1977.

Muller, Eric L. *Free to Die for Their Country: The Story of the Japanese American Draft Resisters in World War II*. Chicago: University of Chicago, 2001.

Nakagawa, Martha. 'Mabel Imai Tomita: How One Family Was Ripped Apart at Tule Lake'. *Rafu Shimpo*, 31 August 2014. Available online: http://www.rafu.com/2014/08/mabel-imai-tomita-how-one-family-was-ripped-apart-at-tule-lake/ (accessed 16 April 2015).

Nakano, Mei. *Japanese American Women: Three Generations 1890–1990*. Berkeley: Mina Press, 1990.

Nash, Lucy. 'Exhibition remembers Dunera Boys 70 Years on'. *ABC News*, 14 February 2010. Available online: http://www.abc.net.au/news/2010-02-12/exhibition-remembers-dunera-boys-70yrs-on/330272 (accessed 2 October 2015).

National Archives of Scotland. 'The SS Arandora Star and the Italian Community in Scotland'. NAS AD57/23 Available online: http://www.nas.gov.uk/about/100630.asp (accessed 10 February 2015).

'National Japanese American Memorial Foundation'. Available online: http://www.njamf.com/ (accessed 16 April 2015).

National Library of Australia. 'The Dunera Boys 70 Years on'. Available online: https://www.nla.gov.au/exhibitions/dunera-boys (accessed 10 February 2015).

National Park Service. 'Honouluili National Monument'. Available online: http://www.nps.gov/hono/learn/historyculture/index.htm (accessed 16 April 2015).

National Park Service. 'Japanese American Confinement Sites'. Available online: http://www.nps.gov/jacs/ (accessed 10 February 2015).

National Park Service. 'Manzanar National Historic Site'. Available online: http://www.nps.gov/manz/historyculture/index.htm (accessed 10 February 2015).

National Park Service. 'Minidoka National Historic Site'. Available online: http://www.nps.gov/miin/index.htm (accessed 10 February 2015).

National Park Service, 'Tule Lake Segregation Center becomes National Monument'. 5 December 2008. Available online: http://www.nps.gov/tule/parknews/new-park-announced.htm (accessed 2 October 2015).

National Park Service. 'Tule Lake Unit, World War II Valor in the Pacific National Monument'. Available online: http://parkplanning.nps.gov/parkHome.cfm?parkID=535&CFID=8551309&CFTOKEN=8943984823429af6-B8C5A5A9-D7A6-E7E0-DD00D94DA6828199&jsessionid=1127B8D1EA09D9FA7D0C32DE70C49984. ParkPlanning (accessed 10 February 2015).

'National Park Service Press Release'. 12 June 2014. Available online: http://www.nps.gov/news/release.htm?id=1600 (accessed 10 February 2015).

Neuman, Gerald L. 'Habeas Corpus, Executive Detention, and the Removal of Aliens'. *Columbia Law Review* 98 (1998): 961–1067.

Ngai, Mae M. "'An Ironic Testimony to the Value of American Democracy": Assimilationism and the World War II Internment'. In *Contested Democracy: Freedom, Race, and Power in American History*, edited by Penny Von Eschen and Manisha Sinha, 237–57. New York: Columbia University Press, 2007.

O'Brien, David J., and Fugita, Stephen S. *The Japanese American Experience*. Bloomington: Indiana University Press, 1991.

Okihiro, Gary Y., and Myers, Joan. *Whispered Silences: Japanese Americans and World War II*. Seattle: University of Washington, 1996.

Otsuka, Julie. 'About Julie Otsuka'. Available online: http://www.julieotsuka.com/about/ (accessed 10 February 2015).

Panayi, Panikos. 'The Historiography of European Immigrants in Britain during the Twentieth Century'. In *European Immigrants in Britain, 1933–1950*, edited by Johannes-Dieter Steinert and Inge Weber-Newth, 29–41. Munich: Saur, 2003.

Panayi, Panikos. *Immigration, Ethnicity and Racism in Britain, 1815–1945*. Manchester: Manchester University Press, 1994.

Panayi, Panikos. 'An Intolerant Act by an Intolerant Society: The Internment of Germans in Britain during the First World War'. In *The Internment of Aliens in Twentieth Century Britain*, edited by David Cesarani and Tony Kushner, 53–78. London: Frank Cass, 1993.

Panayi, Panikos. 'A Marginalized Subject? The Historiography of Enemy Alien Internment in Britain'. In *'Totally Un-English'? Britain's Internment of 'Enemy Aliens' in Two World Wars*, edited by Richard Dove 17–26. Amsterdam: The Yearbook of the Research Centre for German and Austrian Exile Studies Vol. 7, 2005.

Panayi, Panikos. 'Prisoners of Britain: German Civilian, Military and Naval Internees during the First World War'. In *'Totally Un-English'? Britain's Internment of 'Enemy Aliens' in Two World Wars*, edited by Richard Dove, 29–43. Amsterdam: The Yearbook of the Research Centre for German and Austrian Exile Studies Vol. 7, 2005.

Patkin, Benzion. *The Dunera Internees*. Stanmore, NSW, Australia: Cassell, 1979.

Pearl, Cyril. *The Dunera Scandal: Deported by Mistake* (London: Angus & Robertson, 1983).

Pellew, Jill. 'The Home Office and the Aliens Act, 1905'. *The Historical Journal* 32, no. 2 (1989): 369–85.

Personal Justice Denied: Report of the Commission on Wartime Relocation and Internment of Civilians. Seattle: Civil Liberties Public Education Fund/University of Washington, 1997.

Petersen, William. *Japanese Americans: Oppression and Success*. New York: Random House, 1971.

Phu, Thy. 'The Spaces of Human Confinement: Manzanar Photography and Landscape Ideology'. *Journal of Asian American Studies* 11 (2008): 337–71.

Pistol, Rachel. '75 Years after Pearl Harbor, the Threat of Internment Returns'. *The Huffington Post*, 1 January 2016. Available online: http://www.huffingtonpost.co.uk/rachel-pistol/75-years-after-pearl-harb_b_13896910.html (accessed 13 January 2017).

Pistol, Rachel. 'Why Shinzo Abe's Pearl Harbor Visit Comes as Threat of Internment Returns', *Newsweek*, 26 December 2016. Available online: http://europe.newsweek.com/why-shinzo-abes-pearl-harbor-visit-comes-threat-internment-returns-536364 (accessed 13 January 2017).

'Possible Presidential Medal of Freedom to Honor Endo'. *Northwest Asian Weekly* 34, no. 30 (2015), 20 July. Available online: http://www.nwasianweekly.com/2015/07/possible-presidential-medal-of-freedom-to-honor-endo/ (accessed 10 December 2015).

Preston, Julia, Rappeport, Alan, and Richtel, Matt. 'What Would It Take for Donald Trump to Deport 11 Million and Build a Wall?' *The New York Times*, 19 May 2016. Available online: http://www.nytimes.com/2016/05/20/us/politics/donald-trump-immigration.html?_r=0 (accessed 23 August 2016).

Ramati, Alexander. *Barbed Wire on the Isle of Man: The Wartime British Internment of Jews*. London: Harcourt, 1980.

Rao, Maliika. 'These Crafts Made by Japanese-American Prisoners Will Renew Your Faith in Human Ingenuity'. *The Huffington Post*, 15 August 2014. Available online: http://www.huffingtonpost.com/2014/08/15/art-of-gaman-arts-crafts-japanese-interment-camps_n_5655381.html (accessed 29 August 2016).

Rees, Tom. 'Immigration Policies in the United Kingdom'. In '*Race' in Britain: Continuity and Change*, edited by Charles Husband, 75–96. London: Hutchinson, 1982.

Riley, Karen L. *Schools behind Barbed Wire: The Untold Story of Wartime Internment and the Children of Arrested Enemy Aliens*. Lanham, MD: Rowman & Littlefield Publishers, 2002.

Ritchie, Donald A. *Doing Oral History: A Practical Guide*. Oxford: Oxford University Press, 2003.

'Robert Rietti Obituary'. *The Daily Telegraph*, 22 April 2015. Available online: http://www.telegraph.co.uk/news/obituaries/celebrity-obituaries/11555558/Robert-Rietti-voiceover-actor.html (accessed 2 June 2015).

Robinson, Greg. *After Camp: Portraits in Midcentury Japanese American Life and Politics*. Berkeley: University of California, 2012.

Robinson, Greg. *By Order of the President: FDR and the Internment of Japanese Americans*. Cambridge, MA: Harvard University Press, 2001.

Robinson, Greg. *A Tragedy of Democracy: Japanese Confinement in North America*. New York: Columbia University Press, 2009.

Robinson, Greg, and Tajiri, Guyo. *Pacific Citizens: Larry and Guyo Tajiri and Japanese American Journalism in the World War II Era*. Chicago: University of Illinois Press, 2012.

Roxworthy, Emily. *The Spectacle of Japanese American Trauma: Racial Performativity and World War II*. Honolulu: University of Hawaii Press, 2008.

Rushen Heritage. 'Friend or Foe?' Available online: http://www.rushenheritage.org/calendar-item/friend-or-foe/ (accessed 2 June 2015).

Sakurai, Gail. *Japanese American Internment Camps*. Toronto: Children's Press, 2002.

Sammon, John. 'Memorial Planned to Commemorate Tanforan Site'. *Nikkei West*, 12 November 2015. Available online: http://nikkeiwest.com/1/?p=2397 (accessed 2 September 2016).

Sawer, Patrick, Hughes, Laura, Mendick, Robert, and Heighton, Luke. 'Jo Cox's Sister Calls Her "Perfect" and "Utterly Amazing" as Accused Murderer Tells Court His Name Is "Death to Traitors, Freedom for Britain"'. *The Daily Telegraph*, 18 June 2016. Available online: http://www.telegraph.co.uk/news/2016/06/18/jo-cox-mp-shot-thomas-mair-arrives-at-court-following-murder-cha/ (accessed 27 June 2016).

Sewell, Brian. 'Brian Sewell on: Schwitters in Britain, Tate Britain – Review'. *Evening Standard*, 31 January 2013. Available online: http://www.standard.co.uk/goingout/exhibitions/brian-sewell-on-schwitters-in-britain-tate-britain-review-8474403.html (accessed 16 January 2016).

Sewell Jr., William H. 'Marc Bloch and the Logic of Comparative History'. *History and Theory* 6, no. 2 (1967): 208–18.

Sherman, A. J. *Island Refuge: Britain and Refugees from the Third Reich 1933–1939*. Ilford, Essex: Frank Cass, 1994.

Sherwood, Harriet, Dodd, Vikram, Khomami, Nadia, and Morris, Steven. 'Cameron condemns post-Brexit xenophobic and racist abuse'. *The Guardian*, 27 June 2016. Available online: https://www.theguardian.com/uk-news/2016/jun/27/sadiq-khan-muslim-council-britain-warning-of-post-brexit-racism (accessed 27 June 2016).

Simpson, A. W. B. *In the Highest Degree Odious: Detention without Trial in Wartime Britain*. Oxford: Clarendon Press, 1992.

Smith, Bradford. *Americans from Japan*. Westport, CT: Greenwood Press, 1948.

Smith, Harold L. *Britain and the Second World War: A Social History*. Manchester: Manchester University Press, 1996.

Smith, Malcolm. *Britain and 1940: History, Myth and Popular Memory*. London: Routledge, 2000.

Smithsonian American Art Museum. 'Exhibitions: The Art of Gaman: Arts and Crafts from the Japanese American Internment Camps, 1942–1946'. Available online: http://americanart.si.edu/exhibitions/archive/2010/gaman/ (accessed 10 February 2015).

Solomons, Natasha. 'Inspirations – Mr Rosenblum's List'. Available online: http://natashasolomons.com/inspirations-rosenblum/ (accessed 10 February 2015).

Soloski, Alexis. 'Allegiance Review: George Takei Can't Save Broadway's Mediocre Pledge'. *The Guardian*, 9 November 2015. Available online: http://www.theguardian.com/stage/2015/nov/08/allegiance-review-broadway-unexceptional-pledge-george-takei (accessed 16 January 2016).

Spicer, Edward H. 'Review'. *The American Journal of Sociology* 55 (1950): 603–4.

Spickard, Paul R. *Japanese Americans: The Formation and Transformations of an Ethnic Group*. New York: Twayne, 1996.

Sponza, Lucio. *Divided Loyalties: Italians in Britain during the Second World War*. Bern: Peter Lang, 2000.

Sponza, Lucio. 'The Internment of Italians 1940–1945'. In *'Totally Un-English'? Britain's Internment of 'Enemy Aliens' in Two World Wars*, edited by Richard Dove, 153–63.

Amsterdam: The Yearbook of the Research Centre for German and Austrian Exile Studies Vol. 7, 2005.

Sponza, Lucio. 'Italians in War and Post-War Britain'. In *European Immigrants in Britain, 1933–1950*, edited by Johannes-Dieter Steinert, 185–200. Munchen: Saur, 2003.

Sponza, Lucio. 'Italian Immigrants in Britain: Perceptions and Self-Perceptions'. In *Histories and Memories: Migrants and Their History in Britain*, edited by Kathy Burrell and Panikos Panayi, 57–74. London: Tauris Academic Studies, 2006.

'Stamp Honoring Tuskegee Airman to be Dedicated in Special Ceremony at North Carolina Civil Rights Museum'. Available online: http://uspsstamps.com/blog/2014/7/25 (accessed 16 January 2016).

Starn, Orin. 'Engineering Internment: Anthropologists and the War Relocation Authority'. *American Ethnologist* 13, no. 4 (1986): 700–20.

Steinert, Johannes-Dieter, and Weber-Newth, Inge. 'European Immigrants in Britain, 1933–50'. In *European Immigrants in Britain, 1933–1950*, edited by Johannes-Dieter Steinert and Inge Weber-Newth, 7–16. Munich: Saur, 2003.

Steinhauer, Jennifer. 'Senate Blocks Bill on Tougher Refugee Screening'. 20 January 2016. Available online: http://www.nytimes.com/2016/01/21/us/politics/senate-refugee-screening-bill-syria-iraq.html?_r=0 (accessed 3 February 2016).

Stent, Ronald. *A Bespattered Page? The Internment of His Majesty's 'Most Loyal Enemy Aliens'*. London: Deutsch, 1980.

Stewart, Heather, and Mason, Rowena. 'Nigel Farage's Anti-migrant PosteR reported to Police'. *The Guardian*, 16 June 2016. Available online: http://www.theguardian.com/politics/2016/jun/16/nigel-farage-defends-ukip-breaking-point-poster-queue-of-migrants (accessed 30 July 2016).

Stocks, Mary D. *Eleanor Rathbone: A Biography*. London: Victor Gollancz, 1949.

Suyemoto, Toyo. *I Call to Remembrance: Toyo Suyemoto's Years of Internment*. Piscataway, NJ: Rutgers University Press, 2007.

Syal, Rajeev. 'MP Jo Cox Wrote Passionate Defence of Immigration Days before Her Death'. *The Guardian*, 19 June 2016. Available online: https://www.theguardian.com/uk-news/2016/jun/19/jo-cox-passionate-defence-immigration-death-article-eu (accessed 27 June 2016).

Tate Britain. 'Schwitters in Britain'. Available online: http://www.tate.org.uk/whats-on/tate-britain/exhibition/schwitters-britain (accessed 10 February 2015).

Taylor, Jennifer. '"Something to Make People Laugh"? Political Content in Isle of Man Internment Camp Journals July–October 1940'. In *'Totally Un-English'? Britain's Internment of 'Enemy Aliens' in Two World Wars*, edited by Richard Dove, 139–52. Amsterdam: The Yearbook of the Research Centre for German and Austrian Exile Studies Vol. 7, 2005.

'They Deserve a Stamp'. Available online: http://theydeserveastamp.org/ (accessed 16 January 2016).

Thompson, Paul. 'Family Myth, Models, and Denials in the Shaping of Individual Life Paths'. In *International Yearbook of Oral History and Life Studies, Volume II*, edited by Daniel Bertaux and Paul Thompson, 13–38. Oxford: Oxford University Press, 1993.

Tsu, Cecilia M. *Garden of the World: Asian Immigrants and the Making of Agriculture in California's Santa Clara Valley.* Oxford: Oxford University Press, 2013.

'Tule Lake Committee'. Available online: http://www.tulelake.org/ (accessed 10 February 2015).

'Tule Lake Committee Files Lawsuit to Stop the Fence at Airport'. *Pacific Citizen*, 24 October 2014. Available online: http://www.patrickcho.com/pacificcitizen/tule-lake-committee-files-lawsuit-to-stop-the-fence-at-airport/ (accessed 2 October 2015).

'Tule Lake Pilgrimage Facebook Group'. Available online: https://www.facebook.com/groups/5857573804/?fref=ts (accessed 10 February 2015).

'Tule Lake Unit WWII Valor in the Pacific National Monument Facebook Page'. Available online: https://www.facebook.com/TuleLakeNPS?fref=ts (accessed 10 February 2015).

'Tulelake Municipal Airport Stakeholder Engagement Process'. Available online: https://docs.google.com/a/co.modoc.ca.us/viewer?a=v&pid=si tes&srcid=Y28ubW9kb2MuY2EudXN8Y291bnR5LW9mLW1 vZG9jfGd4OjY3M2ZhZTVmZDZiMGZkZGU (accessed 2 September 2016).

Tunnell, Michael, and Chilcoat, George. *The Children of Topaz: The Story of a Japanese-American Internment Camp.* New York: Holiday House, 1996.

Ugolini, Wendy. *Experiencing War as the 'Enemy Other': Italian Scottish Experience in World War II.* Manchester: Manchester University Press, 2014.

Ugolini, Wendy. 'The Internal Enemy "Other": Recovering the World War Two Narratives of Italian Scottish Women'. *Journal of Scottish Historical Studies* 24 (2004): 137–58.

Ugolini, Wendy. '"Spaghetti Lengths in a Bowl?" Recovering Narratives of Not "Belonging" amongst the Italian Scots'. *Immigrants and Minorities* 31 (2013): 214–34.

Ungerson, Clare. 'The Forgotten Four Thousand: Jewish Refugees in Sandwich in 1939'. *Wiener Library Seminar*, 25 January 2011.

'Uprooted: Japanese American Farm Labor Camps during World War II'. Available online: http://www.uprootedexhibit.com/ (accessed 10 February 2015).

Visit New South Wales. 'Dunera Museum – Prisoner of War and Internment Camp Interpretive Centre – Hay'. Available online: http://www.visitnsw.com/destinations/country-nsw/griffith-area/hay/attractions/dunera-museum-at-hay-railway-station (accessed 10 February 2015).

Vulliamy, Ed. 'The Dispossessed Speak to Us Still'. *The Guardian*, 29 February 2004. Available online: http://www.theguardian.com/artanddesign/2004/feb/29/art1 (accessed 10 February 2015).

'Wales Breaks Its Silence . . . from Memories to Memorials'. Available online: http://www.arandorastarwales.us/Arandora_Star_Memorial_Fund_in_Wales/HOME.html (accessed 10 February 2015).

Walker Art Gallery. 'Art behind Barbed Wire'. Available online: http://www.liverpoolmuseums.org.uk/walker/exhibitions/barbedwire/index.aspx (accessed 10 February 2015).

Wang, Frances Kai-Hwa. 'Campaign Urges USPS to Create Stamp in Honor of Japanese-American WWII Soldiers'. *NBC News*, 11 November 2015. Available online: http://www.nbcnews.com/news/asian-america/campaign-urges-usps-create-stamp-honor-japanese-american-wwii-soldiers-n460881 (accessed 16 January 2016).

Wang, Frances Kai-Hwa. 'Oahu's Honouliuli Internment Camp Designated National Monument'. *NBC News*, 21 February 2015. Available online: http://www.nbcnews.com/news/asian-america/oahus-honouliuli-internment-camp-designated-national-monument-n311086 (accessed 16 April 2015).

Wasowski, Richard. *Snow Falling on Cedars Notes*. New York: Wiley, 2000.

Wasserstein, Bernard. *Britain and the Jews of Europe, 1939–1945*. Oxford: Clarendon Press, 1979.

Wax, Rosalie H. 'In and Out of the Tule Lake Segregation Center: Japanese Internment in the West, 1942–1945'. *Montana: The Magazine of Western History* 37 (1987): 12–25.

Weglyn, Michi Nishiura. *Years of Infamy: The Untold Story of America's Concentration Camps*. Seattle: University of Washington, 1996.

Welsh, Anne Marie. 'Theater Review: "Allegiance" Gives Japanese Internment a Soft Focus', *Los Angeles Times*, 20 September 2012. Available online: http://articles.latimes.com/2012/sep/20/entertainment/la-et-cm-old-globe-review-20120921 (accessed 10 December 2015).

Whitford, Frank. 'Sir Eduardo Paolozzi Obituary'. *The Guardian*, 22 April 2005.

Wilson, Robert A., and Hosokawa, Bill. *East to America: A History of the Japanese in the United States*. New York: William Morrow, 1980.

Wong, Curtis M. 'George Takei to Make Broadway Debut in "Allegiance" Musical about Japanese-American Internment Experience'. *The Huffington Post*, 5 February 2015. Available online: http://www.huffingtonpost.com/2015/02/05/george-takei-allegiance-broadway-_n_6624528.html (accessed 16 April 2015).

Wray, Helena. 'The Aliens Act 1905 and the Immigration Dilemma'. *Journal of Law and Society* 33 (2006): 302–23.

Wünschman, Kim. *Before Auschwitz: Jewish Prisoners in the Prewar Concentration Camps*. Cambridge, MA: Harvard University Press, 2015.

Yamada, Gerald. 'Open Letter about "Allegiance"'. *Japanese American Veterans Association*, 10 September 2012. Available online: http://resisters.com/wordpress/wp-content/uploads/2012/09/JAVA_letter.pdf (accessed 20 November 2015).

Yamato, Sharon. *Moving Walls: Preserving the Barracks of America's Concentration Camps*. Los Angeles: Japanese American National Museum, 1998.

Yardley, William. 'Bob Fletcher Dies at 101; Helped Japanese Americans'. *The New York Times*, 6 June 2013. Available online: http://www.nytimes.com/2013/06/07/us/bob-fletcher-dies-at-101-saved-farms-of-interned-japanese-americans.html?smid=fb-share&_r=2 (accessed 20 August 2016).

Yeung, Peter. 'EU Referendum: Reports of Hate Crime Increase 57% Following Brexit Vote'. *The Independent*, 28 June 2016. Available online: http://www.independent. co.uk/news/uk/home-news/brexit-hate-crime-racism-reports-eu-referendum-latest-a7106116.html (accessed 28 June 2016).

Yoo, David. 'Captivating Memories: Museology, Concentration Camps, and Japanese American History'. *American Quarterly* 48 (1996): 680–99.

Fiction

Baddiel, David. *The Secret Purposes*. London: Little, Brown & Company, 2004.

Eberle, Margaret Bane. *The Gem of the Desert: A Japanese-American Internment Camp*. Bloomington, IL: iUniverse, 2008.

Ford, Jamie. *Hotel on the Corner of Bitter and Sweet*. New York: Ballantine Books, 2009.

Guterson, David. *Snow Falling on Cedars*. San Diego: Harcourt, 1994.

Lieurance, Suzanne. *The Lucky Baseball: My Story in a Japanese-American Internment Camp*. Berkeley Heights, NJ: Enslow, 2009.

Mochizuki, Ken. *Baseball Saved Us*. New York: Lee & Low Books, 1995.

Oishi, Gene. *In Search of Hiroshi*. Rutland, VT: C.E. Tuttle, 1988.

Otsuka, Julie. *When the Emperor Was Divine*. New York: Penguin, 2013.

Schwitters, Kurt. *Lucky Hans and Other Merz Fairy Tales (Oddly Modern Fairy Tales)*. Princeton, NJ: Princeton University Press, 2014.

Solomons, Natasha. *Mr Rosenblum's List: Or Friendly Guidance for the Aspiring Englishman*. London: Sceptre, 2010.

Steel, Danielle. *SilentHonor*. London: Bantam Books, 1996.

Stock, Francine. *A Foreign Country*. London: Chatto & Windus, 1999.

Index

CPSIA information can be obtained
at www.ICGtesting.com
Printed in the USA
LVHW080314030519
616524LV00004B/62/P

9 781350 106048